NO LESSONS LEARNED

NO LESSONS LEARNED

The Making of *Curb Your Enthusiasm*

As Told by Larry David and the Cast and Crew

WRITTEN BY LORRAINE ALI

In the Beginning, There Was Larry vi

Curb Rising 14

SUSIE'S EPIC TAKEDOWNS 36

Improv in the Age of Canned Laughter 38

OUTLINE VS. SCENE 74

How Did They Do It? 82

LARRY'S LOS ANGELES 102   SUSIE'S STYLE 116

Curb Imitating Life Imitating *Curb* 120

VOCAB-U-LARRY 154

Jeff, Susie, Cheryl & Leon 156
LEON'S GUIDE TO LOVE 190

Larry vs. Larry 192
ON THE JOB WITH LARRY 212

How Far Is Too Far? 214
WHERE THE SACRED AND PROFANE COLLIDE 232   LARRY VS. KIDS 246

Honey, We Have Guests 248
LARRY'S RULES 270

Pretty, Pretty, Pretty Good 272
REMEMBERING THREE COMEDY GREATS 298

EPISODE GUIDE 302   IMAGE CREDITS 313

Lar

In the Beginning, There Was

Larry at his bar mitzvah, age 13.

Young Larry and his older brother, Ken.

Everyone has to start somewhere, and for Larry David, that day was July 2, 1947, when he was born to Rose and Morty David of Brooklyn, New York. The eldest of two boys, Larry grew up in the middle-class neighborhood of Sheepshead Bay with no plans of becoming a comedian.

"We weren't a funny family," recalls David. "It wasn't like my parents joked a lot. What made me laugh was watching *Abbott and Costello* and *The Phil Silvers Show* where Silvers played Sergeant Bilko. *Amos and Andy* made me laugh, *a lot*. But I never thought of myself as being funny when I was a kid, so the thought of being a comedian never crossed my mind."

David's father was a clothing manufacturer. His mother was a housewife. Certainly they had high expectations for their son's future...

"Not even close. I'm not exaggerating," says David. "There was never talk of a successful future, of what I could be. No big plans. They begged me to take a civil service test to become a mailman. That was their best-case scenario."

Their dreams of Larry going postal never materialized. Instead, he enrolled in college in 1965 at the University of Maryland, College Park, where he majored in history.

"I never felt funny until I got to college," says David. "When I got away from Brooklyn into this new environment where people didn't know me, my personality started to flourish. I was able to tell stories of going on a date and get laughs telling people how badly it went. And when I was asked what I was going to do with a history degree, my stock answer was, 'Something will turn up.' But I really had no idea."

David's BA in history wasn't just useless in the job market, it was also a nonstarter on the dating scene.

"After graduating from college in 1970, I took an acting class because I needed a good thing to say to women when they asked me what I did. I needed something kind of cool because this [points to himself] didn't suffice. My appearance, everything about it, was not going to work. I needed something besides myself. So I thought saying I was an actor could do the trick."

"I NEVER FELT FUNNY UNTIL I GOT TO COLLEGE."

—LARRY DAVID

Larry David's college portrait, 1969.

"The future was bleak."

—LARRY DAVID

As a child, shows like *Abbott and Costello* made Larry laugh.

"Acting also seemed easy. I mean, I grew up watching movies and it didn't look all that hard. Somebody talks, you wait until they finish talking, then you say something. They're just saying these lines. How hard could that be? You're just standing there pretending. So I took a class and realized I didn't really like it very much. I didn't like waiting to talk or saying what somebody else wrote. I wanted to say what was going on in my head. In retrospect, you can see how *Curb* turned out to be the perfect vehicle for me."

But *Curb* was a long way off when David, in his mid-twenties, was struggling to make the rent.

"I did odd jobs as a taxi driver, a private chauffeur, a limo-service driver, stuff like that," recalls David. "But it was a very, very sad time in my life, this period from post college until the first time I did stand-up at age twenty-six. Those four years were awful. I just felt lost. My parents were beside themselves and sent me to a therapist. It was just a very difficult time for me. Bad jobs, no money, living in a dump. By all accounts, I was a failure and the future was bleak."

"Then one day I was taking a break while waiting for the lady I was driving. I had my chauffeur uniform on and I was leaning against the car, and walking down the street was a guy I recognized from college, who was from a very wealthy family. He was dressed immaculately, had on a three-piece suit, and was carrying an attaché case. He spotted me and then quickly averted his eyes, unable to deal with his pity. And that had an impact on me—I thought, 'I really have to do something with my life.'"

Larry's cast portrait for *Fridays*, 1981.

Larry in *Fridays*.

"So I sought out somebody I knew who was getting into stand-up and I sat down with him to find out what it entailed," says David. "So he filled me in: 'You've got to write material. You can't just walk up there.' In retrospect, I think I would have been better off just walking up as opposed to doing material. To this day, I hate doing material. But I wrote some and went to a club in The Village called Gerde's Folk City on what they called a Hootenanny night. I got up for the first time and I was beyond awful. The material was terrible. And then I did it again, like a week later at the Gil Hodges bowling alley in Brooklyn that had a room set up with a little stage. I was terrible, again. Then the third time, I wrote a bit that was kind of clever and auditioned at Catch a Rising Star. The MC liked it and invited me back, so I started going on late at night, sometimes for three people at one o'clock in the morning, when everybody had left except these stragglers. That's what beginners do. From there, you build up your act. Trying to become a comedian really changed my life for the better. I didn't feel lost anymore. And I began hanging out with the other comedians."

One of the folks David began spending time with was a young upstart named Jerry Seinfeld.

"We really enjoyed each other's company and on occasion would write together. We'd walk around Central Park and I'd have my ideas, and he'd have his, and we would help punch up each other's stuff," David says. "But my development as a comedian was fraught with problems. I had many run-ins with the audience. I was ill-tempered up there and if I wasn't going over I did not react well. I would get in arguments with people. But I persevered because there was nothing else. There were no other possibilities."

Finally in 1979, at the age of thirty-two, David got what he jokingly refers to as his "big break."

"I auditioned for this new show that was a rip-off of *Saturday Night Live*, called *Fridays*. The producers came to New York looking for people to cast. It was a good audition and they hired me. I don't remember feeling particularly elated, but I do remember feeling a lack of confidence. 'How am I going to do this? I'm not an actor.' That's why I couldn't get too excited about the whole thing. I was concerned I was going to embarrass myself."

Despite the fear of failure, David moved to Los Angeles for his first big TV job.

"I was on the show for two years," says David, "and I don't think I was very good but I also learned that I'm much more comfortable doing my own material as opposed to material written by someone else. When the show was canceled, I stayed in LA for another two years doing stand-up and writing a film script."

"I just couldn't get the idea of what to do

Bob Weide was the director of development for a production and management company in 1982 when a script landed on his desk called *Prognosis Negative*. "It was one of the funniest things I had ever read," says Weide. "Here's a very brief synopsis: The lead character is named Leo Black. Leo has trouble with relationships. They always blow up. And he's kind of a moaning, complaining guy. Basically, he's Larry David in his thirties. So Leo gets some news, by accident, that a woman he liked and dated years earlier is now terminally ill, but she doesn't know she's ill. So he thinks this is the perfect situation, because he can date her again and really give himself over to the relationship but it won't be a long-term commitment. It was very, very dark. In short, very Larry David. So we called him in for a meeting. I remember my colleague saying to Larry, 'Look, we all think it's a very funny script, but the lead character is not terribly likable. Is there anything you can think of to do to make him sympathetic or more likable?' Larry thought about it, then he said, 'No, I don't think so.' And I thought, 'Oh, I like this guy.' And that's when we started to hang out."

The two would end up working together nearly two decades later, when Weide would direct and executive produce *Curb*. But at the time, they were still making their way in the comedy world.

Weide recalls Larry's early eighties comedy sets at the Improv in West Hollywood. "He would come out onstage and just stare out at the audience with this sour look on his face," says Weide. "There was never any 'Good evening' or 'How are you?' None of that stuff. Then he would say, 'Every morning, I wake up and thank God that I wasn't born a wealthy Spanish landowner.' So already people are looking at each other like, 'What the fuck is this?' And then he'd say, 'Because if I were, I would never know whether to address the help using the *tú* form or the *usted*

ldn't stand being told

—LARRY DAVID

form.' Now people are walking out of the room. 'If I use the *usted* form, I don't want them to feel I'm being condescending. But if I use the *tú* form, I don't want them to feel so familiar that they can just walk into my kitchen and help themselves to anything in my refrigerator.'"

"He would be heckled, 'You're not funny!' There'd be arguments within the audience between pro-Larry factions and anti-Larry factions. But all the comics were lined up in the back of the room, because they loved him and loved watching this kind of ritual."

Other folks outside of LA also had their eye on Larry David, and his second big break came in 1984, when he was hired by *SNL*.

"I was brought on as a writer, and there was no thought whatsoever about me acting or performing on the show. Although my sketches got good laughs at the read-through, I only ever got one on the air at the very end of the show when no one was watching, but I started to develop confidence that I could write. The *SNL* job ended in 1985, when Lorne [Michaels, the show's creator, who had left in 1980] came back the next season and fired everybody."

By the mid-eighties, David had become a master at curbing his expectations. Writing jobs weren't exactly plentiful, and breaking ground as a stand-up was even harder. Still, he braved the comedy clubs once again, which led to a series of events that would change his life—and TV comedy—forever.

"After my stint on *SNL* ended, I did stand-up for the next three years when Jerry [Seinfeld] approached me in November of 1988 and told me that NBC was interested in doing something with him and asked if I wanted to work with him on it. In retrospect, it was a turning point in my life, but at the time, I thought, 'Sure. OK.' The thought was maybe I could make a little money doing this pilot. I didn't think anything was going to happen. But of course, I never thought anything good was going to happen to me. I was conditioned to just get through another day and expect the worst. That way I was never disappointed."

And it was from that sort of hopeful thinking that *Seinfeld* was born.

"I had no sitcom-writing experience. I didn't even know the format," says David. "And the pilot was the flimsiest of premises. It was about Jerry meeting this woman on the road, and she calls him up later to say that she's coming to New York and asks if she can stay with him. Jerry wonders, 'What does that mean, stay? What should he expect? How should he interpret that?' That was pretty much it, but they picked it up for four shows and Julia [Louis-Dreyfus] was added to the cast as Elaine. The pilot aired in July of 1989."

The show wasn't a ratings juggernaut (at first), but it did garner positive reviews. NBC bought four more episodes—and made its first attempt to make the scrappy little sitcom palatable for the masses.

"Larry, you're not funny."
—ROSE DAVID, LARRY'S MOM

Larry poses with his parents and brother.

"They hired somebody to be the executive producer, and he called Jerry and me into his office to give us notes on the first few shows," explains David. "When he finished, I looked at him and said, 'No. I'm not doing one thing. Not one thing.' And I left. Afterward, I said to Jerry, 'Good luck. I can't do this.' I don't know why, but I just couldn't stand the idea of being told what to do. It wasn't that guy's show, it was our show. I don't care how much experience he had. The idea that this person was going to tell us how to do this—I just couldn't live with it. Jerry said, 'Don't worry, I'll talk to the guys at Castle Rock,' which he did. And that was the end of that guy. He never surfaced again."

"And why did the network put up with me? That's a good question. I think they tolerated me because they liked Jerry so much and they were stuck with me because Jerry made it clear to them that he wouldn't do the show without me, and I wasn't going to do it if we couldn't do it the way we wanted to do it. And it was the first time something like that happened, but it certainly wasn't the last."

David's insistence that they do things his way was a lasting theme that would give rise to two of television's best comedies ever, and would afford him a very rare thing in the entertainment industry—a career built upon autonomy. But while David had a staunch belief in his own work, he was taken aback when other folks began to love it, too.

"I remember walking into Catch a Rising Star after the *Seinfeld* pilot aired, and having comedians come up to me going, 'Oh, hey, I saw the show. It was really good. I really liked it.' And I was kind of stunned. 'What?! Are you serious? It was good?' I couldn't believe it. It was startling that someone told me that it was good. I just couldn't fathom it. And it wasn't false modesty."

But not everyone was blown away.

"My mother didn't think me going into comedy was a very good idea to start with," recalls David. "She said to me, 'Larry, you're not funny. I've never heard you say anything funny.' Then when *Seinfeld* was the number one show in the country, she would call me up and go, 'Larry, do they like you? Are they going to keep you? Do they tell you you're doing a good job?'"

"My dad was able to enjoy my success a little more. He also liked when I would buy him stuff, like a new car, [even though] he complained a lot about the air-conditioning and had to return it. When they came out to LA, I flew them first-class. I put them up in a nice hotel on Ocean Avenue, and I called my mother to say, 'OK, I'm going to pick you up at six o'clock. We'll go out to dinner.' She said to me, 'We're not at the hotel.' I said, 'What are you talking about?' She said, 'We've left the hotel. We're at the Days Inn on Santa Monica Boulevard.' I said, 'What? Are you out of your mind?' She said, 'I don't need you putting me up in fancy hotels, flying me out first-class.' My father was perfectly happy in the nice hotel. Imagine that—she dragged that poor guy out of that beautiful hotel. They'd never stayed in a hotel like that in their lives, and she just couldn't handle it."

Seinfeld won multiple Emmys during its nine seasons. David had cocreated and showrun one of the most successful sitcoms ever, and discovered key talent along the way, including writer-directors Jeff Schaffer, Alec Berg, and Dave Mandel (who would later work on *Curb*). But it was in 1997, after seven seasons, that David finally left the NBC sitcom, returning only for the finale.

"When you have a successful show, you start to compete against your previous seasons," says David. "'How is next season going to be better than the season before?' You feel all your great ideas have been done, you've used them all. But it'd also been seven years and I just wanted to try something else…"

Curb Rising Curb Rising Curb Rising

Larry David.

The name was familiar, but the face? Not so much. The *Seinfeld* writer, cocreator, and executive producer was behind one of the most successful sitcoms ever, but by the show's 1998 finale, most folks still couldn't pick David out of a lineup.

Audiences did, however, know more about David than they realized, thanks to a character he based broadly on himself, his *Seinfeld* alter ego, George Costanza. Played by Jason Alexander, the balding, bespectacled New Yorker was insecure and self-centered. He suffered from social anxiety and concocted elaborate lies in the name of self-preservation. His lifelong desire to be admired, while doing nothing to earn such praise, meant no steady job or prospects of a career. And he was paranoid about, well, everything.

George was an expertly crafted sitcom sidekick, but hardly leading-man material. Building an entire production around such a character would certainly equal career suicide. Naturally, Larry David had to try it.

The 1999 HBO mockumentary *Larry David: Curb Your Enthusiasm* featured David playing an exaggerated version of himself: a semi-retired cocreator of *Seinfeld* living comfortably in West LA while attempting to make his way back into stand-up comedy. The one-hour special was envisioned as a singular event—the perfect project for a guy who dreams big but dreads actually having to do the thing that he's dreamed about. If David was lucky, he'd only have to do it once, or maybe not at all if the networks passed on the project.

Larry on set shooting the last few episodes of *Seinfeld* in 1998.

"I don't like pleasing people."

—LARRY DAVID

"I didn't care for stand-up comedy," says David. "I didn't look forward to going onstage the way the other comics did. In fact, if the show was running late and they told me I wasn't going on, I would be relieved. You're walking up there, you're vulnerable, and you have to please people. I don't like pleasing people."

And it was David's apprehension about stepping back onstage as a stand-up that became the basis for the HBO film.

The first inkling of the *Curb* special began with a 1998 conversation between David and Jeff Garlin, who'd later play Larry's manager, Jeff Greene, in the film and the sitcom. The two were discussing potential post-*Seinfeld* projects over lunch when Garlin suggested a documentary that followed David back onto the stand-up circuit as he prepared for his first HBO comedy special.

"I thought about it, me going back to do stand-up with the cameras following the whole thing," says David. "We'd see me onstage. We'd see my act develop over the course of the documentary. But it couldn't all be onstage. What would happen offstage, when I wasn't performing? That seemed boring to me. So I thought I could make it more interesting and funnier if I made up a life offstage. I'd have a wife and kids, because there were originally kids in the special. Then I'd make up funny stories that would have to be improvised to make it seem like a documentary. So that version sounded doable. It didn't sound all that bad."

David teamed up with old friend, writer, and documentarian Bob Weide to help shape his idea into something he could pitch to studios and/or networks. "Larry was thinking about doing a special that would be shot as a documentary and he wanted me to direct it because I made real documentaries," says Weide.

"Larry, Ari Emanuel [Larry's agent], and Gavin Polone [producer], pitched the idea to David's former manager, Chris Albrecht, who was head of original programming at HBO," says Garlin. "Chris said, 'How can we *not* do this?' You never hear that in Hollywood. Ever."

Larry in "The Special Section," S3, E6.

LARRY DAVID PROJECT
POSSIBLE TITLES

Larry David...

Life Be Not Proud
Nowhere Fast
Nothing Ventured
Curb Your Enthusiasm
Kicking and Screaming
Going Backwards
Half Empty
Do Not Go Gently
Out of the Loop
With Friends Like These
Best Foot Backwards
Something So Wrong
Push Comes To Shove
Regrets Only
No Life To Live
The Shame Must Go On
Dead On The Inside

Larry David Vanity Project

Larry:
See if any of these strike your fancy. I'm going to lay a temp title on before Monday.
—Bob

THIS PAGE: Bob Weide and Larry on set for "The Shrimp Incident," S2, E4. OPPOSITE: An early list of possible titles for the special.

Albrecht's eagerness may have been more about his love and respect for David—or morbid curiosity about how such a project might turn out—than any expectation of a hit. Even the film's title warned viewers not to expect much, preemptively signaling failure in the event that things went south.

The name—*Curb Your Enthusiasm*—was floated during a small screening of the unfinished special, where David had invited a group of friends to give their honest opinions of his work. "Larry and I had been brainstorming titles for the show, and I would jot them down whenever he or I had an idea," recalls Weide. "I wanted to call it *Regrets Only*. Larry said it's clever, but it sounds too much like a Richard Lewis Showtime special, and it kind of did. He came up with *Curb Your Enthusiasm*. At the screening, we passed out a little questionnaire with the presumptive titles and asked people to check their favorites. One idea got a few votes, another got some more, and *Curb Your Enthusiasm* got no votes. None. That's when Larry said, 'Too bad. I like that one. *Curb Your Enthusiasm*. That's what we're going to call it.'"

The odds were slim to none that a comedy about a socially challenged industry insider would connect with a mainstream audience accustomed to the humor of shows like *Full House* and *Friends*. *Curb* was irreverent, risky, and behind the paywall of subscription cable television. Most viewers still thought of HBO as a place to rewatch your favorite films long after their run in movie theaters. The platform's early original series like *Oz*, *Sex and the City*, and *The Sopranos* were challenging norms and ideas about what makes for a great drama or comedy, but network TV was still king. It didn't help that the *Curb* special aired at 10 p.m. on Sunday, TiVo was still in its infancy, and, again . . . who the hell was Larry David?

Larry, Jeff Garlin, and Cheryl Hines in various scenes from the *Curb Your Enthusiasm* special.

"The industry knew who he was, but unless you were a hardcore *Seinfeld* fan, it could absolutely escape you who Larry David was," says Weide. "I remember a billboard for the special on Sunset Boulevard. It was Larry's face and it just said, 'Larry David: *Curb Your Enthusiasm*,' and I thought, 'How is that supposed to get anyone to watch this?' It didn't say, 'From the man who brought you *Seinfeld*.' It was just his mug and his name. *Really?*"

"Larry's not really a behind-the-scenes kind of personality," says Jason Alexander, who played George on the NBC sitcom *Seinfeld*. "He's a performer. So I wasn't surprised he was starring in *Curb*. I was however surprised by the format, because with *Seinfeld* he was such a detailed writer who was not happy if a word changed. He scripted carefully, so this idea that he was going to throw caution to the wind and do improv seemed unusual, but I also thought, 'Oh, it's a one-time thing. He's doing an HBO special. If it works, it works. If it doesn't, then no harm, no foul.'"

The special didn't break any ratings records, but no one expected it to. It did, however, generate plenty of praise within the industry and among critics. *Variety*'s Phil Gallo wrote: "No matter how *Larry David: Curb Your Enthusiasm* is interpreted—an indictment of the people within the entertainment industry or a linear delusion of one of comedy's funniest thinkers—it is the work of genius. David shrouds this dark comedy in nihilism and defense mechanisms, distancing it from films that have taken similar tacks (*Waiting for Guffman*, for example) and produced more obviously humorous works. Beyond the intriguing nature of the bizarrely 'normal' David, the big question of what is real and what isn't should definitely add to repeat viewings, transforming this hour-long into the comedic equivalent of *The Blair Witch Project*."

Spontaneity was a large part of the special's appeal. It felt fresh. No canned jokes. No scripted pauses for laughs. "The *Curb* documentary had to be improvised so it would pass as a

An image of Larry that was featured in the promotional poster for the *Curb* special.

documentary, and it did," says David. "I felt like I had a facility for improvisation. I don't know why I felt that confidence, maybe it was from that one improv class I took when I was doing stand-up. I got a compliment from an actress in the class, and, of course, I never forget a compliment."

Handheld cameras followed fictional Larry as he acted upon his terrible instincts, unwittingly offending everyone around him, including his wife, Cheryl. "When we were looking to cast Larry's wife, he didn't know what he wanted," says then-casting director Marla Garlin, Jeff Garlin's former spouse who worked on the *Curb* film and the first season of the show. "I would bring in these shrewish women for him, and he was like, 'No, no, no, that's not what I want.' He was looking for someone who was a great foil, not someone that would beat him down. It also had to be someone that would handle their own with Larry, not somebody he can steamroll over because he's so clever and smart. That's when Cheryl [Hines] came in."

Just as Cheryl found charm in Larry's madness, so too would viewers. There was something cathartic about watching this odd fellow embrace ideas and advice that would send others running. He did and said things that most of us wish we could, or fear we might. His actions throughout the film were liberating *and* hilarious, and David was only just getting started.

"It was after Larry and I had filmed on a Saturday and we were sitting by an empty desk, I remember it clearly," says Garlin. "Larry said, 'Wouldn't this be great to do as a TV series?' I thought, 'He's in the moment. He's happy. But it won't last.' Then he called me after the special came out. It was very under the radar, but it got a lot of respect, especially inside HBO. So he and Ari went to Chris and told him they wanted to do it as a series. And that was the start of the show."

There wasn't anything like the quirky cable series among television's top comedies. *Frasier* and *Everybody Loves Raymond* featured flawed yet lovable protagonists whose personalities were redeemed at the end of each episode. *Curb* would do nothing of the sort. Lessons be damned—Larry would remain a misanthrope. *Curb*'s format was also unique. The series was the first mockumentary sitcom on American television. *The Office* wouldn't debut on NBC for another five years, and blockbusters like *Modern Family* and *Abbott Elementary* were years if not decades in the future.

Larry posing in front of a poster for *Curb's* first season in Los Angeles.

And there was that delightful theme music . . .

"The *Curb* theme is a song called 'Frolic' by Italian composer Luciano Michelini. He wrote it for an obscure 1970s film," says editor and music supervisor Steve Rasch. "Larry had heard it on a bank commercial and asked Laura Streicher [then David's assistant] to track it down, and she did. It was in a production music library called Killer Tracks, and anyone could license it. I knew one of the guys there, so I asked if he could send me all the CDs from that artist. But it turned out to be a collection from an Italian subsidiary of RCA that had all these TV tracks from Italian composers that Fellini had used. They were working on the side doing TV shows. It even included Ennio Morricone's work. The tracks were all in the vein of 'Frolic,' sort of like a circus band, recorded with tuba and classical Italian instruments like accordions. It was the kind of thing you'd hear at the circus when acrobats are performing. So I used them to score montages and transitional elements between scenes."

From *Curb*'s quirky soundtrack to its boundary-breaking humor, Larry David had the sort of creative freedom most showrunners dream of. HBO trusted David thanks to his prior success as a sitcom creator. But that also meant the bar was high for David's new show. After all, how does one compete with the monster success of a comedy like *Seinfeld*?

"I didn't even think about that," says David, "because, like *Seinfeld*, I never expected *Curb* to go anywhere.

One thing was clear when the pilot episode, "The Pants Tent," premiered on October 15, 2000: The half-hour sitcom was not your parents' comedy, or even your uptight brother's. Larry's misunderstandings, social faux pas, and disastrous attempts to fix his blunders were hard to watch, but even harder to turn away from, because they were so damn entertaining. During a night at the movies with friends, Larry wears pants with puffy pleating that cause Cheryl's friend Nancy (Robin Ruzan) to believe he has an erection. Larry also offends Jeff's parents and angers Richard Lewis's new girlfriend, who accuses Larry of looking at her breasts during an argument at the movie theater. He justifies these insults with a string of lies, all of which are exposed by the end of the episode when the storylines converge with pinpoint accuracy.

"I have such a low attention span that, when I'm reading a book, if there's not a compelling story, it's torture," says David. "I need to turn a page. I need to know what's going to happen next. Same with a movie. I want good stories.

Scenes from "The Pants Tent," S1, E1.

EXPECTED *CURB* TO GO ANYWHERE." —LARRY DAVID

THIS PAGE AND OPPOSITE: Ted Danson and Mary Steenburgen played themselves (and started their prolific run as season regulars) in "Ted and Mary," S1, E2.

It wasn't that way at the beginning of *Seinfeld*. I was like, 'We're just gonna talk. Stories are incidental.' But I learned very quickly that, no, you can't do that."

Finding the right performers to flesh out the characters in those stories was just as critical, and many of them came from the stand-up comedy circuit. Susie Essman did not audition for the role of Jeff Greene's high-decibel spouse, Susie. "Larry just called me up one day. I hadn't seen him in about ten years, because I lived in New York, and he had moved to LA to do *Seinfeld*," says Essman. "But I knew him from back in the Catch a Rising Star days, when we were doing stand-up. We were always very friendly, not the kind of friends who go for dinner or anything, but, you know, comic friends. He saw me on a roast I did for Jerry Stiller on Comedy Central. And those roasts are super, super blue. That's what's required. He apparently had a scene in mind where whoever is playing Jeff's wife just goes crazy, [screaming at] Jeff. When he saw me do the roast, I think it was a light bulb moment, like, 'Oh, Susie's perfect for this part.' He called and offered me the job."

"I remember the phone call," says Essman. "I was like, 'Well, what's the character?' He said, 'Don't worry about it. You can do it.' I said, 'Send me a script.' He said, 'There's no script, and there's no money. It's low-budget. You're going to have to fly yourself out and put yourself up.' And I was like, 'Nah, tell them to find the money to fly me out. I don't mind not making money, if I get to work with you, but it's not going to *cost* me money.' So I was in three episodes in that first season, and the first one I shot was 'The Pants Tent.' There wasn't much for my character to do. I was just talking about [my kid] Sammi, who was a boy at that time. He was a boy until season two, when Larry needed Sammi to be a girl, so he became Samantha."

Comedy couple Ted Danson and Mary Steenburgen weren't exactly sold on the idea of *Curb* when they heard about David's plans for the new series. "We met Larry and [David's then wife] Laurie years ago on Martha's Vineyard," says Danson. "We didn't really know each other that well, but we had had a handful of fun evenings together. So he invited a group of about five or six to the rental house, and we had to go up to the attic and sit on the stairs to get a Wi-Fi signal so he could show us the pilot of *Curb* that he had shot in New York with Jeff Garlin. And I thought, 'I really like him, but *oof*. No.' But being the sycophant that I am, at the end of it, I said, 'Hey, fantastic!' I don't think this is my wife Mary's truth, but it was mine. Anyway, we both said, 'If you ever need us just to play ourselves for whatever reason, call us.' I was doing it with the idea that it would never happen. But it did."

Ted and Mary's first appearance on *Curb* was in the show's second episode, aptly titled "Ted and Mary." Danson was certainly no stranger to TV comedy, having starred in *Cheers* for eleven seasons. And his initial reticence about David's new series quickly changed once he'd shot the episode.

"It was so crazy, smart, and bright," says Danson. "It was like guerrilla filmmaking. He called us two days beforehand. For wardrobe, we wore our own clothes. It was kind of like, OK, let's just go have fun."

Curb was referred to inside HBO as the cable network's "little experimental show," a nickname that was at once affectionate and shorthand for a sitcom that would likely be short-lived. After all, how would *Curb* survive, let alone thrive, without scripts or a writers' room? The answer: It probably wouldn't, which would explain why the show operated on a shoestring budget well past its first season.

"I suspect HBO was investing all of their money into the wardrobe of *Sex and the City*. Their costumes, their hair and makeup," jokes co-executive producer Laura Streicher, who started as David's assistant in 1998. "The first few seasons, it was a rogue situation for us at times. We didn't have trailers, so sometimes actors would be getting ready in bedrooms of the homes we shot at or out in the street. It was very fly by the seat of your pants, but there was a beauty to that."

Folks in the entertainment industry also noticed the raw genius of David's latest creation. The show had a field day with the self-centered behavior and fragile egotism that fuels Hollywood. "People in the industry really loved *Curb*, because Larry found a way to make fun of himself, which is a reflection of making fun of ourselves in this industry," says Cheryl Hines. "I remember there was a scene early on where we were trying to get a table at a restaurant, and we said, 'It's for Larry David.' And the maître d' didn't know who Larry David was. I said, 'He created *Seinfeld*.' And she said, 'Oh, I haven't seen it.' Those little moments are pretty inside, or you would think that they would be inside. But then the rest of the country started to get it and thought it was funny."

Behind the scenes of
"Beloved Aunt," S1, E8.

Curb hadn't exactly gone mainstream by its second season, but it was starting to reach a wider audience than David's colleagues, friends, and longtime fans in LA and New York. "We never talked to HBO about ratings or anything like that," says Weide. "We didn't really care. We weren't thinking about it. But there were those early signs that more people were watching the show, more divergent groups than we expected. Like, I'd just come off work and I was in Art's Deli on Ventura Boulevard. There was this older Jewish couple sitting across from me. They said, 'We love your show!' They'd seen the *Curb Your Enthusiasm* Season 1 crew jacket I was wearing. I remember thinking, 'Those people watch the show?!' I mean, we never got, like, *Sopranos* ratings, or even *Sex and the City* ratings, but we had what I used to call a small but disloyal audience. All of that was a surprise, the idea that it would be anything more than a cultish show that a few people would watch, that maybe we'd do a second season."

Another early indication that HBO's odd little series was making waves? The growing usage of "Vocab-U-Larry" (see p. 154) in everyday conversation. Snippets of dialogue from *Curb* began making their way into the national discourse, starting with Larry's "pretty, pretty, pretty good." But it was Essman's breakthrough tirade as Susie Greene that generated one of *Curb*'s first watercooler moments.

"We were six episodes into the first season when Larry David gave me the direction, 'I want you to rip Jeff a new asshole,'" says Essman. "And I thought, 'Well, I could do that. I've been in relationships.' So I go off on Jeff for the first time. Larry kept pulling me aside and saying, 'Go further. Go further, Go further.' And I thought I was going pretty far already. And then he said, 'Call Jeff a fat bastard. Make fun of his fat.' And I said, 'I don't want to do that. I don't like to make fun of what people look like.' That was never my comedy. I always thought that was kind of low. And he said, 'Just do it. He knows you're only acting.' That was the first time I called Jeff a fat fuck. The genie was out of the bottle."

YOU'RE A FAT

FUCKING ASSHOLE!

SUSIE'S EPIC Tak

"BASICALLY, I MAKE A LIVING TELLING PEOPLE TO GO FUCK THEMSELVES," Susie Essman has said of her role as the famously foulmouthed Susie Greene. "I show up, I scream, I rant, they pay me, I go home, and then I get to come back and do it all over again! No one gets hurt, no one is offended, and we have so much fun. It's my dream job."

FAT-FUCK!

Six episodes into season one, in "The Wire," Susie first utters the words she is perhaps most remembered for. Jeff sponsors a child who ends up trashing and robbing the Greenes' home, leaving Susie livid at the loss of irreplaceable keepsakes like her grandmother's brooch. Larry arrives to witness her raging at Jeff: "My wedding video is gone because your fat-fuck manager over here let an asshole kid into our house, OK?"

Get me the head!

Susie refined some of her iconic insults in season two's "The Doll." After finding her "fat-fuck" husband and Larry snooping around her daughter Sammi's room, she realizes the men have taken the head of one of Sammi's prized dolls. She accuses them of being "sickos" and demands they return the decapitated doll's head: "Get me the fucking head . . . you four-eyed fuck and you fat piece of shit. *Get me the head!*"

Bald asshole!

In the season six finale, "The Bat Mitzvah," Susie is screaming at Larry on his doorstep for an undisclosed reason, calling him a "bald asshole!" She is quieted, however, by Larry's new girlfriend, Loretta Black (Vivica A. Fox), who defends her man. Loretta tells Susie to get the hell off their property and promptly slams the door in her face.

Listen, you four-eyed fuck!

Season three's "The Corpse-Sniffing Dog" offered a callback to "The Doll." This time, Susie confronts Larry for accidentally getting seven-year-old Sammi drunk and then taking their family's dog, Oscar. "Listen, you four-eyed fuck . . . you sicko, fucko asshole," she says, *"Get me the fucking dog!"*

WHAT THE FUCK, LARRY?

In the season eight episode "Mister Softee," Susie unexpectedly has an orgasm while riding in the malfunctioning front passenger seat of Larry's car in New York City. Larry is so disgusted by this that he crashes the car into a Mister Softee truck. "What the fuck, Larry?" Susie screams. "Jesus fucking Christ, asshole! What the hell did you do?!"

edowns

"SHAVED HIS FUCKING HEAD!"

In season six's "The N Word," a doctor mistakenly shaves Jeff's "beautiful" head of hair because a man fitting Larry's description—"bald, glasses"—traumatized the Black doctor by using the N-word. The flummoxed doctor then "shaved his fucking head!" Susie screams. "Now he looks like *you!*" When Larry tries to explain himself, he uses the N-word, which is overheard by the Blacks, who rip Larry to shreds and move out of his home temporarily.

"COVID-carrying cocksucker!"

In the season twelve episode "Ken/Kendra," Susie accuses Larry of giving both her and Bruce Springsteen COVID. Quarantining and furious, Susie tells Larry that the whole world hates him because The Boss had to cancel concerts. "You're a walking fucking virus, Larry!" she screams from the top of her staircase. When Larry fires back, she lands the final blow, "You coldhearted, COVID-carrying cocksucker!"

"Rue the day you ever met me."

In the season eight premiere, "The Divorce," when Larry and Cheryl are meeting with divorce lawyers, Jeff suggests to Susie that if they ever get divorced, they should split everything 50-50. Susie vehemently disagrees: "You think we're gonna have a nice divorce if we ever get divorced? No fucking way. I'm taking you for everything you have, Mister. I'm taking your balls and I'm thumb-tacking them to the wall. You're going to get nothing out of it. You mention the D-word once in your fucking life and you'll rue the day you ever met me."

"CAR WASH CUNT!"

Susie arrives late to opening night of Bobo's, the restaurant where Jeff and Larry are investors, in the season three finale, "The Grand Opening." In a bid to normalize the behavior of their chef, who has Tourette syndrome with outbursts of profanity, Larry and Jeff are shouting curse words. Cheryl—who had canceled a lunch date with Susie earlier in the day after a car-wash mishap—joins the cursing, and Susie thinks the words are aimed at her. She tells Cheryl, "Fuck you, you car-wash cunt. I had a dental appointment!"

"Get the fuck out!"

Susie kicks Larry out again in season six's "The Anonymous Donor," this time in response to Cheryl kicking Jeff out of the David house. Cheryl found out that Jeff masturbated at their home during Passover, staining a blanket. Susie lashes out at Jeff ("You have brought your semen outside our home, Jeff?! That's adultery!") but turns her ire toward Cheryl and Larry. "Fuck you, ban him from the house? I will take care of [him] in my own way. If Jeff is banned from your house, you are banned from my house," she tells Larry. "Get the fuck out!"

"Shove it up your fat fucking ass!"

In the series finale, "No Lessons Learned," Larry and Susie team up so she can attest to his character when he's put on trial in Atlanta. But when Auntie Rae (Ellia English) exposes Jeff and Larry for stealing her coveted, secret salad dressing recipe for an anniversary gift to Susie, Susie blows her cover to lash out at Jeff: "That is the lowest form of anything I have ever heard! . . . Take that recipe, Jeff, and shove it up your fat fucking ass!" The show ends with the cast members arguing over one another on the airplane home. The last discernible line of the series comes from Susie, who yells, "Go back to fucking jail, Larry!"

"Take the fucking flowers!"

In the season six episode "The Ida Funkhouser Roadside Memorial," Larry steals flowers from the memorial to give to a private school admissions officer, to sweeten the deal for Sammi as well as the children of the Blacks (the family Larry and Cheryl took in after a New Orleans hurricane). When Larry is forced by Ida's son Marty to get the flowers back, he steals them from the admissions officer's vase and shoves them in Susie's purse. Of course he gets caught in the act and botches the mission. Susie admonishes him for ruining the kids' chances. "You want the flowers?" she says, shoving the bouquet in Larry's face. "Take the fucking flowers!"

Improv
IN THE AGE OF CANNED LAUGHTER

In season nine, Larry dons a disguise after learning a fatwa has been issued against him for an impression he did of the Ayatollah on *Jimmy Kimmel Live!*

Call it

organized chaos or planning for the unplanned. Working on *Curb Your Enthusiasm* was not for the faint of heart—or for those who required a script.

Television's only truly improvised sitcom challenged the status quo with dialogue and action created in the moment, allowing its comedic brilliance to unfurl as the cameras rolled.

For viewers, *Curb* offered a fresh, spontaneous shot of humor unlike anything else on the small or big screen. No matter how outrageous or absurd the set of circumstances—Larry paying a hooker to ride shotgun so he could use the car pool lane, Jeff being mistaken for Harvey Weinstein in a mini #MeToo moment—the situations felt authentic because the characters were truly reacting to one another in real time.

The show's cast, guest stars, and background players knew little to nothing about where the day's shoot would lead, and that's the way Larry David wanted it. He was often the only performer who knew exactly how each impromptu act would figure into an episode or season arc. Once a director like Bob Weide, Jeff Schaffer, or Alec Berg yelled "action," the goal was to provoke and/or enable Larry while keeping up with brilliant improvisers like Richard Lewis and JB Smoove.

But before getting through *Curb*, an actor had to get to *Curb*. The majority of the performers and comedians fortunate enough to make it on to the show faced an audition process that went something like this: Your agent finally proves their worth by booking you an audition for *Curb*. After excitedly calling your mom to tell her the good news and hoping this audition turns into the job that finally pays off your credit card debt, you ask to see the script. But there's no script, just a scant outline, and that's only if David provided it to your agent.

Upon arrival, you're handed a small slip of paper with a few details about your character's situation. You're portraying a head waiter at a restaurant where a rude patron has parked their car in your reserved spot ("The Bracelet," Season 1, Episode 4). Or perhaps your character is the unfortunate shorts-clad airline passenger who's been seated next to Larry on a cramped flight ("The Hot Towel," Season 7, Episode 4). That's all you have to go on.

"Don't try to be funny."
—LARRY DAVID

Feeling woefully unprepared, you enter the audition room expecting to improvise with a fellow unknown actor, or perhaps a casting director. But no. It's Larry David. And, boom, the scene begins. This make-or-break moment comes down to how fast you are on your feet, and how effective you are at provoking *Curb* Larry.

"At my audition, they gave me a little piece of paper, and I opened it up, and it said, 'You're Mocha Joe, the Coffee Guy on the lot. You did Larry a favor and he didn't tip you.' That's it. That's all you get, a piece of paper, like a little piece of origami," says Saverio Guerra, who joined *Curb* as the cantankerous Mocha Joe in season seven.

Guest stars with celebrity cachet such as Bruce Springsteen or Ben Stiller didn't have to audition. But luminaries *did* have to serve the story rather than their ego, and that's a big ask in Hollywood.

There was one standard piece of advice that everyone received when they entered the *Curb* universe: "Don't try to be funny. And above all else, don't tell jokes," says David. "That was the note that I gave more often than any other note. Just do what the scene requires. Act the way you would if this was really happening. If you do that, you'll be funny."

CLOCKWISE FROM TOP LEFT: Audition clips of Dana Lee (Mr. Takahashi), Jillian Bell (Maureen, Larry's assistant), Saverio Guerra (Mocha Joe), and Lisa Arch (Cassie, Cousin Andy's wife).

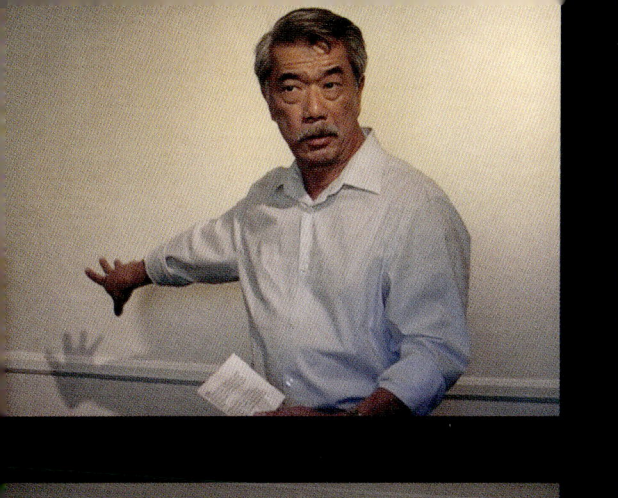

"You can always tell when people come in with a bag of jokes that they're going to lob into the scene," says writer, executive producer, and director Jeff Schaffer, who worked with David on *Seinfeld* before joining *Curb* in its fifth season. "They've seen some of the outline, and they're like, 'I'm gonna get this joke in!' But they don't know where the scene is going because none of us know where the scene is going. So they stick out. What they say feels like a joke joke. It doesn't feel like a conversation. One of the great things about the show is that you don't know what the other person is going to say, so you're actually getting a real, honest reaction. It's not like, 'Oh, I've done this seven times and I'm going to pretend to be angry or surprised.' It's about great, honest reactions because they don't fucking know what's going to come out of Larry's mouth."

Adds David, "Anything can happen, but the worst is somebody getting dramatic, trying to cry, or crying. That's verboten. I would stop them immediately and politely tell them, 'There's no crying on this show.'"

"My goal was always to make Larry laugh," says *Breaking Bad* star Bryan Cranston, who played a recurring role on *Seinfeld* as Elaine's dentist boyfriend before portraying Larry's condescending therapist, Dr. Templeton, in the ninth season of *Curb*. "From a performer's standpoint, you want to please the boss. You want your parent to be happy with your performance. And then Jeff [Schaffer], would go, 'OK, do that again, Bryan. And Larry, you *cannot* laugh. You have to get through this.' And Larry's like, 'I know! I know!' It harkened back to the admonishment that Larry used to give Jerry all the time on *Seinfeld*. 'Jerry. Stop laughing. Don't laugh! Come on. Do it again!' I told Larry, 'This reminds me of what you'd say to Jerry back then,' and he said, 'I know. I didn't realize how hard it was.'"

Bryan Cranston and Larry in "Running With the Bulls," S9, E4.

Actors had no written dialogue, but instead worked from structured outlines for each episode. **ABOVE, LEFT TO RIGHT:** "The Nanny," S3, E4, and "The Ski Lift," S5, E8. **OPPOSITE:** "Chet's Shirt," S3, E1.

"I find improv to be fun and relaxing," says Ted Danson, who, like so many others, played himself—only more so—on the show. *Curb*'s Ted was a congenial guy to whom everything came easy. Though Danson made the transformation into *Curb* Ted look effortless, he admits that bringing the role to life was harder than it appeared.

"The first couple of times I ad-libbed on the show, I thought I sucked," says Danson. "Then Larry, who's so fast on his feet, or Jeff or other people who were part of the early days would go, 'Don't do that. That took us down the wrong hallway. Go this direction.' So by about the fifth or sixth take, you've improvised a script, almost. There were still changes and surprises, but you knew where you were going. I stopped reading the outlines because I found that I was better if I didn't. You have to get out of yourself and pay attention to the other person who's talking. You don't do anything until the other person makes you do it. And I love that."

"We always joke that if *Curb* is improv, then what the fuck were we doing in that office for six months?" says Alec Berg, a former *Seinfeld* writer and director who wrote, executive produced, and directed *Curb* with Schaffer and Dave Mandel from seasons five through eight. "It's improv because there's no written dialogue, but the structures of the outlines are immaculate. You spend weeks and weeks building the outline, tweaking it, and making it rock-solid."

"You can't pull at one string without it pulling at everything," continues Berg. "If you do your job and you outline it correctly, then everything leads to everything leads to everything. And it has to end the way it does because that's the only way that these fibers are braided together. You prepare and prepare so that in the moment, you can just let go. All of the work that goes into figuring out what happens in the story arc is done. Now you can just be funny in the moment."

For *Curb* to work, actors had to lean in and improv their dialogue. That's why many of the show's guest stars were comics.

Leaning in to improv also meant that David didn't have to follow the rules of sitcom television or relive his days as a writer at *Saturday Night Live*. "Improvising prevented us from having the pressure of a writers' room—trying to come up with stuff at two in the morning, you know, eating cold pizza and all that," recalls Weide. "It was just an easier way to do the show. Larry also felt it would simply make it feel more like a documentary, just because of organic speech patterns that aren't written or rehearsed. People could talk over each other and it would be more realistic."

"The joke among the crew has always been that the only reason the show is improvised is because Larry never wanted to memorize lines," says producer Erin O'Malley. "I'm not sure if that's actually true. You'd have to ask Larry."

"I don't like memorizing lines and waiting for my turn to talk," confirms David. "But on this show, I have to listen and can talk whenever I want. I don't know what I'm going to say next. I'm making it up, as are the others. So there's a level of spontaneity that we could never achieve if we all had to memorize lines."

"That's why I think Larry hired a lot of comics, because we're pretty good at coming up with our own lines," says Susie Essman (Susie Greene). "There are actors who are extremely intimidated by not having a script, not having the lines written for them, but Larry would audition with them, and he would see who could handle it, or he'd hire known comedic actors, like Michael J. Fox. I don't think Michael ever did stand-up but his comedic timing, even with Parkinson's, is impeccable."

"It was intimidating for some of the guest stars on our show, because it was a different way of shooting and working," adds Cheryl Hines (Cheryl David). "Because it was improvised, and we were doing it all day, they would come in and do a scene, and then somebody would yell, 'Cut!' and then I'd have guest actors look at me and say, 'I don't know what we just did. Am I going to get fired because I didn't say anything interesting or funny?'"

49

"I don't like memorizing lines and waiting for my turn to talk. But on this show, I have to listen and can talk whenever I want. I don't know what I'm going to say next. I'm making it up, as are the others. So there's a level of spontaneity that we could never achieve if we all had to memorize lines." —**LARRY DAVID**

JB Smoove (Leon Black) said Larry had to take multiple laugh breaks while filming his audition. Here they are together in "You're Not Going to Get Me to Say Anything Bad About Mickey," S10, E4.

"I'd be like, 'No, you're not going to get fired,'" continues Hines. "'You did everything right.' Larry will tell you if he doesn't like something, and also, he's not the kind of person that will come up and fawn over you if you did a good job. He's not that guy who's going to run over and say, 'That was great!' He's just not. So I did have several people come up to me over the series and say, 'I think Larry doesn't like me.' And I'd say, 'Why?' They'd say, 'Well, he hasn't said anything to me during breaks or after the scene.' I said, 'Oh yeah. Then he likes you.'"

Jeff Garlin (Jeff Greene) says that if actors were intimidated by the process, he'd assure them, "The fear is OK. You can make a mistake. Mistakes can be funny. And if not, we'll just shoot it again."

Garlin, Hines, Essman, and others in *Curb*'s core cast had cut their teeth doing improv in comedy clubs from Los Angeles to New York. JB Smoove was no exception. He'd made a name for himself up and down the East Coast as one of the best extemporaneous stand-ups around before becoming a writer at *SNL*.

"When I started doing comedy, the first thing I did was take an improv class, and that propelled everything I've ever done since," says Smoove, who played Larry's forever houseguest, Leon Black. Leon moved into Larry's home in season six... and never left. "From stand-up to my ability to be on TV shows and in films, improv has made me able to go in these different directions and be in the moment. It's one of those things you put in your toolbox to have at your disposal, then you start to use it all the time. But never in a million years do you think it will take you to an improvised show like *Curb*."

"To this day, JB's comedy audition is the single greatest I've ever seen," says Berg. "JB comes in for his *Curb* audition. The scene starts. He's told, 'OK, you're sitting in a chair, you're watching TV. Larry's going to call you over.' So JB is just sitting in a chair and watching TV, but the way he's sitting, the expression on his face. I'm not exaggerating. I don't think Larry could breathe for ten minutes because he was laughing so hard. Every time he wanted to call JB over, he'd just start laughing. It was the funniest thing. Larry eventually pulled it together and called him over and said, 'There is a stain on the blanket.' 'What kind of stain?' asked JB. Larry said, 'Ejaculate.' And JB just went, 'Jackolite?' And it was over. Ten more minutes of laughing. The two of them together—it was just fucking gold."

"After my audition, my agent called and asked, 'How'd it go?'," recalls Smoove. "I said, 'Man, we had so many laughs. If anybody goes in there and gets that role, God bless him.' I mean, we had to take laugh breaks where Larry walked away and stood in the corner."

"Man, we had so many laughs."

—JB SMOOVE

Guest stars had to prove they could improvise, like Isla Fisher **(TOP)** and Jon Hamm and Kaitlin Olson **(BOTTOM)**.

"Anybody who auditioned had to prove they could improvise," says casting director Dorian Frankel, who worked on the show from seasons six through eight. "And a lot of people who wouldn't normally audition did audition for this. [Of course for some,] there were offers. Then there's someone like [former California senator] Barbara Boxer. The crew works with people who are playing themselves, but who aren't actors. They might be given more information than most about what happens on set."

"There was something to the audition process where, yes, there's ad-lib and you have to be able to play with Larry and do the scene, but we also wanted someone authentic," says director Dave Mandel. "We want a doctor who seems like a doctor. We want a cable guy that looks like a cable guy. Sometimes actors have a truth to them. And, sure, you can say, 'Well, anybody can be a cable guy.' But that's not always true. Larry was always very concerned with the truth of the character."

Since most Hollywood VIPs did not audition, how did David know if they'd be able to cut it on an improvisational set?

"I didn't," says David. "In terms of hiring a guest star who didn't audition, only once did I feel like it didn't work. But for the most part, everybody else worked out well. I never had major complaints. They knew how it worked. If they weren't game, they wouldn't have done it."

Hines wasn't a known quantity when, in 1998, she tried out for a spot in the *Curb* special. She'd heard about the new venture from the guy who cocreated *Seinfeld*, and she knew she wanted to be involved. "I went to audition, and the casting director told me that my character had heard it all before from Larry, she doesn't put up with his bullshit, so that's all I knew," says Hines. "But I also thought, 'They're married. She must love him. There must be things about him that she adores and likes.' So, for me, in that character, it was always important to still be able to find what Cheryl loved about Larry. He did make her laugh, and she knows that he's smart and funny. I'm glad I'm married to him, but I also know he drives people crazy, and my tolerance is pretty high for crazy, because I know what he's thinking and I know his intentions, so I can usually float above it. But other people really get stuck when, you know, Larry does something ridiculous."

SHOW 3

Waiter
You are a waiter who has previously waited on Larry David. The last time you served him he gave you a very low tip, while the person with whom he split the check gave you a very generous tip. Now you are serving him again, this time with a bit of attitude. He notices and inquires about the relative tip amounts from the previous meal. He may apologize but you will not let him off the hook.

Julia's Daughter
You are the daughter of a woman Larry knows. Larry thinks you went to a birthday party yesterday and asks you how it was. You tell him you didn't go to any birthday party yesterday. He may ask you if you are sure. You are sure, there was no birthday party yesterday.

SHOW 4

MAN IN SHORTS ON PLANE
You are on a plane from New York to L.A. Larry sits down next to you and notices you are wearing shorts, which irks him. You ask Larry what he was doing in New York. Larry is vague and evasive but you keep pressing him for details. When he finally relents and tells you, you are unimpressed.

FLIGHT ATTENDANT
You are first class flight attendant. At the beginning of the flight you offer Larry a hot towel. Larry burns his hand on the towel. You explain that you did say it was a "hot towel."

MARY JANE PORTER
You are an old girlfriend of Larry's. You two have reconnected over dinner and are now having desert back at your place. Although your cooking has been suspect in the past, you insist that Larry try your home-made dessert. Then the phone rings - you check the caller ID and see that it's your boyfriend. You shush Larry, telling him not to say anything while you answer the phone. Larry tries your dessert - which is terrible - and makes a loud retching sound that your boyfriend hears. You try to convince the boyfriend that it's no one, just the TV, but he's not buying it. You hang up and tell Larry he's coming over so Larry better get out of there fast.

MARY JANE'S BOYFRIEND
You're the jealous type and you suspect that Larry David has been spending time with your girlfriend, Mary Jane. You don't what Larry looks like, but you do know he left a bandage at her place. Coming out of a restaurant bathroom, you bump into a guy and notice his bandaged hand. You put two and two together and ask "Are you Larry David?" Larry starts to flee, you give chase.

Upon arriving at their audition, guest stars were provided with very few details about their character's situation. Here are some examples of character descriptions from season seven.

OPERA SINGER
You sing opera at a fancy Italian restaurant. You start to sing one of your numbers when Larry cuts you off. He doesn't let you sing, and you walk away, feelings hurt.

SHOW 8

Dennis
You and your actress wife Virginia are friends of Larry and Cheryl. Larry shows up at your office to accuse you of inviting Cheryl to participate in a menage a trois. You say Cheryl is single now and free to do what she wants. Larry gets furious as you intimate that Cheryl might have been interested. You also notice that Larry is wearing a pair of pants that are too long and still have the security tag on them. As you argue, Larry trips over his pants cuffs and spills coffee on you.

Lemonade Kid
You are selling lemonade from a stand in front your house. Larry buys some, but after tasting it, says the lemonade is terrible and undrinkable. You argue with him that it is fine. And when he walks away, you call him a bald asshole.

Clothing Store salesman
Larry was trying on a pair of pants at your store when the fire alarm went off. Everyone was forced to evacuate and Larry left wearing the pants he was trying.

Now Larry has returned to get his pants (he left them in the dressing room). But you look and cannot find them.

Incensed, Larry refuses to give back the store pants, which is he still wearing.

You point out that the pants still have the security tag on them. "You can't walk around with a security tag." But apparently, Larry can.

You point out that everyone will think that Larry has stolen the pants. Larry doesn't care.

Officer Krupke
You are an LAPD officer. A fire alarm has gone off at a department store and you are overseeing the evacuation. Larry approaches and mentions the Officer Krupke character from West Side Story. You've never heard of him. Larry even sings a few bars. It doesn't ring a bell. The more Larry explains, the less fascinated with this you are.

Larry wants to go back in the store, you tell him it could be at least an hour maybe more before anyone will be allowed back in.

According to casting director Frankel, actors like Hines who came up with specifics that fit the situation had a better chance of landing a spot in the show. "I remember there was an audition for the role of a lawyer who was meeting Larry for the first time," says Frankel. "One actor just sort of talked in general terms, 'Larry, I can help you out.' But another actor, the one who actually got the job, was very specific, 'Larry, there is a statute that says that this particular thing is illegal.' He threw in a lot of detail—the name of the firm, previous case names—which made it very believable. Actors who are able to play the scene realistically, really engage with him, and not invent a lot of crazy stuff, were the ones who got hired."

"In my audition scene, I had to tackle Larry and take him down to the floor," says Ellia English, who played Auntie Rae to siblings Loretta (Vivica A. Fox) and Leon Black. She and her family move in with the Davids when they are displaced by Hurricane Edna in season six. "My nerves were so raw. I was like, 'Oh God, can I do it? Is he going to be OK?' They told us what the scene would be about, but we would have to create the dialogue right on the spot. Once we started, the director said, 'Ellia, don't be afraid. You can go ahead and take him down.' And I was like, 'Are you sure?' 'Yes, go ahead and tackle him.' So I went for it and took him down to the floor. We did it in one take, and it was wonderful. After they said cut, I was like, 'Are you OK?!' Larry said, 'I'm fine. I'm fine.'"

Scenes from "Porno Gil," S1, E3 **(TOP)**, "The Divorce," S8, E1 **(MIDDLE)**, and "Beep Panic," S10, E9 **(BOTTOM)**.

In season six, the Black family moves into Larry and Cheryl's home after being displaced by the fictional Hurricane Edna.

Once English was hired and they were shooting the scene, she learned why her character was compelled to tackle Larry. Auntie Rae panics when she sees a man in a white sheet descending the staircase in the Davids' home. She doesn't know it's Larry pretending to be a ghost in order to scare Loretta's kids. Rae, who's from the South, instead mistakes the cloaked figure for a KKK member. In a moment of fight or flight, she chooses the former. "It finally made sense why I had to tackle Larry," says English. "Auntie Rae was triggered!"

David had the idea for this detailed scenario before he ever hired English, but transforming his plan into comedic gold came down to her performance. She nailed it.

"After a shoot, Larry would sometimes say that a scene was so much funnier than anything he could have written," says Weide. "There were fewer times when Larry would say, 'It probably would have been a little better if I wrote it.' My answer was always, 'Don't worry, we'll make it work in the editing room.'"

ABOVE: Ellia English's performances as Auntie Rae were comedic gold, seen here in "Atlanta," S12, E1.

OPPOSITE: Larry cracking up while filming a scene with Tracey Ullman in "What Have I Done?" S11, E8.

Richard Kind says he dislikes improvisation, but it didn't stop him from playing Cousin Andy in eight episodes, including "The Black Swan," S7, E7 **(TOP)**, and "The Special Section," S3, E6 **(BOTTOM)**.

"I want somebody else to write the line."
—RICHARD KIND

Even so, editor Steve Rasch recalls that David was always editing scenes in his head, even while he was performing. "Larry's great at recognizing areas that we need to mine and go after," says Rasch, who worked on *Curb* from its inception to its final season. "There'd be take after take. They might do it four times, but once Larry finds what he wants, he knows it. It's not an easy thing to pull off, especially since there was no script. But with Larry at the helm, we found gold in the work of these skilled improv actors. Once the shooting was done, it was then my job to put it all together."

Unlike the editors, the cast wasn't privy to what was being shot when they weren't on set or in the scene. That meant that their character had to fish for clues on camera to understand why Larry had, say, killed a swan with a golf club, invited a sex offender to dinner, or swiped shoes from a Holocaust museum.

"Because things weren't scripted, I often had to figure out what had happened in other scenes when I wasn't there," says Hines. "Like, we're shooting and Larry might turn to me and say, 'Don't look at that guy. I don't want him to see that I'm here.' And I'm like, 'Who? And why?!' He'd say something like, 'I ran into his car so I could get his phone number, but let's not talk about it.' 'What?! Why are you . . . ' 'I don't want to give Lewis my kidney. Listen, let's not talk about it.' I was always trying to catch up to see what happened in the rest of this world that he created."

With a cast and crew who were willing to take risks, David gave rise to a series that challenged the predictability of sitcom humor. "The reason why so many shows have tried improv, and it hasn't worked, is because they don't have Larry's story brain," says Essman. "You see how detailed the outlines are. How intricate everything is. It's all about the callback and weaving stories until everything comes together. It's a big puzzle. It's one of the reasons why I think Larry's such a genius, because I have a comedian's brain, and I would read the outlines, and I would have no idea how he got there. None whatsoever. That sort of genius is transcendent."

Respect for David's storytelling skills was a common thread among the actors who brought *Curb* to life, but not all of the show's performers were fans of improv. Enter Richard Kind, who portrayed Cousin Andy, David's stultifying relative who has no place sitting in the middle seat at a dinner party unless the goal is to bore guests to death. "I hate improvisation," says Kind. "I want somebody else to write the line. The writers are smarter than I am. I'm an actor."

Let me explain something to you, moron, okay?

THE BLACK SWAN: S7, E7

"Larry doesn't write a script, but thankfully, he does write a short story in prose form that's detailed enough so you know what's going on in the scene," says Kind, who admits he leaned heavily on David's outlines for guidance. "Larry describes where you are, what you did that day, what you're talking about, what happens during the scene. You read and then you act it out. And each season has an arc, and each scene adds to the arc of the show. I've done ninety-minute-long movies and the entire script is thirty pages, whereas Larry's outline for a twenty-minute show is seventeen pages. He's brilliant and detailed."

Lisa Arch played Cousin Andy's tactless spouse, Cassie, throughout the show's run. "It could be intimidating, stepping into that world," she says of working with so many talented improvisers. "Once I said something during a scene and as soon as it came out of my mouth, I knew it was wrong. I knew it wasn't funny. When we cut, Larry goes, 'Don't say that again.' But I already knew it didn't work. When I told some friends about it later, they were like, 'Oh, my God, that must have been so awful!' And I go, 'No, it was like your comedy hero telling you he trusted you.' Larry knew that I could handle it and that I would do something funnier next time. So in that way, it felt almost like an exclusive club, like I knew I wouldn't be there if he hadn't found me worthy. And that's all I needed to know. Later, in a scene, I made him laugh really hard, and we had to cut. That was literally the best feeling in the world."

Larry, Richard Kind (Cousin Andy), and Lisa Arch (Cassie) behind the scenes in "Elizabeth, Margaret, and Larry," S10, E8.

"I'M SHOOTING THE SHIT WITH THE GREATEST IMPROV IN THE

The second-best feeling? Being part of a verbal volley that produced whip-smart humor. "There's so much good stuff that it's hard to keep track of what makes it in," says Smoove. "I remember when Leon was fooling around with this dude's wife, and later, he's talking to Larry in a hardware store. I think Larry was there to buy an X-Acto knife. Leon said, 'Man, we fucked up.' Larry said, 'We did?' 'Yeah, Alton found out that I'm tapping his wife. He's gonna fuck somebody up.' Larry said, 'What do you mean *we* are in trouble? I'm not the one tapping, you're the one tapping.' Leon said, 'Oh, we in this together, you and me. We like LEGO. We joined together.' I loved that line."

"I love the scene I did with Larry and Jerry [Seinfeld] in season seven," says Guerra. "I asked Larry to do me a favor and go to get my coffee beans in the Valley, but he came back without the beans, because he said there was too much traffic. And I said, 'You didn't do anything. You didn't do the favor.' Larry said, 'I made the effort.' Jerry goes, 'Well, an effort is not a favor.' And I said, 'Thank you, Jerry.' And then Larry goes, 'I should get an E for effort. E for effort!' I turn around and scream, 'F for favor!' And Jerry goes, 'C for coffee!' That's one of my favorites."

"The vibe on set was more like being part of an extended family," says production designer David Saenz de Maturana. "It was often hard to hold the laughter in when cameras were rolling. There were so many times an improv scene would go off on a wild hilarious tangent and we'd all be laughing our asses off behind the monitors."

"...EATEST SERS WORLD."

—TRACEY ULLMAN

"I remember Larry and Richard Lewis were behind me, improvising away," says Tracey Ullman, the British improv queen who joined *Curb* in season eleven to play councilwoman Irma Kostroski, the most annoying woman in LA. "We were supposed to be in the audience at a Santa Monica political gathering. I was trying to listen to the speech of the politician while Richard and Larry were talking. Richard was not physically at his best. He'd had a lot of surgeries, but he was in great spirits. I remember Richard saying to Larry, 'You never come and see my shows. I'm doing shows in New York. And you don't bother to support me.' And Larry's saying, 'I don't want to go to New York to see you.' And Richard says, 'Well, I came to every *Seinfeld*.' And Larry's like, 'No, you did not!' Richard says, 'Well, you think you'd support me when I'm trying to get out there and do a career.' Then I heard a pause, and Larry said, 'When are you gonna die?'

"I couldn't believe the way they talked to each other. I turned around, and Richard's face, he was trying so hard not to laugh. Then he said something, like, 'You know what? When I'm about to die, I'm going to get a guy to come around and shoot you in the head, and then he's going to come around and shoot me in the head.' And then Larry couldn't stop laughing, and that's when I turned around and went, 'What is the matter with you? Why can't you be quiet? You mid-level celebrities think you're so good.' And then Richard said to me, 'Where did you get your outfit? Substitute Teachers R Us?' And I thought, 'I'm shooting the shit with the greatest improvisers in the world.'"

Richard Lewis and Larry shooting "Affirmative Action," S1, E9.

Outline vs. Scene

Because no take of *Curb* is ever the same, the show outlines often differ dramatically from how the final scene plays out. Following are some examples of the unpredictable magic of improvisation.

The Terrorist Attack

S3, E5: Larry David and Cheryl Hines

OUTLINE

INT. LARRY'S HOUSE — DAY

Larry still can't get over the bathroom ploy, how much the Braudys hate the Reisers, and how terrible he feels about ignoring Mindy. "I could've at least asked her about her perfume shop. She must think I'm the world's biggest schmuck." Cheryl's amused at how Stu always substitutes "freaking" for "fucking." Then the doorbell rings. It's Wanda. She needs to talk to them. It's serious. They take seats in the living room and Wanda tells them how her brother's best friend is in the CIA and has been told from the highest possible source that they should get out of Los Angeles because of some kind of terrorist attack this weekend. Her brother told her she could tell one friend—"so I told you." Wanda says she's going to Palm Springs. Cheryl says they can't go anywhere because of the Alanis Morissette benefit at the Braudys' for the NRDC. Larry, in a bit of a tizzy, tries to convince Cheryl to leave town, but there's no way.

SCENE

CHERYL: I just don't see how we can leave this weekend. I mean, this whole NRDC benefit was my idea. I talked the Braudys into having it at their house. Alanis Morissette is coming to sing. I mean, I just ... I just know I can't leave town.

LARRY: Well, maybe, uh ... you know, maybe I can ... I can go.

CHERYL: And where are you gonna go?

LARRY: I could go golfing at Pebble Beach, maybe?

CHERYL: Mm-hmm. Do you think that's a good idea? For us to be apart if something did happen?

LARRY: Then at least, you know, one of us would ... survive.

CHERYL: It just seems like if we're gonna go, we should go together.

LARRY: Not necessarily. Almost seems a little ... selfish that you would want both of us to ... perish.

CHERYL: So, you'd be fine going on without me?

LARRY: Well, it would be ... very difficult at first, sure. But hopefully I could at some point get back some semblance of a life.

CHERYL: OK ... if you feel good about ... one of us ... dying and the other one surviving, and you can live with that for the rest of your life, then you should go golf this weekend.

LARRY: I'll think about it.

CHERYL: Think about it.

The Ski Lift

S5, E8: Larry David and Susie Essman / Guest Stars Stuart Pankin and Iris Bahr

OUTLINE

INT. SKI LODGE — LIVING ROOM — DAY
On one couch sit Jeff and Cheryl; Heineman and Rachel, his 25-year-old daughter, on another; and the very Orthodox Larry and a kerchiefed Susie on another. Heineman is very curious about Larry and Susie's marriage. Susie tells him how she and Larry met, using every opportunity to mock and belittle him. Rachel, who embodies Orthodoxy, finds nothing about this group remotely entertaining. Larry finally broaches the kidney subject and innocently asks Heineman what he does. He tells Larry about the kidney consortium. Larry, of course, is "blown away" because his friend Richard Lewis is on the bottom of the list. "I'd give him my own kidney," Larry laments, "if we were only a match." And with that, Rachel, who's somewhat suspicious, says goodnight. Jeff and Cheryl quickly follow her lead. Larry doesn't like the idea of those two going off together, though he's helpless to stop it. Then Susie says, "Shall we turn in?"

SCENE

LARRY: She's a wonderful cook, isn't she? My Susie? Isn't she? Isn't she some cook?

HEINEMAN: How did you two meet?

LARRY: Interesting, interesting.

SUSIE: Uh, we met at a Hillel ... mixer, a function.

RACHEL: Oh, in college?

SUSIE: Yes, a singles and he was there trying to pick up every girl imaginable.

LARRY: I was pretty swinging in those days.

SUSIE: Yes.

LARRY: I was in the band, OK? The girls were pretty interested, you know? With the guitar, they liked that.

SUSIE: Not true, not true.

RACHEL: Like a rock band?

LARRY: Jewish folk music, Jewish folk songs.

SUSIE: Folk, folk.

RACHEL: Like what songs?

LARRY: Um, "Gefilte Fish Blues" ... um, "My Freaking Back Is Killing Me and It's Making It Hard to Kvell" ...

CHERYL: Uh, what was the name of your band?

LARRY: The Hipsters.

SUSIE: Yes, it was The Hipsters.

LARRY: Larry David and The Hipsters.

SUSIE: Yeah.

LARRY: And then, I left The Hipsters, and I just became Larry David.

SUSIE: Larry David.

LARRY: And The Hipsters went out on their own and they became quite successful.

SUSIE: Yes. But I was not attracted to him from the band. Honestly, I felt sorry for him.

HEINEMAN: Why?

SUSIE: That was the... Eh, rachmones. It was an attraction out of pity 'cause I'm always the one to take in stray animals, you know, that's ...

HEINEMAN: You remind me a little of my wife ... [speaks her name in Hebrew]

SUSIE: Oh, how lovely.

LARRY: I would like to meet her at some point.

HEINEMAN: Well, she's passed away a number of years ago.

RACHEL: Six years.

SUSIE: Six years? Difficult.

LARRY: Eh. Eh. Eh. So, anyway, enough about us. What do you do?

HEINEMAN: I'm the head of a foundation that finds kidneys for needy recipients.

RACHEL: Global.

LARRY: A very, very dear friend of mine actually needs a kidney and he's ...

HEINEMAN: Sorry.

LARRY: He's on the bottom of the list, Richard Lewis, perhaps you've heard of him?

HEINEMAN: Yes, I have.

SUSIE: Wonderful comedian.

HEINEMAN: Wears black all the time.

SUSIE: Yes.

LARRY: I would give him my own kidney, if only we were a match, but unfortunately ... that's alas, that is not the case.

HEINEMAN: That's God's will. [Speaks Hebrew]

LARRY: [Mimics Hebrew, poorly]

RACHEL: Excuse me?

LARRY: [Again mimics Hebrew, poorly]

Krazee-Eyez Killa

S3, E8: Larry David / Guest Star Chris Williams

OUTLINE

EXT. THE WATKINS' HOUSE — DAY

We open on a racially mixed party. Cheryl is talking to Wanda and her boyfriend, Krazee-Eyez Killa. They have some interaction with an older Black couple, who are Wanda's parents. During all of this, we keep hearing a popping noise that sounds like a cap gun going off. We then pan to Larry and find him stomping on packing bubbles. Cheryl approaches Larry and tells him to cease and desist. He then winds up next to Wanda's father and, desperate for conversation, mentions how he once dated a Black woman and was quite surprised by some of the negative comments he heard when they went out, but he wasn't fazed by it at all. Then Mr. Watkins excuses himself and Larry starts chatting with Krazee-Eyez Killa. Larry asks where he lives, and after going into some detail about its location, Krazee-Eyez Killa abruptly changes the subject and asks Larry if he likes to eat pussy. Larry, a tad thrown by the question, tells Krazee-Eyez Killa that he used to, but now he's too lazy. "It's a lot of work and it hurts my neck. It's a whole to-do." Krazee-Eyez Killa, taking Larry into his confidence, says that he loves Asian pussy. Larry, a little shocked, says, "You mean you used to." Krazee-Eyez Killa says, "Still . . . No way I can give that up." Now Cheryl approaches. Larry tells her that he has to go to Jeff's new house to pick up a script. Cheryl thought Jeff was in a hotel because of the dog, but Larry explains that he's getting allergy shots now and they're helping.

SCENE

KRAZEE-EYEZ KILLA: What's crackin', player?

LARRY: How are ya?

KRAZEE-EYEZ KILLA: I'm all right, yeah, yeah, yeah. I'm chilling, what's up?

LARRY: Chilling. Just chilling.

KRAZEE-EYEZ KILLA: Hey, you a writer, right?

LARRY: Yeah.

KRAZEE-EYEZ KILLA: Wrote some shit this morning. Wrote some shit . . . You know I write my own lyrics and shit, you know what I mean?

LARRY: Yeah, yeah.

KRAZEE-EYEZ KILLA: You want to help me out with it?

LARRY: I've never written rap stuff . . .

KRAZEE-EYEZ KILLA: That's all right. I want to see what you got.

LARRY: OK, go ahead.

KRAZEE-EYEZ KILLA: Check this shit out. It's called "I'm Coming to Get You."

LARRY: "I'm Coming to Get Ya," OK.

KRAZEE-EYEZ KILLA: "So you think you're gonna cross me and mess with my shit, opening your fucking trap and flapping your lip? Don't fuck with me, nigga, or you're gonna get dropped, I'll snap off your neck with a crackle and pop."

LARRY: Oh, I like the Rice Krispies thing, yeah.

KRAZEE-EYEZ KILLA: You got that shit? Yeah, yeah, yeah.

LARRY: "Crackle and pop," of course.

KRAZEE-EYEZ KILLA: Yeah, yeah, yeah. "If you say anything, you'll beg me to die, 'cause I'll make you suck my dick, then I'll nut in your eye. I'll stomp on your world as if my name was Godzilla, I'm coming for you, motherfucker, I'm your Krazee-Eyez Killa." You know? And I'm going to be like this in the video, like . . . you know what I mean?

LARRY: I like it. I got one tiny little comment.

KRAZEE-EYEZ KILLA: What, what, what?

LARRY: I would lose the "motherfucker" at the end, 'cause you already said "fuck" once, you don't need two fucks. You already got the one fuck. I would change the "motherfucker" to "bitch." Because the bitch . . .

KRAZEE-EYEZ KILLA: "I'm coming for you, bitch . . ."

SCENE

LARRY: Yes, because "bitch" is a word that you would use to somebody who you disrespect, right? Isn't that so?

KRAZEE-EYEZ KILLA: You my dawg. You my nigga.

LARRY: I am your nigga. Absolutely.

KRAZEE-EYEZ KILLA: Yeah, that's right. I like that shit. Yeah, I like you. I like you, motherfucker.

LARRY: OK.

KRAZEE-EYEZ KILLA: Yeah, yeah, check it out. You like eating pussy?

LARRY: You know, it's ... I'm a little ... I like it, I like it, but I'm a little too lazy to do it. It's a whole to-do, you know? It hurts my neck.

KRAZEE-EYEZ KILLA: Lazy?

LARRY: Yeah, I'm too lazy.

KRAZEE-EYEZ KILLA: You're too lazy to eat pussy?

LARRY: Yeah, it hurts my neck. I get too lazy to do that.

KRAZEE-EYEZ KILLA: Oh, man, you got to eat the pussy, the cooch. Oh shit, yeah. You know what the best pussy is to eat? Asian pussy.

LARRY: Krazee-Eyez Killa, you're getting married. Wanda's, you know, you can't do that anymore.

KRAZEE-EYEZ KILLA: No, no, I have to do that, motherfucker. You know what I'm saying? I have to eat the pussy.

LARRY: Really?

KRAZEE-EYEZ KILLA: No, I can't live without that shit.

LARRY: You have to eat the pussy?

KRAZEE-EYEZ KILLA: Have to have different flavors of pussy. You got some Thai shit.

LARRY: You got Wanda now. You can't do it. Wanda's ...

KRAZEE-EYEZ KILLA: Wanda ain't gonna find out shit. This is between ... You my nigga, right? This is between me and you.

LARRY: Well, yes, I'm your nigger.

KRAZEE-EYEZ KILLA: So how is she gonna find out? She ain't gonna find out, is she?

LARRY: Not from me. Absolutely not.

KRAZEE-EYEZ KILLA: Yeah that's right. She ain't gonna find out.

LARRY: She's not gonna find out.

KRAZEE-EYEZ KILLA: Right, right, right, right.

LARRY: All right, Krazee-Eyez Killa, I got to take off. I got to pick up a script at my friend's house. Nice chatting.

KRAZEE-EYEZ KILLA: All right, nice to see you. Give me some. Yeah, yeah.

The Table Read

S7, E9: Larry David and Bob Einstein / Guest Star Jerry Seinfeld

OUTLINE

INT. SEINFELD SOUNDSTAGE — DAY

Actors milling before the read-through. Larry is chatting with Julia, who asks how things are going with Cheryl. "Strictly professional," Larry says. "She was hired because she was the best one for the role." Stacy, the producer, walks by and introduces her nine-year-old daughter, Emma. After some small talk, Stacy says she has to take Emma to the doctor because "she has a rash on her pussy." Before Larry has a chance to pursue that, Jason asks to borrow a pen for the read-through—he likes to take notes—so Larry loans him his pen. Then it's on to Michael, who's in a state because he just found out he might have Groat's Disease. Larry tries to calm him down, says he knows someone—an accountant, Danny Duberstein—who had it and is fine. If Michael would like, Larry will have Duberstein call him. Michael's appreciative, would love to talk to him. Larry's on it. Then Larry sees Funkhouser, of all people, walk in. Funkhouser gives him a big greeting. Larry wants to know what he's doing there. He came to support Larry, but Larry's not buying it—tells Funkhouser it's off-limits if you don't work on the show. Funkhouser says to ask Jerry if it's OK, which Larry does, and to his dismay, Jerry's fine with it. Funkhouser then introduces himself to Jerry and tells him a filthy joke, which Jerry loves. The 1st AD yells that it's time to start, and as they walk to the table, Jerry says to Larry, regarding Funkhouser, "I like that guy." Then Cheryl takes Larry aside, tells him she's nervous. "You're going to be great."

SCENE

MARTY: Jerry, Marty Funkhouser.

JERRY: Hey, Marty. How you doing?

MARTY: How you doing?

JERRY: Good.

MARTY: Want to hear a joke?

JERRY: No, not really.

LARRY: He doesn't want to hear a joke. We have a read-through.

MARTY: Yeah ... let me just get right through it.

JERRY: OK.

MARTY: A woman is very afraid of the size of her opening.

JERRY: What is she afraid of?

MARTY: The size of her opening. So she goes to her mother. She says, "What am I going to do? I'm so big down there. When I marry Harry, he's going to divorce me." Her mother says, "Don't worry, sweetheart, it runs in the family. Do what I did when I married your father. Go to the market, get some raw liver, put it in there. He'll never know the difference."

JERRY: Oh my God.

MARTY: So she does. They have eight hours of sex after their marriage. She wakes up at 10:00. He's gone, but there's a note on her pillow. It says, "My darling Harriet, to think that I waited a year to consummate our love relationship makes my heart beat so loudly I'm surprised it didn't wake you up. The only reason I'm not here now, darling, is I'm at work to make enough money to buy you a house, a picket fence. We'll have dogs and children."

JERRY: This is not so bad.

LARRY: Oh yeah, this is great. Will you finish the fucking joke already?

MARTY: "When the 5:00 dinner bell rings, I will be home like the winged gossamer of love in your arms. Your loving husband, Harry."

JERRY: Aw, that's nice.

MARTY: "P.S., your cunt is in the sink."

JERRY: [Laughs]

LARRY: OK. You told your joke. Let's go.

MARTY: How good is that?

JERRY: It surprised me.

MARTY: It's great.

JERRY: I had no idea it would be that revolting.

1ST AD: Ladies and gentlemen, please hold the work. Let's take our places for the table read.

MARTY: OK, let's sit at the table.

LARRY: Go sit in the bleachers.

MARTY: Great meeting you.

JERRY: Yeah, nice meeting you too.

MARTY: Big fan.

JERRY: Thank you, thank you. I like that guy. He's crazy.

Vertical Drop, Horizontal Tug

S12, E3: Richard Lewis, Larry David, Jeff Garlin and JB Smoove / Guest Star Vince Vaughn

OUTLINE

INT. GOLF CLUB — RESTAURANT — DAY

Larry sits with Jeff, Lewis, Leon, and Freddy. Everyone is swapping stories about that repulsive, bulbous misfit the scrotum. People notice Larry's flashy argyle socks. They were a gift from Irma, who—as she's proven—is a terrible gift giver. This leads to more puppy talk, but then Larry gets a text from Sienna Miller, inviting him to join her at a charity function. "Are you kidding?!" Larry grumbles, "I can't do it. Irma! This is the first time in my life women are seemingly interested in me and my hands are tied. Fuck!" Then Freddy gets a text. His friend's wife, whom he's trying to impregnate, is ovulating, but alas, Freddy will be out of town and needs someone to fill in for him. Freddy produces a picture of her and Lewis immediately volunteers. Larry mocks, "You're an old man! You have three sperm left!" Jeff is also game, as is Leon. Larry is curious and throws his hat into the ring too. Freddy takes pictures of Jeff, Lewis, Larry, and Leon, then texts them to the woman. She responds very quickly—Leon gets the nod. They discuss that decision, then Takahashi comes over and warns Larry, "You fight with Jimmy; you no say 'fore.'" Larry tells Takahashi that Troy is deaf. "I waved." "Wave mean nothing. You could be saying hello. One more mistake, there will be consequences."

SCENE

FREDDY: That reminds me. Remember that girl Lydia, the neighbor that I'm helping out? She is ovulating.

RICHARD: Lucky you.

FREDDY: The bad news, though, is I have to go up to Shasta. I got a mattress emergency, so I'm not gonna be able to be in town. But, uh, she's asking if I know anybody. Any of you guys willing to, uh, step in and help my neighbor out, being there for her for her pregnancy needs?

JEFF: What?

LARRY: Seriously?

RICHARD: You're kidding.

LEON: We're on the bench and you sending in a reliever?

FREDDY: Yes. You guys wanna see her? Here she is.

LARRY: Sure. Beautiful.

FREDDY: Yeah?

LEON: Let me see that. Yeah, I'll hit that.

RICHARD: She's fabulous. And I'm in.

LARRY: You're in? I mean, what do you got, three sperm? You could have intercourse with her for the next fifteen years, there's no way you're ever gonna impregnate her.

RICHARD: I'll bet you a thousand dollars I have more sperm than you.

LARRY: You got more sperm than me? In your dreams.

RICHARD: And I will bury you with my sperm.

LEON: The only problem is you can't get someone pregnant on old-ass sperm and shit when it's in powdered milk form. [Laughs]

RICHARD: All right. I'm out, Leon.

LEON: I'll tap that.

FREDDY: Leon's in. Let me get a video here. Hold on. I'm gonna send her this. Make it simple and make it quick. Here we go. Ready? All right.

LEON: I'm Leon Black. You know what it is. I'm looking forward to tapping that ass. Hope you ready. And if you happen to get pregnant, that's a bonus. How about that? Hmm? Yeah, that's what's gonna happen.

FREDDY: All right, there you go. Let's see what she says.

LEON: So just deliver about three or four mattresses, put 'em in front of the house. That way when I wear one out, I'll bring a new mattress, put that shit down too.

FREDDY: Yeah, you gotta have a lot of runway to land the plane. I understand.

LEON: Fuck yeah.

FREDDY: OK, she got back to me. Boy, that was quick.

LARRY: Oh, boy.

FREDDY: And she said yes to Mr. Leon Black.

LARRY: Oh! My God.

LEON: Oh! Fuck yeah.

JEFF: Congratulations.

LARRY: Congratulations.

Ken/Kendra

S12, E9: Susie Essman and Larry David / Guest Stars Bruce Springsteen and Ian Harvie

OUTLINE

INT. JEFF & SUSIE'S HOUSE — KITCHEN — LATER (D2)

Ken, Bruce's manager, reintroduces himself to Larry. "So Larry, it's been a while." Huh? Larry doesn't recognize him. Ken reveals he used to be Kendra. She was at Universal Music a long time ago, when Larry was at *Seinfeld*, and they hooked up back then. Springsteen has clearly already heard about this, but it's all new to Larry and a lot to absorb. As Larry takes this in, there is a little bit of drinking glass confusion between Larry and Bruce over whose drink is whose. Both had set theirs down. Larry is sure he knows. "I follow my glass like a game of beverage three-card monte." Meanwhile, Ken is reminiscing. "We used to have sex on the floor. Remember, Larry?" Larry mumbles, "Yeah, we had sex on the floor." "The hard floor?" Larry says there was a rug. "Why did we always have sex on the floor?" Larry says, "I like having sex on the floor." Ken doesn't believe it. "I think you wanted to have sex on the floor because afterwards you knew it would be too uncomfortable to talk and cuddle."

SCENE

KEN: Larry, good to see you again.

LARRY: Again?

KEN: I'm sorry. I do this all the time. I forget that I haven't told people. It's been like 20, 25 years. I used to work at Universal when you were at *Seinfeld*, and, uh, I used to be Kendra. And now, I'm Ken. Remember Kendra?

LARRY: Mor ... Mor ... Kendra Morris?

KEN: Kendra Morris. Yeah.

LARRY: Hey. Oh. Wow.

KEN: I don't know if you guys know this, but Larry and I used to hook up.

LARRY: Eh.

KEN: Let's just say it. Let's just say it, it's no big deal.

LARRY: Sure, yeah. Yeah, yeah. When you were Kendra. Yeah.

KEN: We had some great times.

LARRY: Yeah. Yeah. Good times. Good times.

BRUCE: It's crazy you guys haven't seen each other in so long.

LARRY: Wait a second. Wait a second. That ... That's my water.

BRUCE: I don't think so.

LARRY: I'm 100 percent positive that's mine. You know, I follow my water like it's a three-card monte game.

BRUCE: I put my water down where I can comfortably reach it.

LARRY: Yeah, yeah, yeah. But as you can see, this is—It's within my hash marks.

BRUCE: It's in your hash marks?

LARRY: It's within my hash marks.

BRUCE: All right, got it. This one's fine.

LARRY: Yeah. That's ...

KEN: It's so good to see you, Larry. It is crazy how long it's been since we've seen each other.

LARRY: Yeah.

KEN: You look great.

LARRY: Oh, that's so nice.

KEN: Still a sexy beast.

LARRY: [Laughs]

KEN: Look at you. Look at you. Doesn't he look great, you guys?

LARRY: Yeah. You—You've changed, uh, quite a lot.

KEN: Yeah. Yeah.

LARRY: Yeah.

KEN: Some people say that I'm as hot as a man as I was a woman.

LARRY: Uh.

KEN: So ...

LARRY: Eh ...

KEN: This guy. We had this little thing. I don't know what it was. Larry would come over to my place—

LARRY: You know, nobody's really interested in reminiscing and going over this stuff. It's boring, really. You know.

KEN: It's not boring.

SUSIE: I am. I'm interested.

BRUCE: [Chuckles] I wanna hear a little more about this.

KEN: Do you remember this? You'd come over, and every time we were intimate, we would have sex on the floor.

SUSIE: On the floor?

KEN: Yeah.

BRUCE: I'll tell you one thing. [Splutters] Sorry. I didn't make you out for a floor fucker. [Chuckles]

The Anonymous Donor

S6, E2: JB Smoove and Larry David

OUTLINE

INT. LARRY'S HOUSE — KITCHEN — MORNING

They're eating breakfast. Leon is not only reading Larry's paper, he's also gotten food stains on it. Larry begins to question Leon as to why he's here. "I'm visiting my sister." "How long are you planning on staying?" "As long as my sister will have me." Then Larry makes a few attempts to engage the kids, which all fall flat, and we can even hear Auntie Rae mumble, "Oh, brother." Now Cheryl enters, takes Larry aside, and tells him that she found a "stain" on a blanket in Leon's room. Larry is appalled. "I can't have some guy staying here, masturbating all over the house." He tells Cheryl he wants to have a word with him. Over Cheryl's objections, Larry signals Leon. He gets up, and Cheryl, wanting no part of this discussion, walks out. Then Larry questions Leon about the blanket, and he emphatically denies it. Not his thing. Loretta's curiosity is piqued and she asks what's going on. Not wanting to be left out, Auntie Rae joins them. When Larry tells them about the stain, Auntie Rae starts gagging. Both women, however, feel that perhaps Larry is merely trying to deflect the blame and that he's really the masturbator. Larry says he's going to take the blanket to the dry cleaner.

SCENE

LARRY: Leon, can I talk to you for a second?

LEON: Excuse me, ladies. I shall return.

CHERYL: Oh my God. I gotta get something over to …

LEON: All right. Man, I'm about to bust.

LARRY: Enjoyed your breakfast?

LEON: Larry, you know how to bring it.

LARRY: That's nice.

LEON: I'm about to blow up.

LARRY: I just spoke to my wife.

LEON: OK.

LARRY: And she said she was putting some flowers in your room. And she found a stain … on your blanket.

LEON: Stain on my blanket, huh? What, like juice, syrup, maybe syrup or something like that?

LARRY: Uh-uh, no.

LEON: Gravies maybe, something in the gravy category?

LARRY: Uh-uh, no.

LEON: What kind of stain was it? Hmm?

LARRY: Ejaculate.

LEON: E-what?

LARRY: Ejaculate.

LEON: Ajackalit.

LARRY: Not ajackalit. Ejaculate.

LEON: Ejaculate?

LARRY: Cum stain. Cum.

LEON: Cum stain. What kind of cum was it, first of all?

LARRY: What do you mean, what kind of cum? Cum's cum.

LEON: Cum is not cum, Larry.

LARRY: Cum's cum.

LEON: It couldn't have been mine. Know why? 'cause I gets mine, Larry. I brings the ruckus to the ladies.

LARRY: OK, so you're denying this. Is that it?

LEON: First of all, look around this place, man. Are there any visuals around here to jack off to? All we have is basic cable, right? What am I doing, jacking off to *Andy Griffith*? Jacking off to Clara, huh?

LARRY: You mean Aunt Bee?

LEON: Aunt Bee, Clara, whoever.

LARRY: Who's Clara?

LEON: Who's the lady who answer the phone?

LARRY: I don't know.

LEON: Is that her name, Clara?

LARRY: I don't know Clara. I know Aunt Bee.

LEON: Nobody wanna jack off to no damn Aunt Bee.

LARRY: I don't remember any beauties on that show, frankly.

LEON: It's not my cum, Larry. OK?

LARRY: OK.

HOW DID THEY DO IT?

roll	scene		take
194	10-18B		1

b

CYE12
curb your enthusiasm

director: jeff schaffer
camera: patrick stewart

Larry David's

character, Larry David, wasn't trying to be funny when he stumbled each week into hilariously tragic situations as if they were unavoidable potholes. He was simply a natural at saying the wrong thing at the wrong time, and even better at screwing up the chance to apologize.

But a great comedy like *Curb* doesn't just wander into ludicrous situations. It takes hard work to create the illusion of effortless humor, which is exactly what the HBO series did over 12 seasons, 120 episodes, and 24 years.

TV Larry's debacles took meticulous planning and skilled execution by the real Larry David, along with a dedicated crew that included writers, producers, editors, and talent. *Curb*'s team brought Susie's rants, Jeff's lies, Cheryl's suffering, and Leon's bad advice to life, scene by scene, set by set, edit by edit.

Each new chapter of *Curb* presented unique challenges, but for the sake of brevity and humanity's shrinking attention span, we'll focus on just one season: 2009's *Seinfeld* reunion story arc, aka season seven. David went to great lengths to reunite the NBC sitcom's original cast and crew, and resurrect the original set on the original soundstage so that the "show within the show" appeared absolutely authentic. But let's not get ahead of ourselves. Here's how the season came to be, from Larry's first scribblings to the show's final edits.

Dawn of a New Season

A collection of Larry David's notebooks, full of plot ideas he has jotted down over the years.

JEFF SCHAFFER, WRITER, DIRECTOR, AND EXECUTIVE PRODUCER (SEASONS 5-12): "A new season usually starts at the end of the season before it, when Larry says '*Curb* is finished! There will never be more *Curb*. *Curb* is done. Dead. Stick a fork in it.' A few months later, he calls and says, 'I'm not doing another season.' We go, 'OK.' Then he says, 'I only have one idea.' 'Do you want to talk about it?' we ask. 'No,' he says, 'it's a waste of time.' Then . . . we'll talk about it. We'll end up working on something that Larry is convinced will never, ever see the light of day. We figure out a season arc, and that's when it's clear that a new season is actually happening."

"Well, it's clear to me. Larry still refuses to think we're actually making the show. It's not until we have seven or eight shows written I tell Larry, 'Hey, we need to call HBO and tell them we are doing another season so we can crew up.'"

LARRY DAVID: "I have these notebooks with ideas, and Jeff [Schaffer] has his own notebooks. We pick through them like the *Mission: Impossible* team for ideas. We're looking to combine stories and ideas that seemingly have nothing to do with each other. The main thing is the premise and the story have to be funny. They have to be ideas that make us laugh, like pee splashing on Jesus in the bathroom and it looks like he's crying. It has to be something that tickles us."

"They have to be ideas that make us laugh."

—LARRY DAVID

SCHAFFER: "Larry is fearless about jumping in and starting, even when we don't know where we're going to end up. He'll say, 'Let's put these things together and see what happens.' And I'll be like, 'Well, where's it going to go?' And he's like, 'I don't know, that's what we're going to find out.' He's great at starting, and I'm always thinking about finishing. We somehow meet in the middle."

DAVID: "From start to finish, it takes around eighteen months to make a season; six months of writing, six months of shooting, and six months of editing."

SCHAFFER: "Each *Curb* episode is actually written three times. The first time is the outline. We throw it up on a dry-erase board (just like we wrote *Seinfeld*) and do comedy geometry until the stories all intersect in a pleasing way that pays off at the end. (That's the toughest part. As a measure of how difficult this part is: In November of 2020 we shot in the middle of the pandemic when there were no vaccines yet, all on location with an older cast. Why? Because we had already written it. Larry was like, we wrote it; we're doing it. And I'll deal with the consequences.) The second time the show is written is on set where these incredible improv actors make magic happen, and every scene is a live rewrite generating lots of funny options. And then the show is written for the third and final time in the edit where we choose which takes and jokes to use."

- get H/biped at a memorial service
- Separate blankets
- Show bad etiquette to sufferer. I'm a patient & give him word
- Traffic accident – get finger – give story wrong ending
- Mispronounce Oregon
- A/p home stain on my coat but I'm late
- Call me when you land
- Grunting during tennis
- I'm a guest in someone's house – the post comes in in the morn. I'm reading the paper. Ask if he wants it. He says yes.

- Annoucing childcare tale; "And she just finished chemotherapy"
- In childcare store I'm shopp/2 women cry/ethnic I'm eavesdrop/ yell at me
- Everyone told to join hands
- People lingering over coffee in restaurant, know you're waiting
- Tom Ash/not invited to Carol King. He hits her on road she has to wear neck brace
- Tch/too many napkins from Chelmark store
- Korean grocer throws you out

Pages from Larry's notebooks, showing rough ideas that he jotted down for possible use in episodes. Many of these eventually made it into the show.

- person ordering they know they're not paying

(OR CATCH TED SIDE-SITTING)

- Abusing free samples
- handy man check out photos
- pick up brother wear shorts in Marie Chef
- being chased in volleyball
- Spell asshole in front of 4 yr old kid tell his parents

Blind man bumps into me "Sorry miss, you smell like a woman"

- Drowning like Cat Stevens - make pact w/ God - then go back

- one conversation split / couple
- wobbly table
- cotton in ear listening to performer still in when they came out
- Man holds funeral for himself
(w/ piñata) Don't stand for anthem cause of bad back
- money remotes
- Dental Hygienist talks gossips about a moth
- Couple invited - I can't go but C wanted to go alone.

1) INT. HULU
- Jewey exec. — "I didn't
- Casting: want to love
  see tape on girl   it"
- Door slam

2) INT. HALLWAY
- What are we   who slammed?
  going to do?
  Acting coach!
  Cheryl.
- Explain door slam → Hooks!

3) Cheryl's — Ask to coach
            M/S - Door Slam

4) INT. RESTAURANT
- Marcos gives notes
- Stealing "Really" "Didn't
- Mention acting coach love
  "Cheryl?"   it."
            - See hot
              dog contest
              in paper
              on table

5) INT. Jeff's Ho[use]
- Discuss Lewis ne[w]
  girl. "Hot dog!"
- Vince buys hote[l]
  LD + Jeff volunteer to s[tock]
  for mini-bar - on[ly]
- Cheryl arrives. L[D]
  asks why she's ma[d]
- "Dinner is serve[d]"
  Andy + Cassie take
  middle.

6) Dissolve:
- LD ate too la[te]
  Not eating. Sus[ie]
  pissed
- Boring chit cha[t]
- LD tells Susie his —
- LD makes a sw[itch]
- Discuss call
  "Guess who I [am]

Each *Curb* episode is thrown up on a dry-erase board to figure out the "comedy geometry," as seen here for "The Mini Bar," S11, E3 **(LEFT)**, and "Thank You for Your Service," S9, E5 **(RIGHT)**.

8) INT. BAR
 "Spoke to chef.
 You undersold face"
 -CD + WAITER ARGUE
 ABOUT FACE

9) INT. TAKA'S OFFICE
 -ASIAN REMARK INSULT. IT WAS a compliment.
 -TAK MAKES FACE "INSCRUTABLE"
 -Is that racist? → will send letter
 PROBATION!

Jeff says disappointed Victor. "Looked up to" time w/ you. (not w/ Jeff)
Hi wants -REENACTMENT!

10) INT. MOVIE
 -DATE w/ MAILMAN DISCUSS "INSCRUTABLE" at POPCORN COUNTER

11) INT. MOVIE
 -LOOK FOR MAILMAN "You didn't beckon."

12) EXT. MAILMAN'S
 -RESET
 -FACE

---

13) INT. ...
 -NO MA...
 -CALL ...

be on possess no mic

14) EXT. Se...
 -CAN'T GE...

15) EXT. K...
 ME...
 -BONDI W...
 -SHOT AT...
 EUGENE
 -RUN AW...
 SPOT TAK

16) EXT. P...
 -CONFRO...
 HASH!

17) INT. C...
 ..."WA...
 some G...
 CLOTHES

18) EXT. GA...
 VICTOR P...

Scenes from the season seven *Curb* finale, "Seinfeld," which Larry felt was the perfect way to do a reunion episode without really doing it.

The Outline

David is renowned for creating airtight outlines that form the scaffolding around each scene, episode, and season. The beams of this sturdy plot structure support the freewheeling improv performances that take place within, allowing for a final seamless narrative where all the disparate subplots converge.

DAVID: "We're always looking for a great story arc, and they're not that easy to come up with. They're more in the vein of a movie premise. That's how the *Seinfeld* reunion came about. We knew it was something we could have fun with . . . and we had no other ideas at the time."

SCHAFFER: "We knew we weren't going to do the *Seinfeld* reunion that NBC wanted. [We wouldn't do] corny. We were going to do a *Curb*-style *Seinfeld* reunion, which meant *Curb* Larry was going to get the cast back together and do a reunion for his own selfish reasons. He wanted to get back with Cheryl. His whole agenda was self-serving. All those things that people wanted in a *Seinfeld* reunion, like, 'Oh, I can't wait for Jerry and Elaine to get together and the show is going to end with a wedding!' We gave it to them, but off-camera, because the two split up before the reunion."

DAVID: "We decided that she'd already had a kid with Jerry."

SCHAFFER: "The choice was to deprive people of exactly what they wanted. It was a very *Curb* choice."

The season seven finale, "Seinfeld," presented unique challenges, even for a comedy as unique as *Curb*.

SCHAFFER: "There was an added level of complexity because it was a *Curb* episode, but it was also part of a supposed *Seinfeld* special. And knowing that *Curb* Larry is only doing the reunion to get Cheryl back, it became logical that he's going to lose Cheryl to Jason. So once we knew that's where we were going to end the season, we had to aim everything toward that conclusion. He was going to almost lose her, then get her back, then lose her for good when he sees the ring stain on Julia [Louis-Dreyfus]'s wood table." (Context: Larry attends a party at Julia's house where he is blamed for leaving a ring stain on her wood table. His defense is that someone else did it because he "respects wood"; he spends the rest of the episode interrogating everyone he encounters: "Do you respect wood?")

Show 10

(1) We watch the tail end of a scene with Cheryl and Jason. (Perhaps the one where fire alarm 4 where LD wondered if he'd have to be with Cheryl for eternity) When the scene ends LD gives some notes. Soon Jason leaves and LD continues conversing with Cheryl, imparting to her all the knowledge and experience the great man has acquired come by to there many years. And to his delight, she's soaking it all up. Yes, it's all working out quite nicely.

EXT. PARKING LOT
Scene 2 - LD walks Cheryl to her car. Some general chit chat, then LD tells her he would love to work with that if she'd like, he would be happy to get together with her later & work on the scene. Cheryl loves the idea, says they could meet after the party for Jason's new book at Julia Hour's house. They discuss the book, which supposedly is about acting for theatre, film, and television. LD notices Jason's car which is nearby and has tinted windows. Wonders why anyone would need that. Seems a little pretentious. It's not like he's George Clooney. Cheryl disagrees. She offers up skin-protection as a reason

might even got them herself. They say goodbye and → go to (A)

(3) EXT. JULIA'S HOUSE —
Jeff & LD are walking outside JLD's house. LD brings Jeff up to date on developments. "The plan is working! They're getting closer every day. He's going over to while on take the beach with her after the party. Should he make a move?" Jeff strongly suggests that LD not make said move. Wants him to wait till the show is done. And there's only a few days to go. "Don't blow this now." Jeff — a deal maker — "It's a single move now, not a married move. Single moves hard at marriage"

Then Mocha Joe, the Coffee passes, wheeling his

coffee cart. LD he says hello, and mentions that he's heading toward the office. LD asks "look if he could you do me a favor." LD asks, "and bring some jumper cables to the office." Mocha Joe says OK, but though he looked something & doesn't seem entirely happy as he walks away.
→ go to 3
#3

Scene 4 - INT. PARTY
LD examines the book. And LD suggests that it's not a book as much as — if not really a book. It's a pamphlet.

- They go back and forth on that, then Terry mentions that he heard Mocha Joe was upset that LD didn't tip him earlier that day. LD explains that it wasn't a tip situation. That he simply asked Mocha Joe to do him a favor. Terry says there's
- no such thing as favors anymore. Even friends tip. Well maybe not friends, but acquaintances. LD and Terry walk away and a moment later Julia approaches LD and informs him that he
- left a ring stain on her beautiful antique end table.

- She greets LD at the table. "Were you sitting here?" LD says he was. "Were you drinking?" LD says he was but he never put it down. Julia isn't buying it. "That is why there are coasters on the table." LD then notices Mocha
- Joe serving coffee in the backyard. LD approaches the cart and tells him that he was upset about not getting a tip. Mocha Joe says it is true. LD's incredulous. "So there is no such thing as a favor?"
- Then Mocha says, "So if I asked you for a favor

you would do it?" LD says of course. Then Mocha proceeds to ask LD to pick up some coffee beans for him in Hillard. LD says that's insane. "It's a favor." "An insane favor." Mocha Joe is not derailed and manages to guilt LD
- into doing it. As LD leaves he runs into Cheryl. Tells her he'll see her later.

Scene 5
INT. CAR – Morning,
LD, Stuck in traffic, barely moving. Looks at watch, picks up cell, calls Cheryl. Crowd cancels. "Mocha Joe!!" Cheryl was there too long. (over

telling her he's going to be late. She tells him it's late, and he should forget about it. Obviously disappointed, he hangs up. "Mocha Joe!!!"

(5A) INT. office –
LD → go to 5A

CURB YOUR ENTHUSIASM
SEASON 7
SHOW 10 OUTLINE
"SEINFELD"

1. INT. SOUND STAGE - DAY (D1)
We watch the end of a scene between CHERYL and JASON (SEE SCRIPT, SCENE H)
When the scene ends, Larry gives some notes. Soon Jason leaves, and Larry
continues conversing with Cheryl, imparting to her all the knowledge and
experience the great man has come by, lo these many years. And much to his
delight, she's soaking it up. Yes, it's all working out quite nicely.

2. EXT. SOUND STAGE - PARKING LOT - LATER (D1)
Larry walks Cheryl to her car. Some general chitchat, then Larry tells her
that if she'd like, he would be happy to get together with her that night
to work on the scene. Cheryl loves the idea, says they could meet after
the party Julia Louis Dreyfus is hosting for Jason's new book about acting
for theatre, film, and television. Larry then notices Jason's car, which
has tinted windows. Wonders why anyone would need that. Seems a little
pretentious. It's not like he's George Clooney. Cheryl disagrees, offers
up sun protection as a reason—might even get them herself. Then MOCHA JOE
passes, wheeling his coffee cart. Cheryl compliments him on the vanilla
decaf latte she had earlier. He mentions that he's heading toward the
office. "Could you do me a favor," Larry asks, "and bring jumper cables to
Tim in the office?" Mocha Joe is not happy, as Larry opens the trunk of his
car and hands him the cables.

3. EXT. JULIA'S HOUSE - DRIVEWAY - EVENING (N1)
Larry brings JEFF up to date on recent developments with Cheryl. The plan
is working! They're getting closer every day. He's going to her house to
work on the script with her after the party. Should he make a move? Jeff
says yes, go for it. Larry says he's nervous about making a move. "The
single move is twice as hard as the married move. There's risk of failure
and shame. It's operating without a net. If the married move fails, so
what. There's always tomorrow."

4. INT. JULIA'S HOUSE - PARTY - LATER (N1)
Larry and JERRY examine Jason's book. Given the size of it, Larry suggests
that it's not really a book; it's more like a pamphlet. They go back and
forth on that, then Jerry mentions that he heard Mocha Joe was upset that
Larry didn't tip him earlier that day. Larry explains that it wasn't a tip
situation, that he simply asked Mocha Joe to do him a favor. Jerry says

1

there's no such thing as favors anymore. Even friends tip. Well, maybe not friends, but acquaintances. Larry and Jerry part ways, and a moment later JULIA appears and informs Larry that he left a ring stain on her beautiful antique table. She leads him to the table and points out the stain. "Were you sitting here?" Larry says he was. "Were you drinking?" Larry says he was, but he never put his drink down. "When I'm in social situations, I'm always more comfortable with something in my hands." Julia isn't buying it. "This is why there are coasters on the table." Larry then notices Mocha Joe behind his coffee cart in the backyard.

5. EXT. JULIA'S HOUSE - BACKYARD - CONTINUOUS (N1)

Larry approaches the cart and asks Mocha Joe if it's true he was upset about not getting a tip. Yes, says Mocha Joe. Larry's incredulous. "Is there no such thing as a favor?" Then Mocha says, "So if I asked you for a favor, you would do it?" Larry says of course. Then Mocha Joe proceeds to ask Larry if he would pick up a bag of coffee beans for him in Hollywood. Larry says that's insane. "It's a favor." "An insane favor." Mocha Joe persists and manages to guilt Larry into doing it. As Larry leaves, he runs into Cheryl, who's talking to SUSIE, and tells her he'll see her later.

6. INT. LARRY'S CAR - LATER (N1)

Larry, fuming, stuck in traffic, barely moving. He looks at his watch, then picks up his cell and calls Cheryl. INTERCUT WITH: A6. INT. CHERYL'S HOUSE - LIVING ROOM - SAME TIME (N1) He tells her he's going to be a while. She tells him it's late and that he should forget about it. "Mocha Joe!" END INTERCUT

7. EXT. COFFEE BEAN STORE - LATER (N1)

Larry pulls up. Knocks on the door, but it's closed.

8. INT. SOUND STAGE - DAY (D2)

As the CAST and CREW are milling about, Larry overhears Jason tell Jerry how well Cheryl is doing. "I worked with her last night." What's that? Larry can't believe his ears. He's asked a question by SOMEONE, but is too stunned to respond. Then Julia tells him that she brought the table in to be refinished, and the estimate was $500. Larry says he didn't do it. "Do you think I would lie about something like that?" "Yes, I do." She tells him to fess up. "I refuse to fess up." Rehearsal starts for the apartment scene (SEE SCRIPT, SCENE I) between Cheryl and Jason. Larry is fixated on Jason and Cheryl, watching for little clues—perhaps he sees a look, a laugh, a playful hit. Lunch is called. As Jerry and Larry sit down in the coffee shop to go over the scene, Larry watches Jason and Cheryl leave together. He is about to get up and follow when Mocha Joe enters and asks

Casting

With season seven, David reunited *Seinfeld's* original cast, wrote a redeeming storyline for Michael Richards (Kramer) after the comedian faced widespread criticism for a racially charged tirade during a 2006 stand-up set, and introduced Mocha Joe (Saverio Guerra) as Larry's new nemesis.

LAURA STREICHER, CO-EXECUTIVE PRODUCER: "Some of *Curb*'s story arcs were reliant on specific guest stars signing on for the season but were written before Larry approached them about it. Mel Brooks for *The Producers* season. Lin-Manuel Miranda for the *Fatwa/Hamilton* arc. Even Jerry, Julia, Jason, and Michael for the *Seinfeld* reunion. And I would say to him, 'Larry, you've written a couple episodes now. Maybe it's time to make the calls and ask if they want to do it?' But he'd never worry about it, he'd just keep writing, and, when the time came to finally ask, somehow it always worked out for him . . . Clearly Larry David is the king of manifestation. I mean, imagine writing a whole season and them being like, 'I don't think so, Larry.' What would we have done?"

DAVID: I don't remember having to talk to the cast about it beyond one or two conversations. It wasn't a big deal. Jerry was onboard immediately, and so once we had Jerry, then getting the others wasn't that hard."

JERRY SEINFELD: "I did think it was a good idea because I knew that doing a conventional network-type reunion show was never going to be appropriate for us. So being on Larry's show was a perfect way to do it."

JASON ALEXANDER (GEORGE COSTANZA): "Initially I had concerns that a reunion show wouldn't be a good thing to do, or a fun thing to do. We hadn't worked as a group in ten years. So we're all ten years older. So the first thing I'm thinking is, what was barely charming on characters in their thirties and forties may be completely devoid of charm in their forties and fifties, and that may be a mistake. Would we be able to resurrect that sense of ensemble play that we had so effortlessly on our show? But then also just the pure technicality of, it's hard enough to improvise a scene when it's two people, but when you've got six people?! 'My turn, no, my turn.' I thought this was a daunting task that could show us as being less than we were. But the experience was glorious; the ensemble feeling that we had, the affection that we had for each other, it was immediate. And walking back onto those exact replicas of our sets was like a time tunnel. It was just astonishing."

"BEING ON A PERFECT

DAVID: "I have to give credit to Jason. He was playing a really prickly version of himself, which he did the whole season. Remember the scene in the restaurant where he wouldn't coordinate the tip? It still makes me laugh."

ROGER NYGARD, EDITOR (SEASONS 6-8, 10-12): "Larry needs someone who's going to fight back and fight with him, so the actors from *Seinfeld* are the perfect foils [for him] and they work with whatever you give them. They're good at creating conflict. I remember asking Julia Louis-Dreyfus, 'What does it take for you to make a scene funny?' And she said, 'I need to have something to push back against, then I can make it funny.' And that's what Larry does, he pushes back against stupid social mores or somebody's dumb rule and he gets to have the arguments. So they were the perfect match for Larry."

SCHAFFER: "Obviously Larry has a long-standing relationship with all of those guys. So the improv always felt pretty natural. Jason's playing a fun-house version of himself. Julia is playing a version of herself that is more irascible. Everyone just sort of amped it up to make Larry uncomfortable. You're following a lot of people and a lot of stories at the end of the season; they're coming together on a show that Larry and Jerry had to write. It was really complicated."

DAVID: "I wanted to do something for Michael [Richards]. Like a little gesture for him in that episode because he was coming off of that horrible stand-up set [that went viral]. I just wanted to put him on the show. So we ended up pairing him with JB, who was playing Leon playing Danny Duberstein."

SCHAFFER: We also brought back the crew and our staff from *Seinfeld* to play the people on *Curb*'s "Seinfeld" set, like our producer Susie Mamann Greenberg, writers assistants, our former AD [assistant director] Randy Carter. It was exhilarating to see everybody back there, and for this one brief shining moment, it was like we were on *Seinfeld* again."

Most of the *Curb* audience had no idea that the crew portrayed on the *Seinfeld* reunion set were in fact the original *Seinfeld* crew. Why did the team go to the trouble of bringing them back when no one but *Curb* insiders knew?

DAVID: "Well, if we were shooting on the *Seinfeld* stage with the *Seinfeld* cast, why not the *Seinfeld* crew?"

SCHAFFER: "And we're only making the show for us. I've always said, if Larry was making this show as a home video for himself, nothing would be different."

ARRY'S SHOW WAS WAY TO DO IT."

—JERRY SEINFELD

The Location and Set

Curb traversed the city of Los Angeles for the majority of its twelve seasons. The various homes of the Greenes and Davids were actually rented properties in Malibu, the Hollywood Hills, and Brentwood. Angelenos may have noticed that Larry's dining spots included Canter's Deli and Don Cuco's Mexican Restaurant. The *Seinfeld* reunion season moved the show back onto the original lot and soundstage where the nineties sitcom was shot. But for authenticity's sake, Larry pushed it a step further.

ERIN O'MALLEY, PRODUCER (SEASONS 5-8), DIRECTOR OF "THE SURPRISE PARTY": "Larry wanted me to get the original *Seinfeld* set, so I said, 'Sure, where is it stored?' And he's like, 'I don't know, call somebody.' It became a quest. There were rumors that the set was at the Smithsonian. I checked; it wasn't. So I called NBC, and they said to call Castle Rock. It took a while, but somebody at Castle Rock finally narrowed it down to a storage facility way out in the San Fernando Valley. I sent my production designer to this giant warehouse. We're on the phone as he's in this facility walking, walking, walking. He finally sees this strip of wood, and it says "Seinfeld" on it. And there it was, literally tucked away in a corner."

"We set it up back on the CBS Radford lot. I didn't have all the little pieces, because the guys from *Seinfeld*—Jerry, Julia—said that everyone took pieces when the show ended, as keepsakes. But Larry also wanted to update the set, so we were taking this iconic set and modernizing it. But it was such a bizarre thing to actually stand on that set. It was like touching history."

SCHAFFER: "We re-created Larry and Jerry's office in the same space where their actual office used to be, in Building 5. And we had their two desks facing each other, because that was how it used to be arranged. There's also a dry-erase board on the wall in those reunion scenes, and you'll see ideas written on there. Those were actual ideas that Alec [Berg] and I had pitched when we worked on *Seinfeld* that Larry said no to, so we never used them. It's like we finally got to use them. You'll also see that building in "The Bare Midriff" [Season 7, Episode 6], when Larry catches his assistant's stomach to keep from falling off the roof. That's the roof of the building where *Seinfeld* was written."

ABOVE: Larry and Jerry's *Seinfeld* office was re-created in the exact same space and layout for season seven, complete with an old dry-erase board filled with actual scene ideas from the *Seinfeld* days.

OPPOSITE: The *Curb* team used this schematic, called a "spotting plan," of the original *Seinfeld* set as a guide to bring Jerry's apartment back to life for the season seven finale.

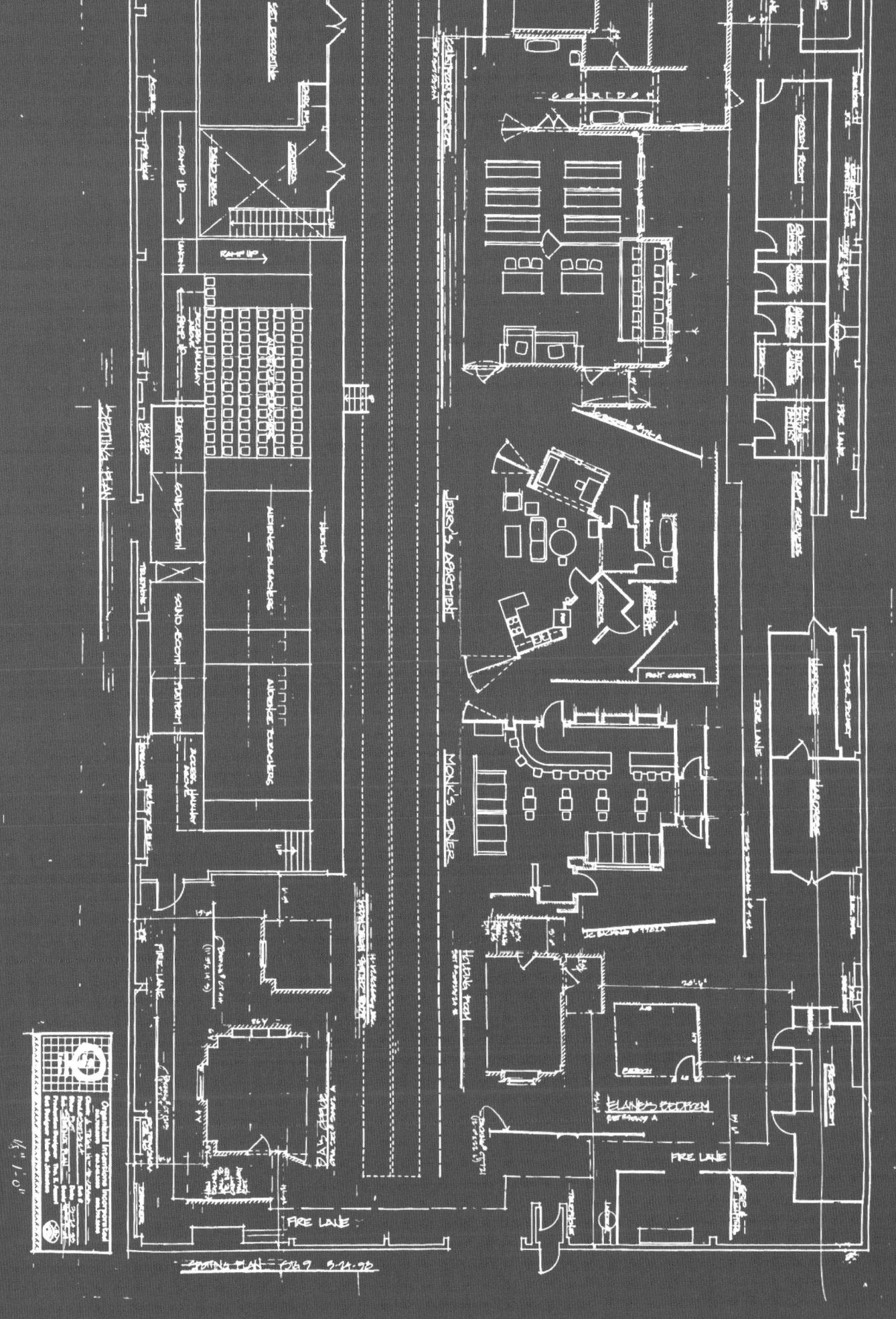

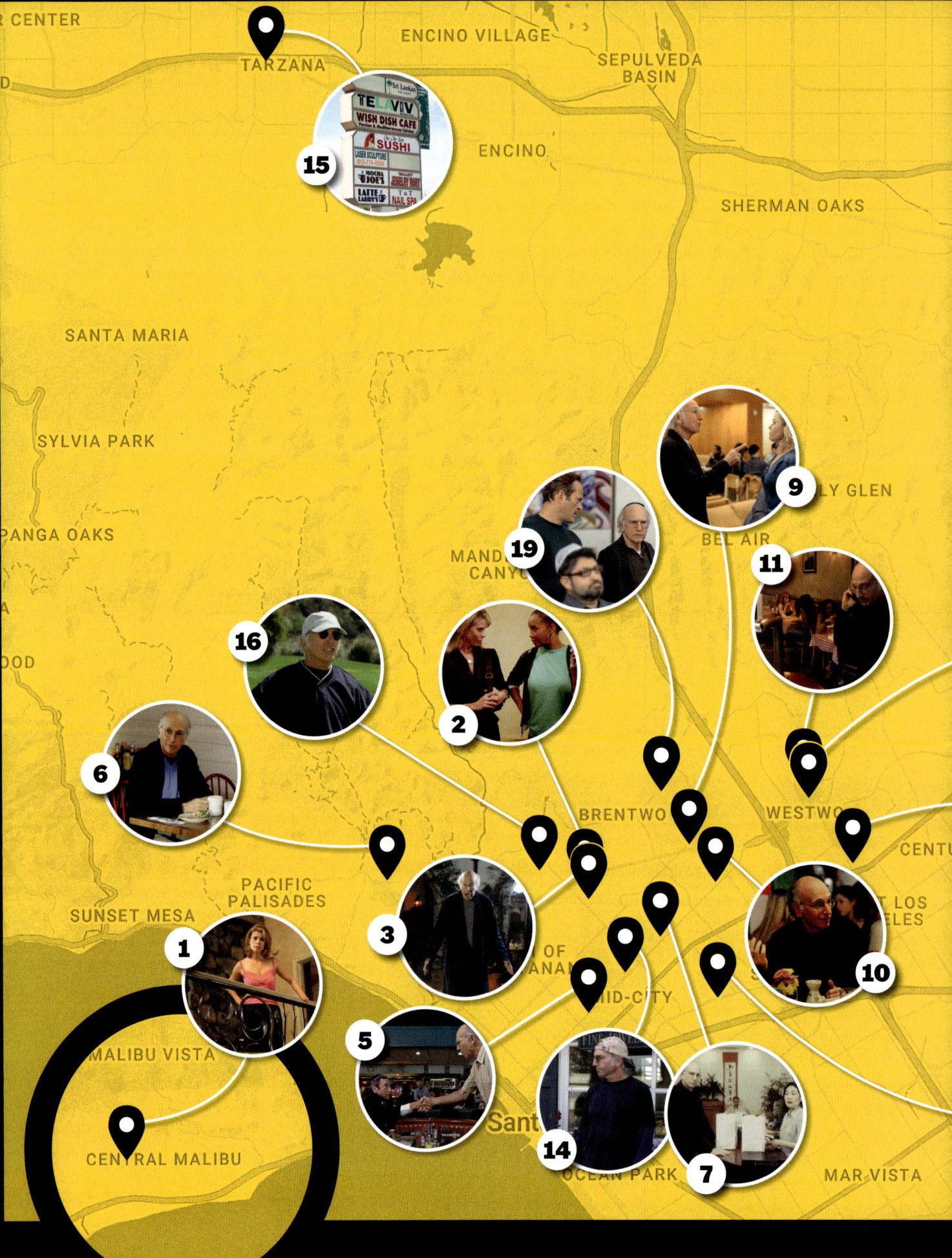

LARRY'S LOS ANGELES

Most of Larry's feuds took place in LA's wealthiest neighborhoods, like Pacific Palisades, Brentwood, and Santa Monica. Jesse Cole, the locations manager who joined the show in season five, says he chose the sites to fit the joke: "It had to feel real to Larry. He hated the idea of cheating anything." Directives for location scouting? Everything should be west of the 405 freeway since *Curb* loosely mirrored David's real existence in the Palisades. "It was a combination of him wanting to be in places where he actually goes, and also logistics. In general, he didn't want to have to schlep. Who can blame him?" adds Cole. "Places would often tell us, 'Normally we don't allow filming, but we love the show and we love Larry.' I was amazed how many places said we could film there because they were fans of *Curb*." (Sadly, many of these locations, particularly in the Palisades, were lost to the January 2025 California wildfires.)

The David Homes

Cole says Larry had a couple of directives about his homes on the show, including that he wanted a two-story foyer for interactions when people came in and out of the house. "It also had to be believable that it's a place he would live," says Cole of the upper-class locations they picked on the Westside. "Familiarity and the ability to take over the neighborhood were hard to come by. It was kind of like a puzzle. We needed a location that we could film at a lot."

Larry and Cheryl's first house
CENTRAL MALIBU

Where Larry turns away teenaged trick-or-treaters, who seek revenge by toilet-papering the house and graffitiing "Bald Asshole" on the front door.

Larry and Cheryl's second house, with the Blacks
BRENTWOOD

Not long after opening their home to the displaced Black family, who overstay their welcome (only temporarily moving out after they hear Larry using the N-word in a misunderstanding of hilarious proportions), Cheryl separates from Larry and moves out.

Single Larry's house with Leon Black
BRENTWOOD

After losing his home in the divorce, Larry moves with perma-houseguest Leon to a location down the road on Moreno Avenue. It's here that a burglar drowns in Larry's pool (sparking his crusade against Santa Monica's five-foot-fence rule), leading to Larry being blackmailed by the burglar's brother.

Larry's Office

The Lantana campus in Santa Monica, Building 3
3000 OLYMPIC BOULEVARD

The location for Larry's office in the series was in a working office building where David's real office is also located. This office on *Curb*, which Larry shares with his loyal assistant Antoinette in the early seasons, is the site of many feuds with Richard Lewis, including when Larry regrets giving Richard's girlfriend a job because she reports back on his frequent bathroom activity.

The Delis

Izzy's Deli
1433 WILSHIRE BOULEVARD, SANTA MONICA

It's at this now-shuttered deli that Larry poses as an Orthodox Jew in hopes of impressing the religious head of a kidney consortium, so he will help with Richard's transplant (getting Larry off the hook for donating his own kidney). Larry's plan goes sour later, when the man's daughter has to jump off a ski lift to distance herself from Larry as Shabbat nears.

Mort's Deli
1035 NORTH SWARTHMORE AVENUE, PACIFIC PALISADES

This former Palisades deli stood in for the fictitious Leo's Deli, where Larry gets a sandwich named after him and feuds with Ted Danson and Richard Lewis over their sandwich contents. *Curb* filmed at many Pacific Palisades locations that were affected by the 2025 L.A. wildfires, including places on Swarthmore Avenue and at Tallula's restaurant, where Larry and Richard have squabbled over the bill.

The Restaurants

Royal Star Seafood
3001 WILSHIRE BOULEVARD, SANTA MONICA

In a callback to the 1999 TV special that launched *Curb* the series, Larry again feuds with an HBO exec in season two's "Shrimp Incident" over a Chinese food mix-up. After Larry accuses the exec of eating his takeout shrimp, HBO passes on doing a TV show with Larry and *Seinfeld* star Julia Louis-Dreyfus.

Sunnin Lebanese Cafe
1776 WESTWOOD BOULEVARD, LOS ANGELES

Larry's antics lead to a protest between Al-Abbas, the fictional Palestinian restaurant in "Palestinian Chicken," filmed at Sunnin Lebanese Cafe, and the neighboring Jewish deli, Greenblatt's. For Greenblatt's, *Curb*'s location team used a neighboring daycare center, dressed as a deli with exterior signage.

Katsuya Brentwood
11777 SAN VICENTE BOULEVARD, LOS ANGELES

Larry offends the sushi chefs at this trendy Japanese restaurant where the show filmed often when he borrows their greeting of "Irasshaimase," which means "welcome to my restaurant," and uses it to greet others.

Hana Sushi
11831 WILSHIRE BOULEVARD, LOS ANGELES

In season five's "Kamikaze Bingo," the staff at this since-closed Japanese restaurant scream "chicken teriyaki boy!" whenever Larry arrives, and the greeting is misunderstood by Yoshi (Greg Watanabe), a friend of Larry's friend (Kevin Nealon). An argument ensues between Larry and Nealon after Yoshi runs out of the restaurant over the perceived insult. Hana Sushi's management let *Curb* film at their restaurant only because they were fans of the show, and gave the team strict filming times.

Enzo's Pizzeria
10940 WEYBURN AVENUE, LOS ANGELES

Larry orders the shop's famous chicken sub and helps himself to too many napkins, leading to an argument with the owner and then to his arrest.

The Sports Venues

Staples Center
1111 SOUTH FIGUEROA STREET, LOS ANGELES

Larry is nearly canceled by all of Los Angeles when he sits courtside and accidentally trips and injures Shaquille O'Neal during a Lakers game, which was partially filmed at a real Lakers–Minnesota Timberwolves game (pre-game and during commercial breaks) at the Staples Center. Shaq, a big *Seinfeld* fan whose favorite episode is "The Contest," ends up forgiving Larry.

Dodger Stadium
1000 VIN SCULLY AVENUE, LOS ANGELES

Larry picks up a prostitute (Kym Whitley)—at 555 West 23rd Street—as a passenger so he can use the car pool lane to get to a Dodgers game on time. *Curb* filmed at Dodger Stadium, with some shots during real games. Hijinks ensue and Marty Funkhouser gets arrested after borrowing Larry's jacket, which has marijuana in the pocket for Larry's father to treat his glaucoma. Cheryl, meanwhile, thinks he has picked up a prostitute for his tenth-anniversary adultery present.

The Stores

3rd Street Jewelers
2319 WILSHIRE BOULEVARD, SANTA MONICA

Early inclusions of businesses would lead to a "*Curb* bump" for the real locations. The founders of this shop, sisters Mary Kelley and Diane Allen, said real Larry came into their store back in 2000 to buy his wife a Christmas present and pitched them on filming there. The resulting season one episode, "The Bracelet," features Larry and Richard wrestling in the security vestibule over a bracelet. "It was like our $1 million commercial," Kelley told *Los Angeles* magazine. The shop closed in 2019.

Latte Larry's
19024 VENTURA BOULEVARD, TARZANA

Larry opens a "spite store" called Latte Larry's next to rival Mocha Joe's that ends up burning down. The biggest accelerants to the blaze? The germophobe's excessive hand sanitizer supply. Latte Larry's was filmed at a real strip mall in Tarzana, where Cole and team leased the storefronts for the season.

Other

Riviera Country Club
1250 CAPRI DRIVE, PACIFIC PALISADES

The golf course at this Pacific Palisades country club inspired Larry's fictional club, where he constantly clashes with owner Mr. Takahashi (Dana Lee). *Curb* occasionally filmed at Riviera, including during the pandemic for season eleven, but Cole says most of the country club scenes were an amalgamation from other golf clubs, including El Caballero Country Club, Woodland Hills Country Club, and Braemar Country Club in the Valley.

The Paramour Estate
1923 MICHELTORENA STREET, LOS ANGELES

A new friendship with Wanda's fiancé, Krazee-Eyez Killa (Chris Williams), has Larry touring the rapper's home, filmed at the Paramour Estate, in a scene similar to an episode of *MTV Cribs*. The friendship goes sour after Krazee-Eyez Killa confides in Larry about his adultery and later arrives at Larry's home to confront him when the secret gets out.

Westwood Village
1067 BROXTON AVENUE, LOS ANGELES

The site of Larry meeting his greatest enemy: a selfie stick, which he promptly breaks in half. This was real Larry's way of striking back at constant fan requests for pictures, and everyone on the crew approved.

University Synagogue
11960 SUNSET BOULEVARD, LOS ANGELES

The temple where Larry scalps High Holiday tickets, asks a rabbi for advice about committing adultery for his tenth-anniversary present, and bribes another rabbi with Palestinian chicken were all filmed at this Brentwood place of worship. (For the latter, Cole says they used the rabbi's real office.) Larry's biggest comeuppance here was getting kicked out of Rosh Hashanah services for scalping those tickets, after a kid ratted him out.

CBS Studio Center
4024 RADFORD AVENUE, STUDIO CITY

Two episodes of the *Seinfeld* season were filmed at the original lot and soundstage where the nineties sitcom was shot: "Table Read" and "Seinfeld." The season reunites Larry with the *Seinfeld* crew and stars Jerry Seinfeld, Julia Louis-Dreyfus, Jason Alexander, and Michael Richards, and the reunion is successful up until Larry's jealousy over Jason and Cheryl's relationship leads him to quit the show.

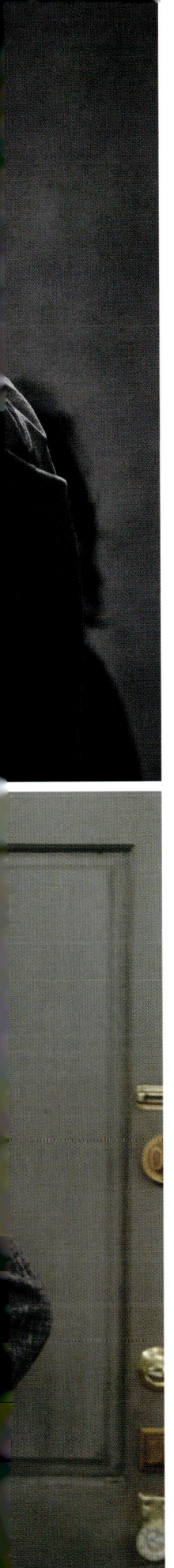

TOP: Jeff Schaffer on set during season twelve. BOTTOM: Larry and Michael Richards in "Seinfeld," S7, E10.

Production

DIRECTING

When *Curb* and *Seinfeld* collided for the reunion storyline, directors Jeff Schaffer, Alec Berg, and Dave Mandel had to manage a show within a show. It wasn't always easy.

SCHAFFER: "It was surreal to work back on the old set on Stage Nine, on the Radford lot in Studio City. We'd be shooting a *Curb* scene where Larry was watching and giving notes on a *Seinfeld* scene. There were the *Seinfeld* cameras, and then behind that were the *Curb* cameras where Alec and I were directing. Once, when the take-inside-a-take ended and *Curb* Larry walked up to give notes to the *Seinfeld* cast, I also had notes on the *Seinfeld* scene just like I used to back in the nineties. I started to walk out on set to give them, and Alec literally had to grab me by my belt, and say, 'Idiot, you're going to ruin the shot!' We were still in the scene! It was so instinctive to think, all right, the *Seinfeld* scene's over. Larry's got some notes and I've got some notes. It was a real mind-bending situation."

"We also wanted to show the set from different angles for viewers who watched *Seinfeld* but didn't get to go behind the scenes. So we had the cameras follow Cheryl going behind the set, past our set PA actor (Eric André, in one of his first roles ever) and all over the place on the lot."

"I'm doing him, doing me."
—LARRY DAVID

PERFORMANCES

In the reunion season, fictionalized Jason walks out of the production and *Curb* Larry steps into the role of George Costanza to keep the show going. But since the fussy *Seinfeld* character was initially created as an elevated version of David himself, this sowed understandable confusion on the *Curb* set.

DAVID: "I was uncomfortable because he was doing me on the show *Seinfeld*, and now I'm doing him, doing me. It was weird and crazy."

SCHAFFER: "You were really uncomfortable. All I could say is, 'But it's going to be so funny.' You were squirming around trying to figure out if there was another way to get to the same spot in the story arc without playing George. It was supposed to look like a big mistake, and it did."

DAVID: "Jason was giving me George lessons. He was taking me through it. I would say to him, 'How do you say this?' And he'd go, 'George is getting upset!' But think about how crazy that was. There's going to be a *Seinfeld* reunion, and Jason's not going to be in it, but TV Larry is going to be playing George. Very odd."

SAVERIO GUERRA (MOCHA JOE AND LAWYER JOE D'ANGELO): "When they were working on the reunion, *Curb* Larry thought Cheryl was having sex with Jason in the back of his car out on the lot. So Larry opened the door, and Jason's got these two killer dogs in the back. They chase me [as Mocha Joe] down the lot, and they bite me. So Larry comes over to my cart. I've got a bandage on my hand. I say, 'I'm going to have Jason's dogs euthanized.' He said, 'You can't do that.' I said, 'Not only am I gonna have them euthanized, but I'm gonna have it televised!' Then the director said, 'No, no, that's too much.' And [the real] Larry said, 'No it's not. Leave it in.' That's when I realized he edits in his head, even when he's acting."

A portrait that Larry gives Susie for her birthday suffers a series of unfortunate events in "Side Sitting," S10, E2.

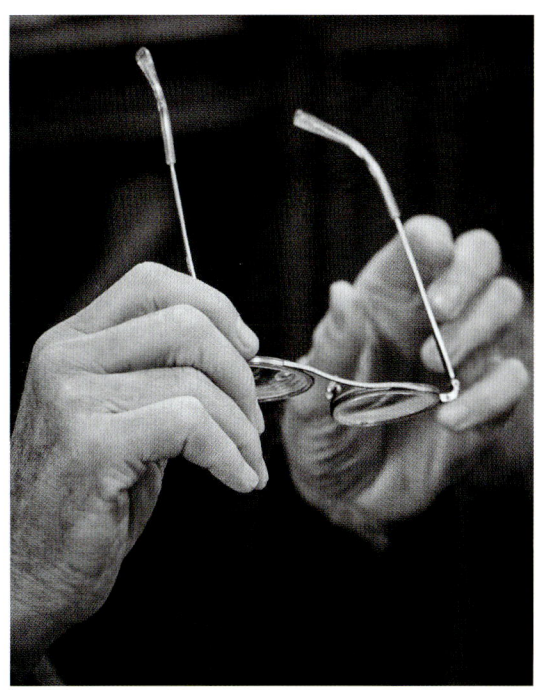

Props

DORT CLARK, PROPERTY MASTER (SEASONS 1–9): "The glasses on the show were the real glasses he wore. They were a certain style of Oliver Peoples frames from the 1990s. He only had two pairs, one that was transitional and one that was clear."

ROSE LEIKER, PROPERTY MASTER (SEASONS 11–12): "Larry's glasses were the property department's daily heart attack. I was only on the final two seasons and by that time, the glasses protocol was already established, but what I can say is that it is impossible to get the exact frames today. What I was told was that a few seasons before me, a producer went down the rabbit hole in search for the manufacturer of the exact pair of glasses. She was able to find someone in a small cabin in Switzerland to make four pairs, which Larry inherited. So every day, the prop department was in charge of his personal irreplaceable glasses. Remember, in some episodes we even had to drop them in a toilet or bend them!"

Wardrobe

LESLIE SCHILLING, COSTUME DESIGNER (SEASONS 9–12):
"Everyone always says Larry just wears his own clothes. This is a bit of a misconception. Larry likes to be Larry. When I first started the show, I went to his house to 'shop' his closet. It was clear to me not a lot of shopping had been done in the years when the show was on a break [a six-year gap between seasons eight and nine]. Styles had changed. Larry's taste had not. Larry likes a simple silhouette. Slim but not tight. Fitted but not structured. I bought him new versions of the same things and maybe every gray and blue cashmere sweater in town. James Perse had a modern version of his corduroy jacket. The AG Tellis became the perfect five-pocket pant. At the end of each season Larry took his closet home so at the beginning of the next season I would 'shop' his closet and supplement with newer pieces as we filmed. When I see Larry in public, I like to spot the pieces I bought him."

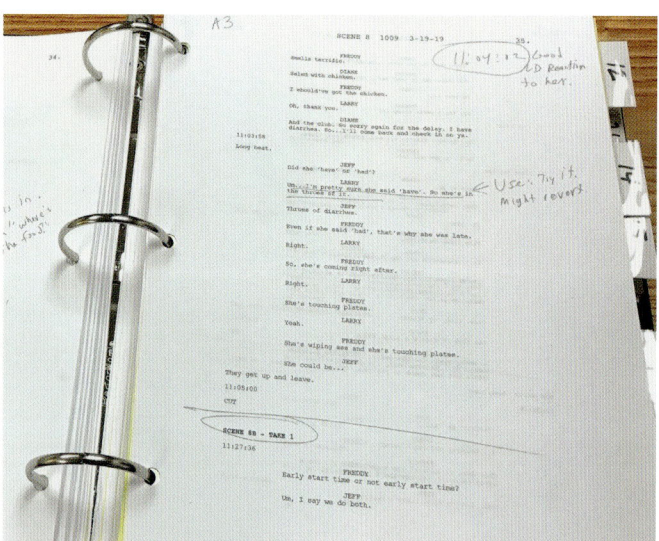

TOP LEFT: Editor Roger Nygard's notes after watching raw footage with Larry during "Beep Panic," S10, E9.

TOP RIGHT: Roger Nygard during an editing session for "Beep Panic," S10, E9.

BOTTOM: Multi-cam images from the final episode of *Curb Your Enthusiasm*, "No Lessons Learned," S12, E10.

Post Production

EDITING

It took more than six weeks to edit one *Curb* episode. That's about six times longer than it generally takes to edit a standard, scripted sitcom episode. The last three seasons of *Curb* required two editors to split up the work since the series had expanded in scope and budget, and there was more footage to wade through. David would often be in the edit bay, working over the shoulders of his editors.

STEVE RASCH, EDITOR AND MUSIC SUPERVISOR (SEASONS 1-12): "One of the biggest challenges of editing this type of material is when you have two or three people arguing, and they're overlapping in different ways. Say Susie's yelling at Jeff and Larry's interceding. The order is not scripted. So do you take the first part of the argument from take three, and the second part from take seven? Trying to attach them together is my job. And improv can wander all over the place. You have to get into Larry's headspace to figure out what works best."

NYGARD: "Faster comedy is funnier comedy. Generally I could take a scene and make it 15 percent funnier simply by going through and pulling out all the pauses, the *ums*, the *you-knows*, the *uhs*. I'd lean it up and clean it up. When you make it concise and faster, it just gets funnier. And the *Seinfeld* season was really funny."

MUSIC

Curb offset Larry's disruptive etiquette with lighthearted, carefree music, often culled from old stage productions and film scores. The theme song, "Frolic," for example, is an instrumental by the Italian composer Luciano Michelini, written in 1974 for the film *La Bellissima Estate*. Or Gilbert and Sullivan's "Three Little Maids" might pop up as interstitial music that set a mood or connected scenes.

RASCH: "We don't necessarily score in the traditional sense of supporting the emotion of the scene. It's more transitional or a montage. The tuba sound is primary in a lot of scenes, and I think it really helps because it's such a silly, clowning sound. It takes the edge off Larry's anger and cues the listener like a laugh track. Like, don't worry, it's just a comedy show. If a scene gets hot and we get out of the scene, a little bit of a tuba or accordion draws you back into the comedy world so it doesn't get too dark. It's a trigger to say, 'We're having fun, don't worry.'"

THE NETWORK

DAVID: "HBO gave us everything that we needed, and they never interfered at all. They just let us make the shows, so we never had any network pressure, ever. It was quite a luxury."

SCHAFFER: "Alec used to say, 'There's no *They*.' On regular shows, we're always asking, 'Are *They* going to like it?' *They* could be the network. *They* could be the audience. But we never had to worry about *They* with *Curb*. *They* left us alone."

CASEY BLOYS, CHAIRMAN AND CEO, HBO AND MAX CONTENT: "First of all, there's no one like Larry, he's a comedy icon. *Curb* had the staying power to become our longest-running scripted series because people continued to confound Larry and that remained hilarious to watch. Frustrated Larry is funny. But it's not that simple; there's a strong architecture to the writing that Larry and Jeff Schaffer did to crack every season and arc out each episode."

O'MALLEY: "HBO trusted Larry emphatically. There was so much autonomy, it was unreal. I've never had it like that on any other show, and I never will again."

Susie's Style

The indomitable fashion sense of Susie Greene was a character unto itself over *Curb*'s twelve-season run. From the top of her equestrian-themed hat to the tips of her fuzzy pink Uggs, Susie's assaultive style was always on brand with her larger-than-life personality.

"Before we say action, everybody just looks at me and starts laughing. I put on the outfits and I just become her. I don't have to think about it." —Susie Essman

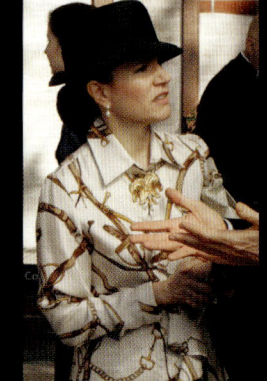

"It was like a party. We would just go crazy. But we were also really trying to find the balance of that woman who has money and who loves extravagant things but doesn't really have the best taste." —Christina Mongini, costume designer

"For the finale, we originally had Susie at the hotel being mistaken for a hooker because of the way she dresses. She has an altercation with the hotel manager."
—**Larry David**

"We didn't get approvals on her outfits. We would do these fittings and just send her to set. And a couple times Larry would be like, 'No, you look too crazy.' But my favorite was when she would walk on set and he would just look at her and start laughing. It was the best." —**Christina Mongini, costume designer**

"It's truly wonderful when an actor really wants to play and have fun with their character's wardrobe."
—**Leslie Schilling, costume designer**

"Susie completely believes she has the greatest taste in the world. And who's gonna argue with her about it? No one."
—**Susie Essman**

"With each new season, the costume designers and I would say, 'What's our fashion theme for Susie?' Sometimes it was hats, or like an animal print theme, or lots of accessories. But we would never tell anybody about it. We'd just do it." —**Susie Essman**

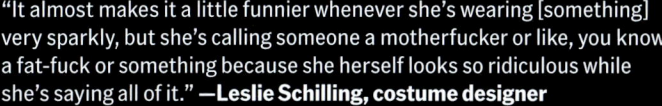

"It almost makes it a little funnier whenever she's wearing [something] very sparkly, but she's calling someone a motherfucker or like, you know, a fat-fuck or something because she herself looks so ridiculous while she's saying all of it." —**Leslie Schilling, costume designer**

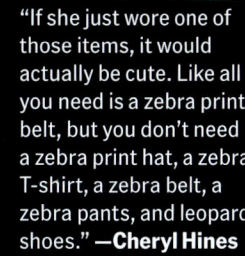

"If she just wore one of those items, it would actually be cute. Like all you need is a zebra print belt, but you don't need a zebra print hat, a zebra T-shirt, a zebra belt, a zebra pants, and leopard shoes." —**Cheryl Hines**

Curb ImitaLife ImitaCurb

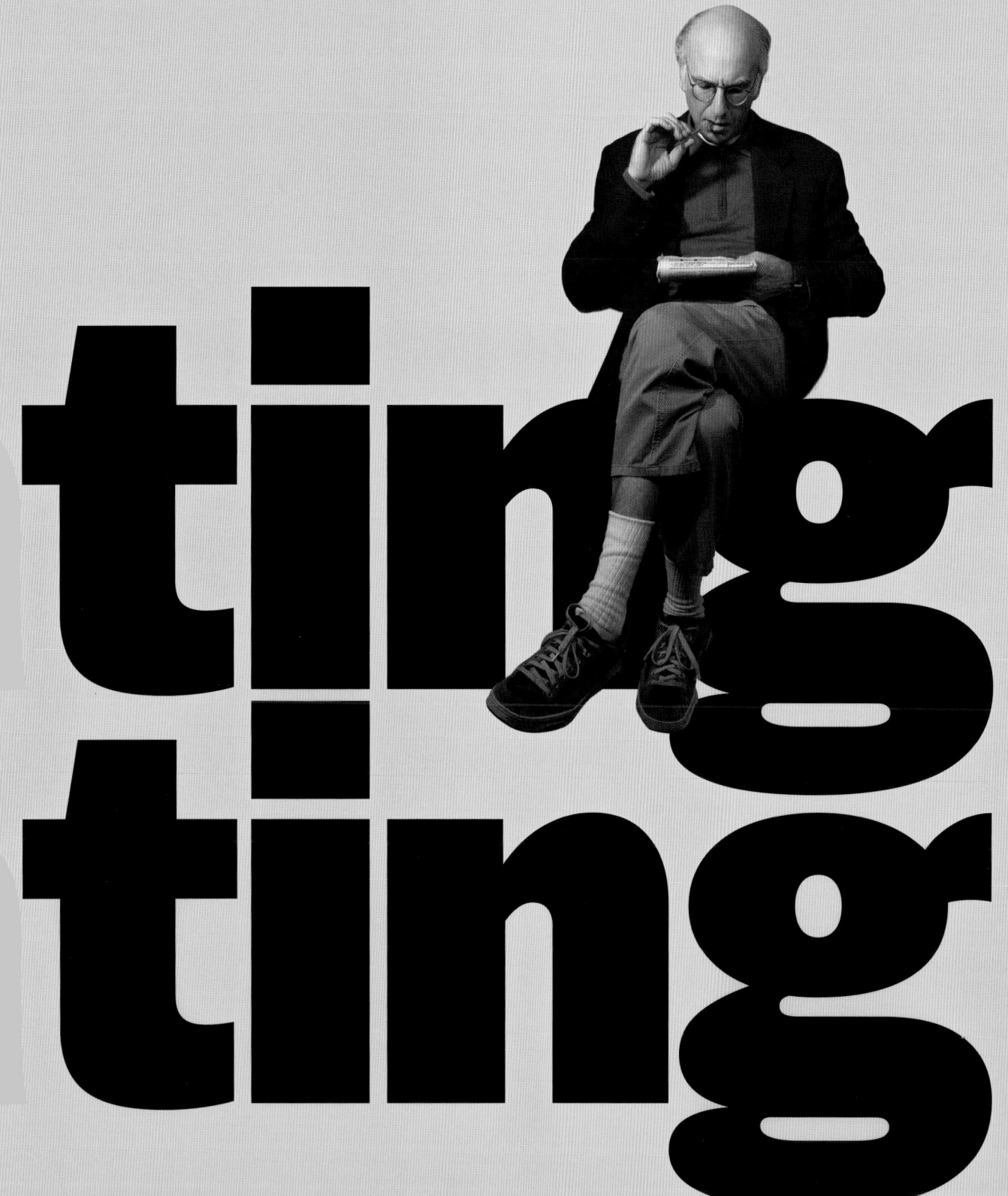

Curb

Your Enthusiasm spanned multiple decades, filtering a rapidly changing world through Larry's prescription lenses. From George W. Bush to Joe Biden, water-cooler talk to social media chatter, iPods to AI, the series mined humor from news events, fleeting trends, politics, pop culture, and even the personal lives of those on the show.

A hit musical by the name of *Hamilton* inspired Larry's season nine musical, *Fatwa!* A Christmas tradition long practiced by Cheryl Hines's family became the basis of Larry's season three nativity scene brawl. And Trump's real-life presidential impeachment saga laid the groundwork for a whistleblower exposing Larry's wrongdoings in season eleven. The absurdity of real life was *Curb*'s greatest muse.

"We weren't truth seekers," says director and writer Bob Weide. "That was never the intent. You just look at the world around you, observe it, then put it through the comedy meat grinder and something funny comes out the other side."

If something became a cultural fixation, it would eventually make its way onto *Curb*. The world refracted through Larry always made us laugh, and it also told us a little something about ourselves. "Generations from now, people will look back on *Curb* as a kind of reflection of its time, in the same way that *All in the Family* was reflecting the country in the 1970s, or *Saturday Night Live* through different eras," says Weide. "*Curb* shows where we were at in the first two decades of the twenty-first century."

Larry before rehearsal for his daring new musical, *Fatwa!* ("Fatwa!" S9, E10).

THIS PAGE AND OPPOSITE: Larry in "The Blind Date," S4, E3.

The show was still fairly new when America was attacked on September 11, 2001, but *Curb* succeeded in finding humor in the unthinkable in the aptly titled "The Terrorist Attack." In season two, Wanda Sykes learns of a planned attack on LA through a confidential CIA informant, and warns Larry and Cheryl that they should leave town. Cheryl can't because of her involvement in a benefit event, so Larry suggests she stay while he gets out of LA. Cheryl questions if he could live with himself if she died and he survived, and he says he'll think about it. Larry said the quiet part out loud, assuring viewers that they weren't the only ones whose better angels abandon them in times of crisis.

America's ensuing war on terror in places like Afghanistan and Iraq, and the Islamophobia it engendered here at home, informed season four's "The Blind Date." In the episode, Larry tries to fulfill his blind friend's wish to date a woman whom no other man can see when he sets him up with the Muslim, burqa-clad Haboos (Moon Zappa). Through an only-on-*Curb* series of events (spilled deli sauce is involved), Cheryl winds up wearing Haboos's burqa to a Halloween party. But on the way there, a group of young men pull up next to the Davids' car and shout, "Hey Osama, go back to your own fucking country," pelting him with an egg.

"We're always taking input from what's happening in the world around us," says director and executive producer Jeff Schaffer. "It's our job to take these real events and twist them around until they're funny. Anything and everything is on the table. It's all in the execution."

Season five's "The Christ Nail" did just that when it tackled the country's passion for *The Passion of the Christ*, the Mel Gibson–directed dramatization of Jesus's last days. The film became the highest-grossing R-rated film of all time. In the episode, Cheryl's dad (Paul Dooley) wears a nail-pendant necklace that he bought after seeing the movie. Larry tells his father-in-law that he's "gay" for worshipping Jesus because Jesus is a man. Larry eventually uses the nail to hammer in his mezuzah—an encased verse from the Torah that Jews often affix to the doorpost outside their home. It was hard to see a mezuzah without thinking of Gibson, who'd be caught on tape the following year screaming antisemitic slurs at a policeman.

You can't make this stuff up, which is exactly why *Curb* had such success pulling its best gags from pop culture. The series weighed in on the early 2000s obsession with reality TV competitions when it merged a horrific chapter of history with a trashy binge watch. In 2004's "The Survivor," two men labeled "survivors" meet over dinner at the Davids. It's soon discovered that the term is being used in very different ways. Larry's father is accompanied by a Holocaust survivor friend. But the rabbi at the table has brought along a contestant from the wildly popular reality competition series *Survivor*. Runner-up contestant Colby Donaldson and the Holocaust survivor Solly (Allan Rich) get into an argument for the ages.

"'The Survivor' episode didn't pound the ugliness of antisemitism into people's heads, making them so uncomfortable or sad that they had to stop watching," says producer Erin O'Malley. "It got the point across by making them laugh. Part of Larry's brilliance is shining a light on really hard stuff inside of really good comedy."

Hurricane Katrina was no laughing matter when it devastated New Orleans in 2005, killing and displacing thousands. Many felt the government was slow to respond because a majority of the storm's victims were Black. The national debate around systemic racism, and the plight of the displaced, found its way into season six of *Curb* when Cheryl took in a family affected by the fictional "Hurricane Edna." But when Larry picked up Loretta Black (Vivica A. Fox), Auntie Rae (Ellia English), and kids Keysha (Carla Jeffery) and Daryl (Nick Nervies) from the airport, he wasn't exactly a source of comfort: "Your name is Black?" he said. "That's like if my last name was Jew. Larry Jew." Man-made disaster Larry strikes again.

One episode later, in "The Anonymous Donor," Leon Black (JB Smoove), Loretta's mysterious brother, moves in with the Davids. Leon, one of *Curb*'s funniest characters, brought with him multiple opportunities to explore national tension around issues of racial justice.

"Giving Larry somebody who shows him a different way of life and a different way of thinking was a big part of Leon," says Smoove. "Leon introduced this older Jewish guy to a whole different way of doing things. Larry needed new ways to combat the things he was going through with people. He needed that dude."

Barack Obama's presidential candidacy leading up to his 2008 White House win uncovered the disturbing reality of racist rhetoric in American discourse, evident in the content of leaked emails, social media chatter, and hot mic mishaps. In season six's "The N Word," fictional Larry is disgusted when he overhears a white man using the slur while complaining to his friend. Later, Jeff's Black doctor (Wren T. Brown) walks by as Larry is recounting the story. He reprimands Larry for using the "most vile word in the English language," calling him a "bald son of a bitch!" The doctor heads into surgery in such a rage that he accidentally shaves Jeff's head. While consequently apologizing to the Greenes, he explains he made the mistake after being victimized by Larry's usage of the abhorrent term. Larry explains himself to Jeff and Susie, using the N-word again, which the Black family overhears. They're incensed: "Fuck you, Larry!"

"Larry did that show called 'The N Word,' which is like the ultimate thing that can't be touched in comedy or elsewhere," says Weide. "But he found a way to do it, and in turn commented on how a lot of the country still hasn't dealt with centuries-old racial issues."

COLBY: So here we are, in a region of Australia where, out of the world's ten most deadly snakes, nine of them inhabit this region. It  was harrowing. You come across a taipan on the trail, you get bit, you're dead in thirty minutes flat.

SOLLY: Oy, I'll tell you. That's a very interesting story. Let me tell you, I was in a concentration camp! You never even suffered one minute in your life compared to what I went through!

COLBY: Look, I'm saying we spent forty-two days trying to survive and we had very little rations, no snacks.

SOLLY: Snacks? What you talking 'snacks'? We didn't eat sometimes for a week! For a month! We ate nothing...

COLBY: I couldn't even work out when I was over there. They certainly didn't have a gym!

THE SURVIVOR: S4, E9

"HE'S WE

Stills from "Happy New Year," S10, E1.

AS A REP

ARING IT

Enter Donald Trump and the culture wars between the left and the right. By the time 2020 rolled around, Larry—like many politicians—had found a way to leverage the polarization to his advantage. By season ten's "Happy New Year," he was donning a red MAGA cap. Why? Because wearing it around liberal LA made him a pariah, fulfilling his antisocial dream to have everyone leave him alone. The MAGA accessory was all the funnier since Larry's politics on the show leaned left, yet the real David's lampooning of America's partisanship cut both ways.

"The MAGA hat in season ten, he's wearing it as a repellent," says Susie Essman. "It's clearly a comment on MAGA, but he's also commenting on the liberals who are repelled by it. It's an example of the depth of Larry's equal-opportunity takedowns."

ELLENT."

—SUSIE ESSMAN

The fraught 2020s were a playground for *Curb*. Example: The selfishness inspired by COVID-19 pandemic supply-chain shortages rivaled even Larry's self-interest, when in season eleven's "The Five-Foot Fence," it's discovered that the Davids' friend Albert Brooks is a COVID hoarder. His stockpile of hand sanitizer, antibacterial wipes, and other scarce items is uncovered when Larry accidentally opens up a storage closet in Brooks's home. Jon Hamm spoke for pandemic-weary viewers everywhere when he screamed at Brooks: "First responders could have used this stuff!"

As for the political turmoil of the 2020s? *Curb* had that covered, too. In "The Mormon Advantage," whistleblower Alexander Vindman appeared on the show. Vindman, whose testimony led to the first impeachment of President Trump, overhears Larry trying to bribe a local councilwoman. Vindman exposes Larry's attempt at a quid pro quo, and in another example of art imitating life, his testimony does not result in putting anyone behind bars.

Stills from "The Five-Foot Fence," S11, E1, where Larry discovers a drowned burglar in his pool.

FIRST RESPONDERS COULD HAVE USED THIS STUFF!

—Jon Hamm, after discovering that Albert Brooks is hoarding supplies during the COVID pandemic

TOP: Larry being arrested for violating the Election Integrity Act in "Atlanta," S12, E1. **BOTTOM:** Cheryl, ignoring Larry while scrolling on her BlackBerry, during "Kamikaze Bingo," S5, E4.

The twelfth and final season aired in 2024, just ahead of a contentious election. The season managed to squeeze in send-ups of Georgia's suppressive voting laws and Trump's infamous mugshot (episode one's "Atlanta") when Larry is arrested for violating the law at a polling place, and grimaces just like Trump in his mugshot. Rudy Giuliani's hair-dye-melting press conference is also replicated, except it's a white lawn jockey who must endure the humiliation of hair dye melting down his face rather than the former mayor of New York.

But *Curb* wasn't always about capital-I issues. The show was as adept at grabbing on to cultural commonalities that were just plain annoying. A growing addiction to technology animated season five's "Kamikaze Bingo," when Cheryl ignores Larry at dinner because she's too busy typing away on her new BlackBerry. Larry's limited grasp of his TiVo's functionality in 2007's season six is the beginning of the end for his marriage. In season eight's "Palestinian Chicken," he confronts a friend's wife about using text abbreviations in verbal conversation when she says "LOL" to a disgusted Larry. "If you're going to laugh out loud, why aren't you laughing out loud?" he complains. "Why say it? Why not just laugh?" Later in the series, he embodies the frustration caused by annoying new gadgets when he snaps a pedestrian's selfie stick in two, knocks over a row of electric scooters, and screams obscenities at Siri.

"We needed to include Siri," says Jeff Schaffer. "The same with the vacuum-sealed packages, when Larry struggled with the shampoo bottle in the shower. You can't open those! Larry's got to speak for those who have no voice."

As heroic as that sounds, Larry's actions in season eight's "The Hero" were anything but valiant—but they *were* ripped from the headlines. During a flight, he trips over his shoelaces and accidentally knocks over an abusive airline passenger who happens to be berating a flight attendant. He's hailed a hero by news outlets, just like Captain "Sully" Sullenberger, the pilot from the 2009 "Miracle on the Hudson" plane landing two years earlier.

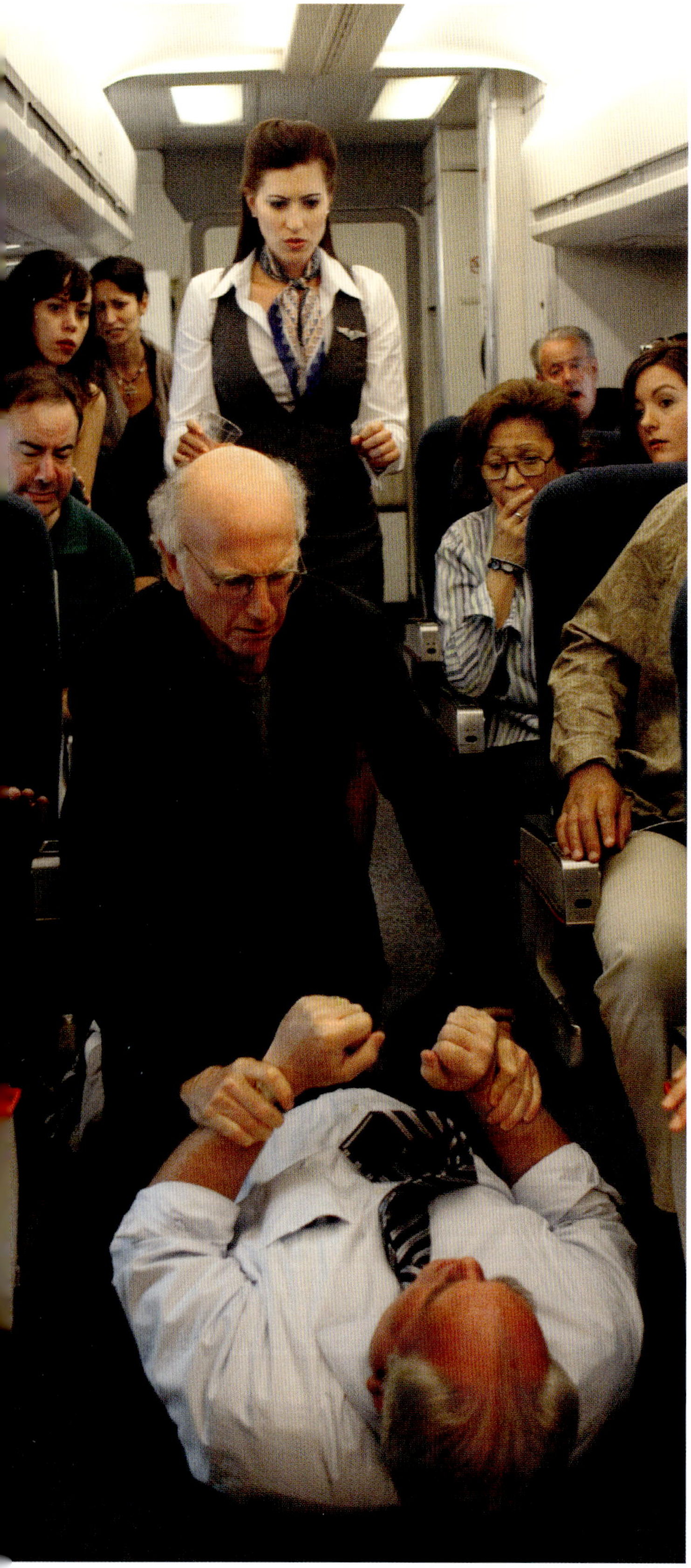

Larry is applauded as a hero when he accidentally trips a passenger abusing a flight attendant in "The Hero," S8, E6.

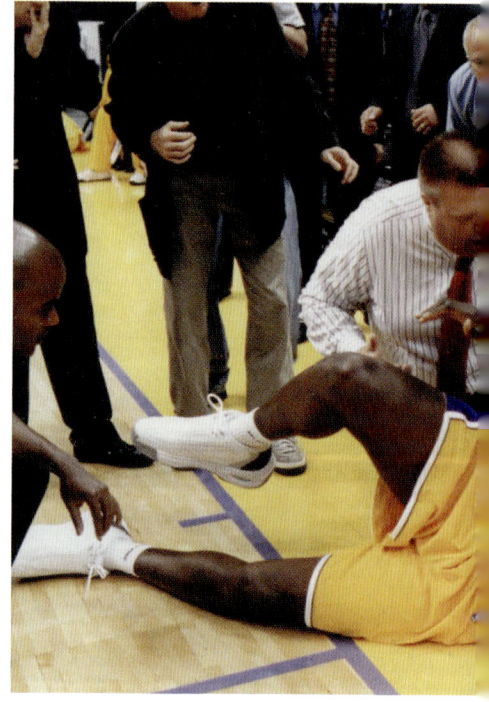

ABOVE: Larry accidentally trips Shaq during a Lakers game in "Shaq," S2, E8.

The cultlike way in which sports had become central to people's lives by the turn of the century was also grist for *Curb*'s comedy mill. When season two's "Shaq" aired in 2001, the Lakers were in the middle of the second of what would be three straight championship wins and Laker fever was at an all-time high. During a game in LA, Larry accidentally trips and injures

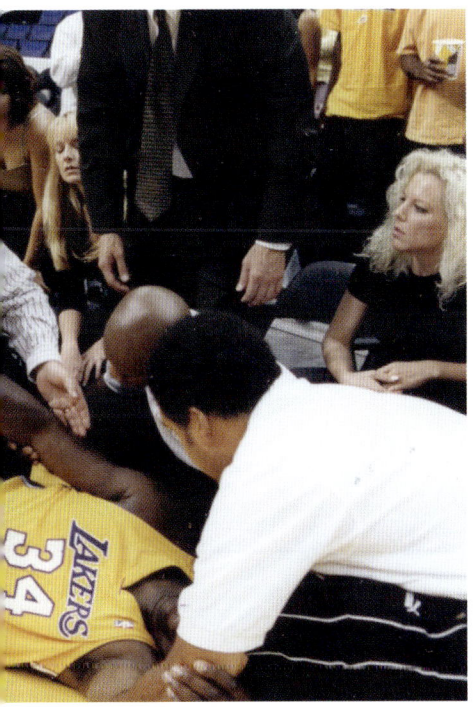

Laker Shaquille O'Neal while stretching out his legs from his courtside seat. The incident (which was partially filmed at the Staples Center during a real Lakers–Minnesota Timberwolves game) generates citywide scorn toward Larry—a stigma that works to his advantage when friends stop asking for favors and his in-laws end their visit early.

In season eight's "Mister Softee," Larry derails his softball championship game when a painful childhood memory is triggered by the tune blaring from a Mister Softee ice cream truck. He freezes and makes an error in the last inning, costing his team the win. His manager (who earlier in the episode invokes a motivational speech by Yankees owner George Steinbrenner, whom David famously voiced on *Seinfeld*) accuses Larry of "Bucknering him," referring to Red Sox player Bill Buckner's infamous error that led to his team losing the 1986 World Series. Later, the real Bill Buckner shows up and is redeemed when a woman trapped in a burning building throws her baby down to the firemen below, the baby bounces off their safety net, and Buckner runs twenty feet, making the perfect catch that saves the infant.

"Larry loves baseball and sports like he loves women. He's a guy," says Richard Kind, who played Cousin Andy. "He just happens to be more observant about life than the average guy."

And it wasn't just our collective reality around major events and trends that informed some of *Curb*'s finest moments. The off-screen lives of David and the cast also offered a wealth of material for the show.

Season twelve's "Ken/Kendra" features a scene in which a restaurant downgrades its posted health rating from an A to a C while Larry is dining there. The scenario was based on a lunch David had with Schaffer and writer-directors Dave Mandel and Alec Berg, where they watched as the restaurant owner swapped the letters in the window. "It was just too perfect," says Schaffer.

THIS PAGE AND OPPOSITE:
Larry is triggered by the Mister Softee truck during his softball team's championship game in "Mister Softee," S8, E9.

"IT'S CRAZY WHAT GOES THROUGH LARRY CRAN...

"Sometimes stories just fall into your lap," says Schaffer. "I remember I was with my family in Europe in the summer. It was crazy hot and the waiter was sweating like a fiend. We had ordered this branzino which we didn't realize was ridiculously expensive. As the waiter set the dish down, he was hovering over it, and on the tip of his nose was a gleaming bead of sweat. I've never watched anything more intently in my life, and I thought to myself, 'If that drop of sweat falls into that fish I'm throwing the whole thing in the trash.' I called Larry right after and it immediately went in the show ['Beep Panic,' Season 10, Episode 9]."

The impetus for an improvised gag also included whatever the performer brought in from their personal life when they walked onto the set that day. "The night before we shot the 'Palestinian Chicken' sex scene, I watched this old movie, *The Scarlet Pimpernel*," says David. "And there was a line in the movie that really stuck out, that I kept repeating: 'They seek him there. They seek him there. Those Frenchies seek him everywhere... Is this heaven? Is this hell? Damn that elusive Pimpernel!' So when we filmed the scene after I had sex with [Shara], I had to walk downstairs in my bathrobe, and for some reason, I started repeating that idiotic little line from the movie."

"It's crazy what goes through Larry's cranium and gets right out onto the show," says Schaffer.

"One of my favorite episodes was based on a true story from my family," says Cheryl Hines (Cheryl David). "I'm from Florida and when I went home for the holidays, my family had baked a nativity scene; all the figures were cookies, the hay was toasted coconut. My sister-in-law was walking around saying, 'Nobody eat Baby Jesus!' I called Larry and said, 'If you were at my house, you would eat Baby Jesus and my family would lose their minds.' He said, 'I gotta do this! Tell me everything. What else is happening there?' And I said, 'Well, besides the baked nativity scene made of cookies and toasted coconut, there are also live nativity scenes, where people are doing it in their yard.' He didn't know what I was talking about. I said, 'People dress up like Mary and Joseph, and they stand in the yard and re-create the scene.'"

"So on *Curb*, we do an episode where my family comes to LA, they make the nativity scene, Larry eats Baby Jesus and Mary, and my family is so mad. To get back in their good graces, he hires actors to do a live nativity scene at our house. Then when he's talking to Joseph, he remarks on how hot Mary looks. They get into a fistfight, and the whole nativity scene burns down."

Y'S
IUM
AND GETS RIGHT OUT ONTO THE SHOW."
—JEFF SCHAFFER

Scenes from "Mary, Joseph, and Larry," S3, E9.

Curb didn't just take from reality, it also gave back. The series contributed much to the zeitgeist, more often than not in the form of new descriptors and sayings for every type of situation. Don't want to wait in line? Chat 'n' cut. Need to tell somebody something without taking responsibility for what is said? Accidental text on purpose. Use a coaster under your drink? Respect wood!

As early as season one's "Porno Gil," Larry's iconic phrase, "pretty, pretty, pretty good," was launched into the TV-verse when he sarcastically uttered the three words during a car ride with Cheryl where the two are lost. The phrase's meaning would later flip, becoming a common refrain for Larry—and his fans—to describe a positive situation.

"Isms are a strong early indicator of a comedy's success," says Amy Gravitt, head of comedy programming at HBO. "If we're quoting something, it means it's resonating. As with everything else, *Curb* is the standard-bearer of isms in the halls of HBO."

One of Gravitt's favorites? "Foisted." It came from the eponymous season nine episode in which Jimmy Kimmel unloaded—ahem, *foisted*—his useless personal assistant onto Larry. Who of course foists her onto Susie. It didn't matter that few of us in the general public had personal assistants to foist, after *Curb* foisted the word upon us, it would be applied to a myriad of situations. As Gravitt says, of all of *Curb*'s isms, "'foisted' is the handiest."

Larry promotes his new musical on *Jimmy Kimmel Live!* in "Foisted!" S9, E1.

YOU AND YOUR FUCKING LITTLE SOCCER SHOES IN MY HOUSE!

—Porno Gil's wife to Larry, after he refuses to remove his shoes and breaks her lamp

ABOVE AND OPPOSITE: Comedian Kym Whitley as Monena with Larry in "The Car Pool Lane," S4, E6.

Life relied on art with season four's "The Car Pool Lane," when outtakes from *Curb* footage saved baseball spectator Juan Catalan from spending his life in prison after he was arrested for a murder he didn't commit. Catalan was watching the Dodgers play a home game when a drive-by shooting occurred across town. He was fingered for the crime, and when his ticket stub wasn't enough to prove he was inside the stadium during the time of the murder, his lawyer set out to find video footage from the venue that might serve as an alibi. *Curb* happened to be shooting at the same game, in the same section where Catalan was seated with his daughter. Raw footage from the shoot went on to show that Catalan was indeed there in the stadium, proving his innocence. David commented afterward, "I've now done one decent thing in my life, albeit inadvertently."

Larry befriends a local city councilwoman, played by comedian Tracey Ullman, to help him get a city ordinance repealed in "Irma Kostroski," S11, E7.

In one instance *Curb* contributed material to politics rather than pulling from it: The show was mentioned during a debate between Senator Ted Cruz of Texas and Senator Bernie Sanders of Vermont when both became contenders in the presidential primaries of 2016. It began when David was recruited by his former employer, *SNL*, to play Sanders on the sketch show. Later during the debate, Cruz told the real Sanders to "*curb* his enthusiasm." (David would later find out while appearing on the PBS genealogy show *Finding Your Roots* that he doesn't just look and sound like Sanders, but the two are actually related.)

Election season and *Curb* were linked again when in season eleven's "Irma Kostroski," Larry shirks his civic responsibility to vote in the local Santa Monica City election and his candidate loses by one vote. Larry's crime is discovered and he's publicly shamed for failing to cast his ballot. The episode birthed a social media meme that was reshared at large during the 2024 election: "Don't be Larry. Vote!"

Curb's infiltration of our world beyond the screen wasn't just reserved for cautionary election tales. When a billboard Susie purchased on Santa Monica Boulevard in season twelve for her caftan business is graffitied with an image of two large penises, fictional Larry finds it highly amusing. In reality, when HBO erected the same billboard (minus the graffiti) on the same LA thoroughfare to promote the new season, motorists derived their own amusement from the billboard. The sign was defaced with the image of two large spray-painted penises within a week of the episode airing, and it wasn't a network publicity stunt.

But as much as the show trafficked in send-ups of the world at large, perhaps its greatest acknowledgment of cultural conversations was when it referenced Larry David's own work. After all, the series finale culminates in a court case over Larry's violation of the Georgia voting law, but it's really a nod to the zeitgeist-iest of all previous zeitgeist shows: *Seinfeld*.

Curb had parodied its creator and main character's connection to the sitcom classic from the very beginning. In episode one of season one, "The Pants Tent," Larry name-drops himself as cocreator of *Seinfeld* to a restaurant hostess to try to get a seat. The hostess tells him maybe she's seen one episode.

And of course, *Curb* later dedicated a whole season to reuniting *Seinfeld*'s main cast. After a year of honoring, and skewering, Larry's previous show, the season seven finale featured a *Seinfeld* reunion episode. And it got in one last dig at that show's failures: "C'mon, we already screwed up one finale, we can't do another," Jerry Seinfeld says, giving Larry a critique of his hasty rewrite of the reunion episode's ending. Larry pushes back: "We didn't screw up the finale. It was a good finale!" The cast replies in unison, "Eh."

Susie Greene launches her fledgling caftan business with a billboard in "The Gettysburg Address," S12, E6.

Vocab-U-L

Accidental Text on Purpose
THE ACCIDENTAL TEXT ON PURPOSE, S9, E6

Purposefully sending a text to someone while pretending that it was meant for someone else in order to get out of a sticky situation. Usage: *Freddy's girlfriend was upset when Larry offended her, so Freddy pretended to scold Larry in a text, but knowingly sent said text to Marilyn to prove that chivalry is not dead.*

Big Goodbye
HAPPY NEW YEAR, S10, E1

An exaggerated farewell when one departs a social gathering after avoiding that person all night on purpose. The feigned gesture helps the departing avoid a real conversation while ensuring that those left behind feel appreciated.

> It's the greatest move in history.

> I know a chat and cut when I see it.

Chat and Cut
VOW OF SILENCE, S8, E5

Striking up a conversation with a person in line whom one vaguely knows, or doesn't really care to speak with, in order to cut in said line. Can be used anywhere, but best suited for buffets and crowded amusement parks.

Hallway Hog
THE SURPRISE PARTY, S10, E6

One who causes a jam-up in a corridor or tight pedestrian thoroughfare by walking too slowly. Their actions are also known as "bad walker etiquette."

Middler
THE MINI BAR, S11, E3

One who's asked to sit in the middle of the table at a social gathering because they're adept at facilitating conversation and including others in the discussion. Usage: *Cousin Andy is not a middler so place him at the end of the table where he won't bore everyone.*

> You can't handle the middle. You're not a middler!

Outfit Tracker
FATWA! S9, E10

One who regularly notices when others wear the same articles of clothing multiple days in a row. Usage: *When F. Murray Abraham asked Larry David if he was wearing the previous day's clothing, Larry replied, "Nobody likes an outfit tracker... I just feel like I'm living in some kind of clothing police state, like it's 1984. Big Murray's watching me."*

> I have never seen a bunch-up like this in my life.

Pants Tent
THE PANTS TENT, S1, E1

The unfortunate gathering of fabric that occurs in the crotch area of one's pants when seated. Oftentimes, it resembles an erection once one stands. Usage: *Though Larry was happy to see her, he swore the unseemly bulge in his slacks was no more than a pants tent.*

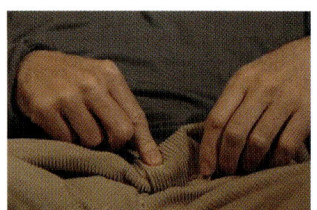

Pig Parker
VOW OF SILENCE, S8, E5

One who fails to park their car within the lines of their allotted space, in other words, every other motorist in Los Angeles. Usage: *A pig parker made it impossible for Larry to fit his Prius in the adjacent parking space, thus ruining his trip to the mall.*

Larry

Larry birthed dozens of new terms for old annoyances, fresh irritants, and the evergreen awkward situation. Decades from now, when linguists are struggling to find out where it all went wrong, they can turn to this handy guide for clues.

Plopper
THE FIVE-FOOT FENCE, S11, E1

One who flops down heavily on a couch, causing reverberations throughout the cushions. Usage: *After Larry spilled his glass of wine on Mary's couch, he blamed it on Susie when he accused her of being a "plopper."*

Schmohawk
MEET THE BLACKS, S6, E1

A reductive term for a bad driver, or anyone else whose behavior can be labeled foolish or stupid. Possibly derived from the Yiddish term schmuck.

Side Sit
SIDE SITTING, S10, E2

The act of two people sitting side by side at a restaurant instead of across the table from one another, giving the impression of intimacy. Usage: *The couple at the table by the window side sat, disgusting Larry with their wanton display of adoration.*

Stop and Chat
THE MASSAGE, S2, E10

The expectation to engage in meaningless conversation when one spontaneously runs into a friend or acquaintance. Usage: *Larry was forced to stop and chat when a simple "hello" or "goodbye" would have been sufficient.*

Premature Honey
THE ACCIDENTAL TEXT ON PURPOSE, S9, E6

Calling a romantic interest "honey" when it's too soon in the relationship, signaling a premature sign of commitment that may scare off said date.

Secondhand Semen
VEHICULAR FELLATIO, S7, E2

When someone (Richard Lewis's new girlfriend) has recently performed a blow job, avoid giving them a kiss goodbye because such an exchange may transfer secondhand semen from them to you.

> ## "So you're operating this place just out of spite?"

Tip Coordination
THE REUNION, S7, E3

The coordination required when two people split a check. It's important to tip the same amount so that one person doesn't look like an asshole. Usage: *Larry would not have been deemed an asshole by the waiter if Jason had agreed on tip coordination.*

Sample Abuser
THE IDA FUNKHOUSER ROADSIDE MEMORIAL, S6, E3

One who abuses their sampling privileges at an ice cream or frozen yogurt shop, holding up the line for everyone else behind them. These offenders may force others to "chat and cut" (see left).

Short Fly
RUNNING WITH THE BULLS, S9, E4

A pant zipper that doesn't provide enough room for the wearer to reach his hand in the opening and access his penis in order to urinate. Usage: *Larry had to pee but a short fly made the task more daunting.*

Spite Store
THE SPITE STORE, S10, E10

An establishment that one opens with the sole intent of putting a neighboring establishment out of business. Usage: *Larry opened his spite store, Latte Larry's, next to Mocha Joe's because he hated Joe and wanted his coffee shop to fail.*

Ugly Section
THE UGLY SECTION, S10, E7

The belief that a restaurant (specifically Tiato in Santa Monica) seats its attractive customers in one section and ugly customers in another.

Jeff, Susie, Cheryl & Leon

The best

moments on *Curb*–Cheryl's emergency run through a car wash, Susie's discovery of her daughter's beheaded doll, Jeff's questionable stain on Cheryl's blanket, Leon's "dick dial"– were made possible by a core cast of talented actors whose characters were Larry's closest antagonists and enablers. Together, Cheryl Hines, Susie Essman, Jeff Garlin, and JB Smoove helped elevate the series from a cult mockumentary to a must-see comedy for the twenty-first century.

Candid and on-set shots of Larry with costars Cheryl Hines, Susie Essman, Jeff Garlin, and JB Smoove.

Jeff Garlin

Jeff Garlin played Jeff Greene, Larry's longtime pal, talent manager, and bad-behavior buddy. Jeff often found himself cleaning up after Larry's social catastrophes, and Larry often found himself covering for Jeff's serial infidelity. Both gave each other terrible advice because in *Curb,* that's what friends are for.

PLAYED: **JEFF GREENE**   YEARS: **2000–2024**   EPISODES: **120**

Who is Jeff Greene, according to Jeff Garlin?
Jeff is someone who only wants to protect his friend, get away from his wife, and move forward. He has no moral compass, but he is affable.

How much are you like that other Jeff?
Except for the affability? Zero.

Jeff Greene is Larry's number one enabler. Do you agree with that description?
I'm more like a creator of havoc for him. Often when I tell him to do something, it turns into shit. So my job on the show is either to send him on a self-destructive adventure. It's like, "Hey, let's do this." I'll put it this way . . . Larry wrote me a card a few years after we started the show, where he thanked me for laying the pipe, because a lot of exposition comes out of my character. The exposition person is not the one where people say, "Oh, look what he did!" It's about setting things up for everybody else. But, for me, it was about Larry. So my job was twofold, to send Larry to do shit and lay the pipe for it all to happen.

Why does Jeff do everything to protect Larry?
He's Larry's manager, but, more importantly, he's Larry's best friend. He has to protect him because his relationship with Larry is much better than his relationship with his wife. I'm much closer with Larry than I am with Susie.

Jeff is a busy man. Where does he find the time to cheat on Susie?
Larry always asks Jeff, "How do you do this? How do you pull this off?" He's mystified by it. I've always got something going. But I can't divulge Jeff's secrets.

Describe Jeff's relationship with Susie.
If he gets divorced, he knows how much it'll cost him. If you remember that one season [Season 9], we had to move into a new house because I was fucking the realtor. When Susie got wind of this, she made me buy the biggest house the real estate person sold. And that was horrifying. So I know it's not good for me to cheat, but I still do.

Susie is terrifying. Her tirades, even though make-believe, seem like they'd be traumatizing on set.

When Susie [Essman] first joined the show and was told what she had to do, she went to [director] Larry Charles and Larry David and said, "I don't want to say this to Jeff." And they said, "Do it. Go nuts." And so she went nuts. I was amazed. I knew she had it in her. I didn't laugh, at least until after the take. But during the take, I never felt like laughing once when she yelled at me because it made me feel very sensitive, like, "Oh my God, I'm fucked!" And there's no time in my performance to find something amusing so I didn't laugh. Plus I'm really good about not breaking. It's Larry who can't look at her. We all get enjoyment from Larry breaking, and we might laugh based on that. But Susie and I are good at staying in character and sticking to what's going on.

You've been with *Curb* since the beginning. How has it evolved?

For the first three seasons or so, HBO called us their "little experimental show." I'm using that exact phrase because that's what they said. But the show would go on to be the longest-running scripted comedy in the history of the network. We tied with *Cheers* and *M*A*S*H* for the most "Best Comedy" Emmy nominations. Those shows won at least once. We never won. I don't know what the Academy had against us. Anyway...

Jeff and Larry crack up while shooting "You're Not Going to Get Me to Say Anything Bad About," S10, E4.

Jeff and Larry over the years. Jeff provides occasional wisdom (and frequent comic relief) in response to Larry's antics.

Larry David is notorious for saying the show was done at the end of each season, but then it would come back. How did you plan around that kind of uncertainty?

Larry is who he is. I waited until he had five or six ideas, and he was happy with the storyline, before I was like, "OK, we're gonna do it." I don't know how other people felt, but the uncertainty was great for me because it kept me on my toes. I knew I couldn't rely only on *Curb* income. That's why, in the offseason, I got a job on *The Goldbergs*. And I ended up doing other things, like *Never Have I Ever*.

Do you have any favorite *Curb* scenes?

There's too many to count. But every time I was in a scene with Larry, when it was just him and I, it was so creatively fulfilling. I felt like my voice was much larger than it is in other scenes that I was helping to mold. I love when there's a dinner scene and I don't say anything until I need to say something. I'll be quiet for a long time, and then it's like, "Oh, all right, I'll say this!" I love being quiet, and I can tell you this: In the entire history of the show, whenever I've tried to shoehorn anything funny in, it has never once worked.

By "shoehorn" do you mean planning your dialogue ahead of time rather than responding in the moment?

Yeah. It's better to just react to what's going on with Larry. It's the easiest form of improvisation. Just being able to relax and react—that's where the funniest stuff comes from.

Let's go back to the very beginning. When did you land the role of Larry's manager?

Right from the get-go, Larry said, "I want you to play my manager." I was like, "OK, but what about directing?" [*Garlin impersonates Larry.*] "No, I have an idea for something else." He loves my impression of him; whenever I do it, people laugh, so I do it as a matter of habit. Anyway, I was kind of disappointed. But I was also naive about how everything worked. I learned a lot from Larry and *Curb*.

Susie Essman

Susie Essman played Susie Greene, Jeff's wife, known for her abominable fashion sense, ear-shattering tirades, and lyrical lines such as "Get the fuck out of here, Larry!" or "Jeff, you fat fuck!" Susie was a fierce protector of her daughter, Sammi, and a frequent host of dinner parties that Larry often ruined. Above all, Susie was a force. Everyone feared her, particularly Larry. Her entrance into a scene was often accompanied by foreboding music, such as the spaghetti Western showdown anthem "For Whom the Bell Tolls."

PLAYED: SUSIE GREENE **YEARS: 2000–2024** **EPISODES: 92**

Are you like the other Susie?
No. I'm not one of these people who wants to play themselves. I'm with myself 24/7. I wanted to play a fun character, and I loved her. The thing about Susie that really resonates—people think that it's her language—but I think it's her comfort with her own anger. She's so completely comfortable and unapologetic in her rage.

Susie is renowned for her individualist style. Was there any particular inspiration behind her fashion choices?
We were shooting in this house up in the Hollywood Hills that was supposed to be where Jeff and Susie lived. It was very modern and decorated with all this black leather furniture. I was walking around, taking it all in, and it just came to me who this woman was—what her taste was, how she dressed. I had this vision of a woman who was so secure in herself and in her taste. She thinks that everything about her is absolutely right. She's the opposite of me. I'm a comic. I question everything, and I'm insecure about everything. Susie Greene is completely secure about everything she thinks. When she responds to something, she never second-guesses her behavior. She's always sure she's right. And she's sure she has the greatest taste in the world. I remember these girls in high school who seemed so mediocre, and yet they were so secure. I always marveled at them, like, there's nothing to be so secure about. But I guess they had mothers that really loved them.

Describe Susie's fashion sense.
She wears really expensive stuff but it just looks like crap. A lot of times with her outfits, there's one thing that's fine, but it's the combo platter that kills it. Like you could wear a nice zebra print top with a pair of jeans and look like a normal person. But Susie Greene adds a pair of leopard pants, and then accessorizes with all the jewelry and the bags . . . it's a lot. I was the one who came up with her look, and Larry just let me go with it. The Susie outfits eventually became a thing where I'd come to set in wardrobe and it would be the reveal of the day.

Scenes from "The Nanny," S3, E4 (**ABOVE**) and "Vertical Drop, Horizontal Tug," S12, E3 (**OPPOSITE**).

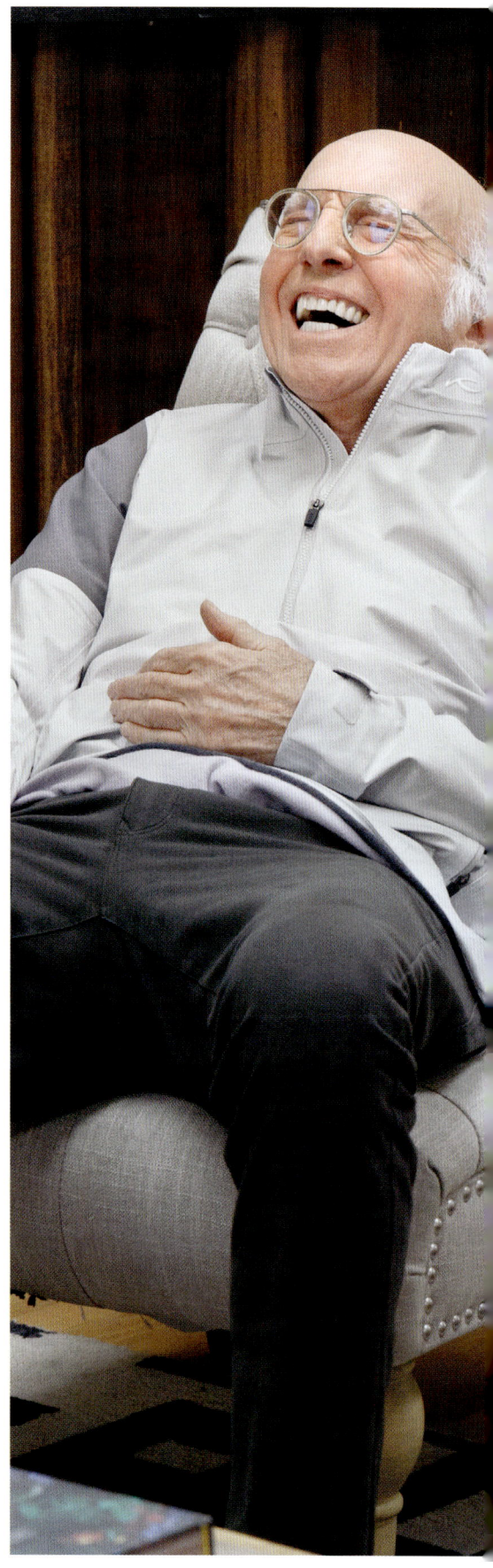

Did the clothes help you get into character?
Oh yes. I would put on the outfits and become her. Some actors work from the inside out, I worked from the outside in. I wouldn't even have to think about it once I had those outfits on. That was it. I *was* Susie Greene.

How did your castmates or guest stars keep a straight face when Susie was ripping them a new one?
Larry was the worst with breaking [character] because he loves to be yelled at. For some reason, when he's being yelled at, he gets the giggles. So I would do take after take where he just couldn't get through it. [Director] Jeff Schaffer used to say that Susie Greene was Larry's kryptonite.

When do you rein Susie in, or do you?
A lot of it depends on what's going on in the episode. In the morning, I'd always read the outline of what we were doing that day because I'd needed to know the flow of the episode. Is somebody else yelling and screaming at Larry in the scene right before mine? If that's the case, then I'm going to downplay it. I always look at what the scene needs. Where does it have to go and how can I drive it to that place? It's not just like you show up and start making up shit. There's a method to the madness.

Susie and Larry in "The Five-Foot Fence," S11, E1 (LEFT); "The Freak Book," S6, E5 (MIDDLE); and "The Surprise Party," S10, E6 (RIGHT).

What is one of Susie's better qualities?

She's very protective and loyal to her family. I was an unprotected child. I did not have a protective mother at all. So, when I'm playing Susie, I get a chance to act out that fantasy. It's just how I would want a mother to behave towards me if I was a kid. To protect me.

Susie is always berating Larry, but Larry often does something to deserve it. Does the real Larry David inspire that kind of anger in those around him?

No. I love him so deeply. He's one of my favorite people. The only man I love more than him is my husband . . . oh, and my dog. Having said that, he's clearly unusual. Just look at what's coming out of that brain. It's not normal. And I say that in a good way.

What is it about *Curb* that made it different from other comedies out there?

Curb has no script, it's all about the situation. So it's really a sitcom in the truest definition of the word. If Larry created a scene that was meant to be funny, it would be funny just by the situation that he created because he's such a genius. I completely trusted his comedic instincts. I never had to think about being funny. I just had to think about being in character and what my relationships were, what information I had to get, or what I needed in the scene. It was such a great way to perform and act. I just put on those crazy fucking outfits and followed the intention of the scene. It was the most creative way to work. I will never have that much fun acting again.

Did you *ever* prepare lines ahead of time?

Only once. I believe it was season three, an episode called "Grand Opening" [Episode 10]. It's the restaurant opening in the finale. I had a scene where I walk into the restaurant late and find the other characters are all cursing away. They're trying to make the chef with Tourette's feel comfortable, but Susie doesn't know that. Cheryl shouts, "You goddamn motherfuckin' bitch!" and I think that she's saying that to me. I say, "Fuck you, you car-wash cunt! I had a dental appointment!" I remember we shot that at like six o'clock in the morning, and I had been there since six o'clock at night. I was sitting in my trailer, it was taking so long, and I was just thinking about the line and what I was going to

say. Susie really likes alliterations like "four-eyed fuck" or "fat fuck." So I came up with "car-wash cunt." It's the only time I ever used that word across all the seasons.

Did you feel toxic after screaming at other actors in scenes?
No. It was like primal therapy. I would have scenes where I would scream and yell, and then I would go back to my hotel room and I'd sleep like a baby. I was so relaxed.

Describe a pivotal *Curb* moment for Susie.
I think it was in "The Doll" [Season 2, Episode 7], when it was established that Jeff and Larry live in fear of Susie. That is still one of my favorite episodes. It's a perfectly crafted half hour of comedy.

Susie kicks Larry out of her house all the time, but he's always back there by the next episode.
That's the thing about Susie. She will ban him from the house. She'll tell him, "Get the fuck out of my house!" Larry and I were trying to figure out how many times Susie kicked Larry out. And then the next day she'd be like, "Hey, Lar, wanna come to a dinner party?" All is forgiven. They have this relationship where they're kind of like brother and sister, where they're fighting and fighting, and then the next day they're playing Monopoly together.

When people see you out in public, are they afraid of you?
No, they want me to curse at them. Or they shove phones in my face and say, "It's my husband. Can you call him a fat fuck?" The only good thing about it is, if I'm in a restaurant and the service is bad, they expect me to not be nice. It's not a bad thing for people to have a little fear.

I live in New York and people stop me in the street all the time. I see people's faces drop when they say something to me and I'm gracious and kind to them. I see them get visibly disappointed. I never knew that this is what my life was going to end up being. That I was going to be beloved for telling people to go fuck themselves.

THE DOLL: S2, E7

Get me the the head!

—Susie to Jeff and Larry, demanding a replacement head after they cut the hair off a doll belonging to a TV executive's daughter

Cheryl Hines

Cheryl Hines played Larry's long-suffering wife, Cheryl David. The character endured her partner's irksome idiosyncrasies with steely grace and unimaginable patience. She also possessed the rare ability to see through Larry's bullshit while rising above it. The two split after Larry tested her limits one last time in the season six finale, but she remained in his orbit until the very end.

PLAYED: CHERYL DAVID **YEARS: 2000–2024** **EPISODES: 110**

Why did people relate to Cheryl David?
People come up to me all the time and say, "My husband's just like Larry David," and "I'm just like Cheryl David." I think they relate to her because they might be living with someone who does things like Larry does on the show, where he will say the wrong thing but he would never think that he's saying the wrong thing. It may even be the truth, but it's not something that needs to be said at that moment. People have said that I'm the voice of reason on the show.

Cheryl did appear to be the most grounded character in Larry's world.
Yeah, and I think she represented how the audience was feeling. She needed to know why he's doing what he's doing, and what his thought process was. Like why would you pick up a hooker and take her to the Dodgers game? Why?! Then he'd say something like, "I wanted to use the car pool lane." She needed to make sense of his actions.

How much did you know about Cheryl David, or the 1999 *Curb* HBO special, before auditioning for the role?
I didn't know anything about the project. I was told something about a one-hour stand-up special that Larry David was doing, and that it was going to be in the style of a documentary—basically a mockumentary about Larry going back to do stand-up. I didn't really know who Larry David was other than he created *Seinfeld* with Jerry Seinfeld, and that was a big reason for his success.

Why do you think you were chosen for the role?
One of the reasons I was cast is because I was an unknown actress. Larry wanted to blur the line of what's real and what's not real. In that special, you had Richard Lewis playing himself. Everybody knows, that's Richard Lewis. You had Larry David. It's really Larry David. Jerry Seinfeld was in it. A lot of famous people were in it. I think Larry wanted to create the illusion that, "Oh, this must be his wife because I've never seen her as an actress." That's how it started. He wanted people to identify with the actors and comedians and say, "Oh, these are real people."

But as the show gained popularity, your anonymity waned.

It was really interesting for me because it was the first big show that I was part of, and my character's name is my real name. So at first it was very confusing to me when people would come up and say, "Cheryl!" then start talking to me like they knew me. I just assumed that I somehow knew them. It wouldn't be until they referenced something from *Curb*, or until they talked about Larry, that I realized, "Oh, it's that!" It took a while for me to acclimate.

They always ask me where Larry is. I'll be in an airport, running for a plane, and they'll say, "Cheryl, where's Larry?" I was shooting something in Canada, and a guy said, "Hey, Cheryl, how's your vagina?" It took me a second. Then I [remembered], there's an episode with Wandering Bear asking me how my vagina is. So, yeah, they ask for things from the show.

Celebrity guests were a constant on *Curb*, including luminaries like Bruce Springsteen and Martin Scorsese. Was it intimidating to work with people like that, particularly in the beginning?

I never felt intimidated. I mean, when we started, I didn't know if I had even seen a picture of Larry David. It was back in the dark ages when you couldn't just Google somebody and find out everything about them. So I wasn't intimidated. I bonded with Larry so quickly and easily; I felt like I'd known him for years. The same with the rest of the cast—Jeff, Susie, Richard. We were so comfortable with each other. Even when we had people like Dustin Hoffman on the show, I never felt intimidated. It felt like they were coming into our little world.

Scenes from "The Mini Bar," S11, E3 **(TOP)** and "What Have I Done?" S11, E8 **(BOTTOM)**.

Timothy Olyphant (Mickey), Kimberly Shannon Murphy (Sasha), Cheryl, and Ted Danson in "You're Not Going to Get Me to Say Anything Bad About," S10, E4.

The real Larry David often tests the limits of tolerable human behavior through his character on the show. Did you ever think he, or the show, went too far?

I remember there was one season when Larry was writing the story outlines. We weren't shooting yet, but we were talking, and he said, "I think I'm going to write a show where my mother dies and my dad doesn't tell me, and I miss the funeral." I said, "That's not funny." He said, "No, it's funny." And I said, "No, that's sad." Then he took that as a challenge and said, "You watch. It'll be funny." And it was.

Why does fictional Cheryl put up with Larry?
Her tolerance was pretty high for crazy because she knew his intentions, so when everyone else got offended because he did something ridiculous, she could usually float above it all.

Name Larry and Cheryl's most epic fight.
Of all of the fights we've had? Wow. There were a lot… The episode when I leave him was based on a story that I told him [in real life] about a friend of mine who was on an airplane. It looked like the landing gear wasn't working properly, so the pilot started circling to dump fuel because he thought it was going to be a really rough landing. Everybody on the plane started calling their loved ones to tell them the landing gear is not working and that they were bracing for the worst. My friend called her husband and he said, "I gotta call you back. The cable technician is here. I've waited all day for this guy. He just walked in."

Larry thought that story was so funny. In the scene [from "The TiVo Guy," Season 6, Episode 7], Cheryl calls Larry from the plane, but the TiVo guy is there with him. TiVo—that's how long ago it was. Anyway, I'm on the plane in turbulence. The plane is rocking, and everybody's scared. I call Larry and say, "I just want to tell you that the plane might go down." He asks, "What shows do we need to worry about saving?" When I get home later, I'm so mad at him, that was the final straw. I say, "I can't do it anymore. I always tell people there's another side of you that they don't see, but there's not another side of you." That's what finally ended our marriage.

Larry and Cheryl in "Funkhouser's Crazy Sister," S7, E1.

You cut your teeth as a performer with the improv group The Groundlings. Can you describe what "winging it" meant as a regular on *Curb*?

For the first three seasons, I never had a story outline to read. I would show up on the set and say, "What can somebody tell me? What is going on in this show?" Larry would always keep me on a need-to-know basis. I was really glad that he finally let me read outlines for the fourth season and beyond, because I do remember reading a scene where it said, "Cheryl's in her bathing suit at the beach, and Larry's fully clothed." I was like, whoa. As an actor, I need a minute to think about being in my bathing suit on-screen. Even the story outlines are just skeleton outlines, so he would not really tell me what was going to happen in the scene. It might just say, "Larry comes home. Cheryl tells Larry her parents are staying for two weeks," and that's all we get. But I already know just by reading that, that he's not going to want my parents to stay for two weeks.

Cheryl David often had no idea what Larry was up to. She'd find out after the fact, when people were screaming at him and he'd begrudgingly confess.

That's true. He would go and do something stupid and come back and tell me about it and I would ask, "Why in the world would you have a water bottle in your pants when the little girl hugged you?" But I wasn't usually with him in the moment or I would have tried to stop him. That's who I was on the show. It was usually Jeff or JB or somebody that would go along with whatever he was doing.

So you, too, were learning in real time about what happened on set when you weren't in the scene?

I never knew what was shot in other scenes. People in the improv world would make fun of me for asking questions [on the show] because when you're doing live improv, you don't ask, "Why would you do that?" But on *Curb*, I had to, because I often didn't know what Larry was talking about. Like, there was a scene where he and Richard Lewis asked me to bake some brownies with Benadryl in them. What?! Why would I do that?! I had to ask what was going on. There was a season when Larry tripped Shaquille O'Neal accidentally at the Lakers game. Whenever he went anywhere in LA after that, people would boo him. But I wasn't with him when he tripped Shaq. So when we walk into Starbucks and people are booing us, I had to ask, "What happened? What's going on?" It made for an added element of surprise.

***Curb* was unparalleled at elevating the element of surprise to masterful levels.**

It made the show so special. Like, Larry and I are in a scene, and he's talking to my mother, and she asks, "Do you have a mint?" Larry says, "A mint?" He reaches into his pocket, and he pulls out a mint and gives it to her. And she says, "This is a loose mint." And he says, "Well you should be thankful I even found a mint." She says, "I don't want a loose mint that's been in your pocket." I am biting the inside of my cheek because I don't want to ruin that moment by laughing, but it's so specific and surprising, the two bickering about a loose mint in his pocket. You don't get those little moments on other shows.

JB Smoove

JB Smoove played Leon, the uninvited houseguest who'd eventually replace Cheryl as Larry's foil. Cheryl invited Leon's family, the Blacks of Louisiana, to stay with her and Larry after they were displaced by a hurricane. Leon, however, lived in Los Angeles and wasn't affected by the natural disaster, making it all the more curious when he inexplicably showed up and moved in. Even after the rest of Leon's family left, he stayed, eating sugary cereal and dispensing terrible advice to Larry.

PLAYED: LEON BLACK   **YEARS: 2007–2024**   **EPISODES: 56**

What are Leon's talents?

He's good at math and fucking. That's his whole thing. Leon always says he has a black belt in fucking, like, "I've been kung fu-ing that ass for a while now." Even in "Denise Handicap" [Season 7, Episode 5], when Leon finds out Larry couldn't perform with her, he says, "Give me her number. I'll go over there and break that ass in two pieces. I'll bend that ass like Beckham. I'll have a wheelchair-bound lady tap-dancing."

Larry and Leon develop a codependent relationship. How did you nurture that fantastic dysfunction?

Leon's argument was always that he's giving Larry something. "I'm helping your ass out, Larry! And what are you giving me? You don't give me anything." Leon's role is that when Larry has decisions that he can't make his mind up about, he comes to Leon. Leon doesn't go to Larry. Leon says, "Larry, you don't know how to handle yourself. You need somebody who's been through a whole lot, to set you straight and point you in the right direction." Leon's really good at giving Larry bad advice. Then they became dependent on each other. They needed that yin and yang.

Leon first appears in the season six premiere, but part of the joke is that he arrives with almost no explanation.

Leon had no origin. You don't even know where he came from. All you knew was his sister, Loretta [Vivica A. Fox], lived there with Larry and the family. And you knew that Leon lived in LA. So you're thinking, "Why would he come over to Larry's if he has a place in LA already? His family is from New Orleans." So we started building this story of why he's in Larry's house. First, the questions: "So he's been displaced by Hurricane Edna and he's from Louisiana?" My sister answers, "No, he's my brother, Leon. He lives here in LA." It's like OK, that makes no sense, but everyone rolls with it.

So who is Leon?

Larry never knows who the fuck Leon is. No one does! I tried to give Larry something he didn't know about Leon every time we did a scene, but still left enough mystery so he didn't know where the hell he came from. Did he skip out on the rent at his place? Larry still doesn't know his complete background. He still can't prove if half the stories that Leon tells are true.

> "HE'S GOOD AT MATH AND FUCKING. THAT'S HIS WHOLE THING."
>
> —JB SMOOVE ON LEON BLACK

Larry and Leon in "The Table Read," S7, E9 **(TOP)** and "Artificial Fruit," S10, E3 **(BOTTOM)**.

Then once Larry and Cheryl's marriage broke up, that opened the door for Leon to step in and build a relationship with Larry. It was obvious Larry needed somebody, but he also can't get rid of Leon. He won't leave.

You began your comedy career in stand-up and had recurring roles on *Everybody Hates Chris* and *SNL*, where you were also a writer. *Curb*, however, really tapped your improv skills. You clearly thrive in a scriptless environment.

Being that *Curb* is improvised, we did get outlines, but a lot of times I never read them because I felt like it would take me someplace different. I didn't want to overthink what I was going to say as opposed to just giving a natural reaction of how Leon might address Larry in a scene. I didn't want to be a robot. I wanted to really address how I thought the character would react to him.

Leon's wardrobe almost rivals Susie's in the what-the-hell-is-he-wearing department. How did you develop his playa-meets-couch-potato look?

All that came from just vibing with the wardrobe person to figure out what Leon would wear. Like with the durag—I said, "Get a bunch of them in different colors. I'm gonna change it up all the time." Then the tank top, and the shirt over the tank top. The socks up to his knees. It was like I was building a uniform that he would wear constantly. The flip-flops. Even the robe he would wear—I told wardrobe, "I don't think he should have a belt for the robe. I want him to hold it closed with his hand all the time." There's something really funny about the fact that he lost that belt a long time ago.

Why does Larry listen to Leon?
Leon elaborates to the point where he's got you hooked on what he's telling you. But at the same time, he's trying to give you good, sound advice on how to handle things based on what he's been through. Larry has never been through half the shit that Leon's been through. Larry's like, "Yeah, you're right. Good idea. Good idea." But it's a horrible, horrible idea. Still, Larry does it because he's caught up in Leon, even though he doesn't know if this dude's being truthful or not. That's the foil people need: "Should I do it this way? Or should I do it that way?" It's like a fork in the road, and Leon is the fork.

Do you have a favorite Leon-ism?
It's always about "gettin' that ass." Like, "You gotta defend yourself, Larry. You can't let another man belittle you like that and bring you down. You gotta defend yourself!" And Larry says, "What am I gonna do? The guy will kick my ass!" You gotta verbally fuck somebody up—that's Leon's philosophy. Gettin' that ass is an anthem for not letting people take advantage of you or put you in a fucked-up position where you can't defend yourself. And there's, like, five different versions of gettin' that ass. One involves lighter fluid and matches, like an ass arsonist or something.

You chose for Leon not to know anything about *Seinfeld*. Why?

Because that gives Larry something to play with. Leon never even knew what the hell *Seinfeld* was. In the *Seinfeld* season of *Curb* [Season 7], during the run-through of the show, Leon's on set asking, "Who's that guy right there?" Larry says, "That's Jerry. You've never seen the show?" "Nope," Leon says, "I dunno who the hell these characters are. And who's she?" Larry says, "That's Elaine." Leon says, "Oh OK, so Jerry and Elaine—they fucking, right?" Then Newman walks in and now it's, "Who is this little fat bastard?"

Just like Leon had no business being on the set of that reunion, he also has no business staying with Larry in New York.

Right. Larry goes to New York, and Leon just shows up. Larry's walking up to the building and it's, "Hey, what's up!" Now Leon's in New York. He drove Larry's Prius across the country with no goddamn license. And Larry said, "Why didn't you fly?" Leon says, "I need an ID for that." They go up to the penthouse and Leon's like, "Where's my room at?" Leon livin' large now, talking about classy shit like champagne-filled croissants.

I loved when Michael J. Fox was our [upstairs] neighbor because that's when we find out that Leon thinks Larry can't fight. Larry was getting irritated because of the noise upstairs, so Leon said, "Man, that's a good fight. You versus him. That's even Steven." Larry asks, "What do you mean even Steven?" Leon says, "You old, and this motherfucker got the shakes. That's an even fight. If I go up there, it's Michael J. Fucked Up."

What is Leon's greatest achievement?

I feel he got Barack Obama elected. When the man was just running for president, Leon said, "I'm like Barack Obama, I'm the president of hittin' that ass." The man wasn't even president yet. But then he was elected. Leon did that.

Larry and Leon in various hilarious (and absurd) situations through the years.

LEON'S GUIDE TO LOVE

1. BRIN[G]
2. WHEN IN DOU[BT]
3. DON'T BE A M[OPEY DICK]
4. ASS IS ASS
5. YOUNG.
6. RE-TAP THA[T]
7. SOME NEW AS[S]
8. IS A GOOD FU[CK]

1. In Leon's first-ever episode, he is accused by Cheryl of ejaculating on a bed in the David home. He denies the accusation, memorably explaining to Larry that the stain can't be his because "I gets mines, Larry. I brings the ruckus to the ladies." (The "jack-off suspect" turns out to be Jeff.) **2.** In season eight's "The Bi-Sexual," Larry finds himself in competition with Rosie O'Donnell when they date the same woman (played by Amy Landecker). Larry feels that Rosie has the lesbian advantage, but Leon argues the opposite: Rosie doesn't have a penis. "What dangles below your bat?! We got bat and balls, what do ladies have?! What do gloves do? Catch the goddamn balls. Bats and balls run the fucking world." He then suggests a grand-slam idea and offers Larry Viagra. **3.** Larry is depressed over his split from Cheryl in the season six finale, "The Bat Mitzvah." Leon says Larry is moping around the house like a "Mopey Dick" and encourages his pal to find a date for Jeff's daughter's bat mitzvah, since Cheryl will be there with a plus-one, and to "focus on the ass." Leon tells Larry that he needs to adopt a new persona to reenter the dating world: "Grow a mustache, grow a goatee, grow sideburns, become another motherfucker right now." **4.** Larry learns more about Leon, including his open door policy on sleeping with married women. ("I hit it and I quit it!" he tells guest star Tim Meadows during a season six mix-up about sleeping with Meadows' character's wife.) In season seven's "Vehicular Fellatio," Larry accidentally tips off a friend to Leon having an affair with his wife. "I'm tappin' that ass. I've been kung fu-ing that ass for a while now," admits Leon to Larry. When Larry asks Leon why he has to fool around with married women, Leon has a simple explanation: "Ass is ass." **5.** In the season eleven premiere, "The Five-Foot Fence," Larry is dating Lucy Liu, and she witnesses him walking into a glass door. Leon warns Larry that it's his second feeble act and sure enough, Lucy tells Larry she doesn't view him sexually anymore. When a similar situation happens

G THE RUCKUS.
BT, VIAGRA.
OPEY DICK.
5. STAY
AP THAT ASS. 7.
ASS. 8. GET
S. 9. AN HOUR
CK WINDOW.

with Leon's girlfriend, he compares himself to an ostracized pigeon when explaining to Larry why he blew it. "You can't unsee that shit," he says. **6.** In season eight's "The Mini Bar," Leon pitches Larry an idea for the hotel mini bar that Larry is planning on curating at Freddy Funkhouser's new hotel: Tap Water. "People go to hotels to fuck," he says. "So I take all the elements of an ED pill and infuse it into a beverage called Tap Water, based on tapping that ass. It's like an energy drink for your dick." Larry calls it one of Leon's best ideas ever. **7.** In season ten's "Happy New Year," Larry comes home late at night and is cagey about where he was. Leon assumes it's because he was with a woman. "This right here is called tappin' hours," he says. "These are the hours when people are tappin' ass. Older white men should not be out this fucking late. There's not late-night yacht club or late-night garage sales." Larry takes his time before finally revealing to Leon that it's his ex-wife Cheryl he's been seeing. Leon is thrilled that he's "re-tapping that ass." **8.** In the season eight premiere, "The Divorce," Larry and Marty Funkhouser are both getting a divorce. Leon suggests they drive around honking their horns like when people get married with a "Just divorced" sign to signal their availability. "Get out there and get some new ass," he tells Marty. Later, when Larry loses the house in the divorce, Leon confesses that he has had sex with women in Larry's bed. In his defense, he asks, "How you gonna fuck two bitches in a twin bed?" **9.** In season nine's "Namaste," Larry is eager to have sex with his new girlfriend, an NBC censor named Bridget (played by Lauren Graham). She invites Larry to her house to seal the deal, saying she has an hour, and Leon comments that an hour is a good fuck window. But Larry doesn't have his car, so Leon suggests Larry use the guest house that he stays in at Larry's home. Larry refuses, calling it a "scum shack" where Leon must have "ejaculated 10,000 times in two years." Leon says his room is broken in: "It's primed and ready to fuck."

Curb

Your Enthusiasm should have arrived with a disclaimer when it premiered on television a quarter century ago: *The stories you are about to see were inspired by true events, but certain characters, incidents, and details have been altered or fictionalized for maximum hilarity.*

The new series wasn't a wacky family sitcom, a jokey roommate comedy, or even a witty workplace satire. It followed Larry David, playing a character named Larry David, in storylines that straddled the line between reality and fiction.

Take season three's "The Grand Opening." It featured a snooty food critic who looked suspiciously like the film critic Roger Ebert, and both men used the thumbs-up or thumbs-down symbol to describe their feelings about a restaurant or movie. For example, Ebert gave David's 1998 film, *Sour Grapes*, a thumbs-down, writing, "Scene after scene crashes to the floor. I can't easily remember a film I've enjoyed less." David appeared to later take his revenge in *Curb* when his character hit the fictional food critic with a dodgeball, breaking both of his thumbs.

There also seemed to be little daylight between *Curb* Larry and real-life Larry. Both men cocreated a hit show called *Seinfeld*. Both men were semiretired. Both men drove a Prius. In short, they pretty much seemed to be the same guy. But were they?

It all depends on whom you ask...

In "The Grand Opening," S3, E10, Larry is forced to feed a food critic spaghetti after he breaks the critic's hands during a dodgeball game.

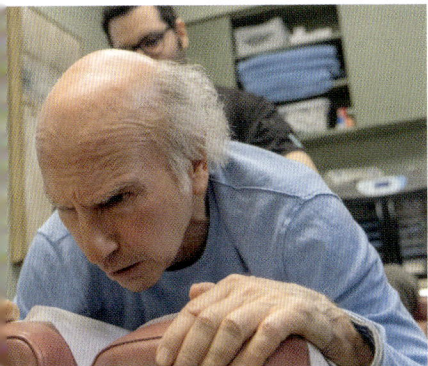

The many looks of Larry David.

Larry venting his frustrations in "Affirmative Action," S1, E9 **(LEFT)** and "The Shrimp Incident," S2, E4 **(RIGHT)**.

Bob Weide

Director (Seasons 1–5, then periodically thereafter)

I've known Larry for a long time, since back when he was much more like TV Larry; so before marriage, fatherhood, and success mellowed him. I remember we were at the bank, standing in line, and he wanted to make a deposit or something simple. He said, "Is it my imagination or has this line stopped moving? We've been standing here for like ten minutes." He was looking at the people at the teller windows and zeroed in on one guy, "It's that one. Why are they chitchatting? You can't chitchat in the bank." I recall Larry saying, "Excuse me, are you gonna be here all day chitchatting? We all like to chitchat, but some of us have to be somewhere!"

Larry was a frustrated guy who was prone to speak out. He must have known he was brilliant and he was not getting acknowledged for it. And when you become that wealthy and successful, it's hard to complain that nobody respects you anymore. Once *Curb* became known, he couldn't act like that in public anymore, because he's Larry David. He had to keep all that stuff inside. But TV Larry got to speak up. That's why we all admire that character. He vents his frustration, whereas we all tend to just swallow it and grow a tumor.

THE SURPRISE PARTY: S10, E6

Is that your top speed on this thing?

—Larry to Wally, regarding his poor hallway etiquette

Larry and Sean Hayes (Christopher Mantle) crack up during a take for "Fish Stuck," S12, E5.

Jeff Garlin, Bryan Cranston, Larry, and Susie Essman on set for "Running with the Bulls," S9, E4.

Jason Alexander
Curb guest star who played David's alter ego, George Costanza, across all nine seasons of *Seinfeld*

Most people only see the side of Larry that says, "I'm more than this situation. I'm the smartest guy in the room. I know what's right and wrong. I'm not afraid of social mores." That's the side that Larry capitalized on to create the Larry of *Curb*. I believe that Larry himself, and he's going to say I'm wrong, spends a good deal of time having to get to that place because the other part of him really is considerate and generous. He feels an awful lot. And so it is possible that Larry would enter a circumstance similar to something he does on *Curb* and thinks the things that *Curb* Larry does, but real-life Larry goes, "No, I can't treat somebody like that." He suppresses that. And *Curb* was his outlet to let the biggest part of his id go crazy. So to me, they're very different guys.

Ted Danson
Cheers and *Becker* star who guest-starred on *Curb* across all twelve seasons

The only regret the world should have that *Curb* became so popular is that it gave real-life Larry license to be more Larry. There was no need for him to even pretend anymore. In real life he had rules like, "I'll never go out to other people's houses for dinner because I can't get up and leave whenever I feel like it without catching a lot of flak." Whereas now, if he goes out to dinner with you at a restaurant, he can do that. He can leave. *Curb* did that.

Jeff Schaffer
Writer, director, and executive producer (Seasons 6–12)

So many *Curb* situations are based on things that happen to Larry outside the show, so people always ask us, "Was that scene because of me?" And because it all takes place on LA's Westside, everyone's conceited enough to think it was about them. Often the answer is, "No, but it was someone like you. Surprise, surprise, there's another asshole in LA."

Cheryl Hines
Cheryl David

He was talking to me about bringing a new character in who'd be Cheryl's sister. I was like, "OK, what's her name?" He said, "Well what's your sister's name?" I told him it's Becky. He said, "OK, then that's her name. Becky." The real first name thing did get confusing at times, especially when people I didn't recognize would call my name. It's like, do they know me, or the other Cheryl?

Jimmy Kimmel
Late night host of *Jimmy Kimmel Live!* who guest-starred on *Curb* and fraternized with David outside the show

We were at a party at someone's house, I think it was Conan O'Brien's. Larry was standing in front of the fireplace trying to decide whether it was OK for him to throw his gum in the fireplace. He had assembled a group of people around him to debate the gum question, and I happened to walk into the middle of the conversation. People were actually arguing. Someone asked what I thought. I said, "I think if it's a wood-burning fireplace, it's OK to throw gum in it. If it's gas, it's not." The matter was settled to Larry's satisfaction, otherwise we may have been there all night.

Another time I invited him to come to dinner at my house on a Monday night, and he accepted the invitation. A week before the date of the dinner, I get a text from him, asking, "How do I get in?" I wrote back, "Get in where?" And he texts, "I'm in front of your house." I'm like, "Larry, the dinner is next week. I'm at a funeral." He was very happy because he'd made the effort by accepting the invitation and showing up, but he didn't have to go to the dinner. It was a big win for him all the way around.

THIS PAGE: Larry and Cheryl in "Meet the Blacks," S6, E1. **OPPOSITE:** Larry grins over a giant plate of hot dogs in "The Mini Bar," S11, E3.

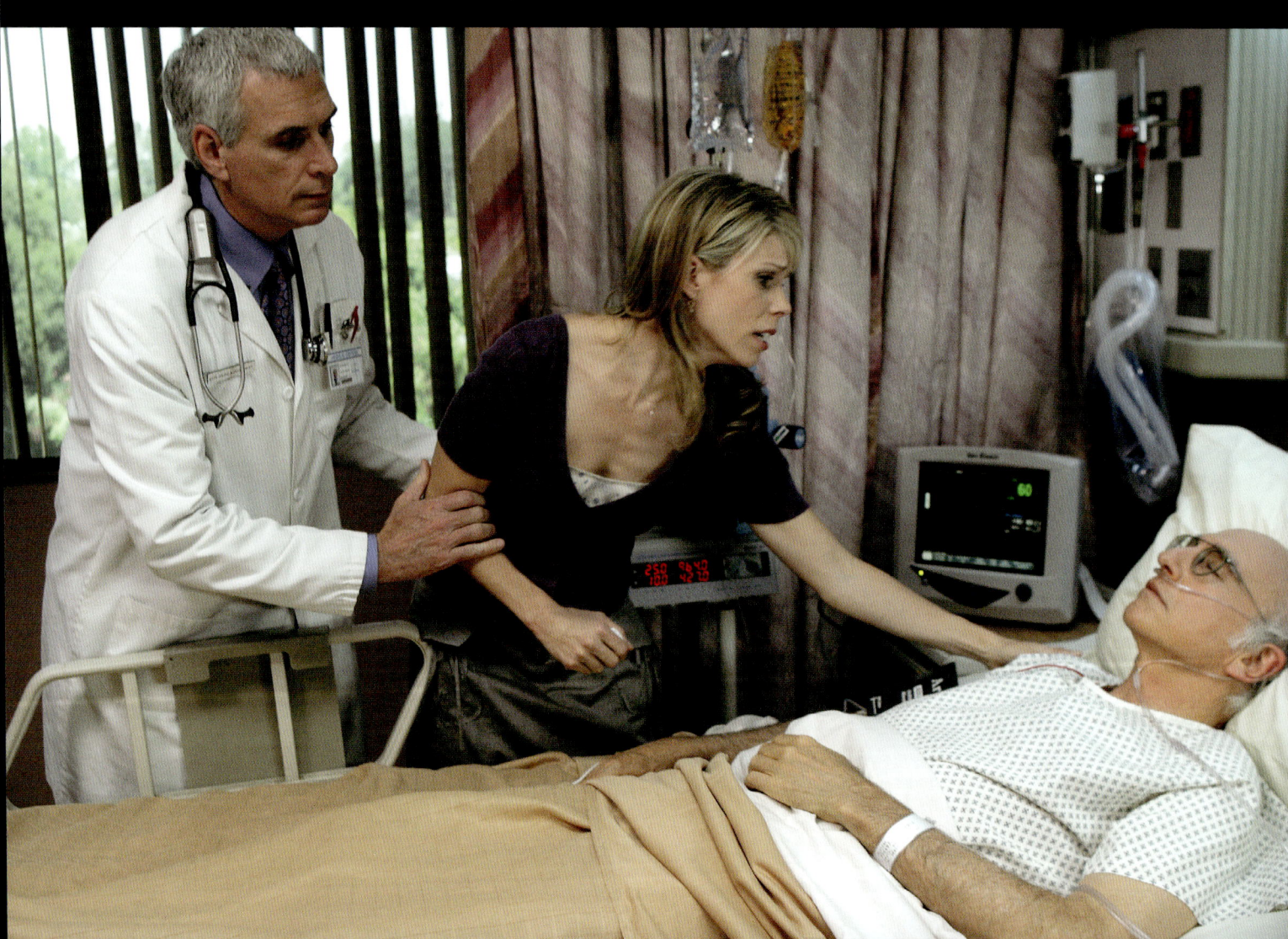

SO WOULD IT BE OK IF I FOOLED AROUND

A LITTLE UNTIL YOU GOT THERE?

—Larry to Cheryl, when he nearly dies after donating a kidney to Richard Lewis

Erin O'Malley
Producer (Seasons 5–8), director of "The Surprise Party"

The real Larry is not at all like the Larry you see in *Curb*. Here's an example: In the season we did with Mel Brooks [Season 4], the character of Mel's assistant was supposed to be a lesbian and she and her partner were adopting a baby. There was a whole improv where Larry's asking her how on earth can she have a baby. And then there's something about adopting a baby from Africa. Naming the baby. Larry was basically touching on cultural appropriation, and it was really funny and ahead of its time.

I'm gay, and I was married to my wife, and we had two young daughters. Between takes, he came up to me behind the monitors and said, "Hey, is this too offensive?" He was asking me earnestly. He would be mortified that I'm telling you this right now. Anyway, he earnestly asked me, and I said, "It's fine. This is great. This is really hilarious." He's like, "You sure?" I was like, "Yes, it's fantastic." The point is that he actually really does give a shit. He actually cares.

Jason Alexander

Larry might disagree with me vehemently, but I always saw what was so lovely about him. I saw his shyness, where his vulnerabilities were, what he was insecure about. Larry has this wonderful thing that he was able to write into George, and once I understood it, I could really take advantage of it. He lives in this strange dichotomy, where he feels that he's not terribly talented, not terribly attractive, not terribly interesting, not terribly important. He really undervalues himself. At the same time he thinks, "I don't understand why I'm not getting my due. I should be getting respect. I should be successful. Why don't people listen to me?" They both live in equal measures inside him, often side by side, and I always found that so charming.

Mel Brooks invites Larry to audition for *The Producers* during "Mel's Offer," S4, E1.

"As curmudgeon he seems to be, is a lovely guy."

—BRYAN CRANSTON

Susie Essman
Susie Greene

Not all shows are happy sets, but *Curb* was always a happy set. Not to say there weren't times when there was tension [or when] we had ridiculously long days and things went wrong. I mean, that happens. But in general, it was a place where everybody was glad to be there and wanted to be there. It was an incredibly loyal crew who would come back year after year because they loved working with Larry so much. Larry set the tone for that.

Bryan Cranston
Breaking Bad star who guest-starred on *Curb* and *Seinfeld*

Larry is that guy who sees things and goes, "Why is there a doggie [poop] bag? Dogs don't pick up after me. Why should I pick up after them?" He explores the mundane and the microcosms of life to its nth degree, and that, of course, is the essence of *Curb*. But he also loves to laugh, and I think he truly loves to perform. As curmudgeonly as he seems to be, Larry is a lovely guy.

Christina Mongini
Costume designer (Seasons 5–8)

Larry's going to be rolling his eyes when he reads this, but there is an understated, casual elegance to him. He carries himself tall and lean, with a subtle grace. I'm of course dealing with what he wears, and his look is very streamlined. It's comfortable, casual, long drapey lines. Soft corduroys and soft, well-made jackets. He is this entity that glides through the room, and his attire reflects that.

Richard Kind
Semi-regular *Curb* cast member who played Cousin Andy

Larry doesn't compromise. He goes, "I know this is good. I know this is funny. You like it? Good on you. If not, then go fuck yourself. But I know this is good." I think that's a great way to live your life. He knows what's good and what's funny. And you know how the famous stand-up story goes: Larry's up onstage doing jokes, and he walks off because he's like, "I'm too good for this audience. You're too stupid." That's how he lives his life and I appreciate that. But on the flip side, even though he appears selfish and self-consumed, he's a very good man.

y as Larry

Larry taking a break during shooting.

Vince Vaughn
Freddy Funkhouser (Seasons 10–12)

When Freddy is figuring out what goes into the minibars for a hotel he just bought, he finds Larry's got a fascination for minibars. He didn't really see that coming. You might predict Larry dispelling a minibar as something of no interest, but instead, his light goes off. Then you realize that for years, Larry's held on to these ideas of what he wishes was in a minibar. He's really turned on by the fact that he might get to create one now. And then it becomes this thing about having his creative process thwarted when his ideas have to go through a committee, like what's testing well? It's not a process he's into. It takes the fun out of following his instincts when his minibar ideas get dragged down by this corporate, please-everybody point of view. It's the story of Larry David.

Jerry Seinfeld

In comedy you always just use the parts of yourself that you think will be funny. Sometimes they're real, sometimes they're made up.

Steve Rasch
Editor and music supervisor (Seasons 1–12)

For *Curb*, we would hire editors for their skill, but [we'd also ask], "Are they good in the room?" We wanted them to gel and be part of a team, and also know how to deal with Larry. He's from Brooklyn, and when he's shouting at one of the other producers, he may sound angry, but he's not. He's just from Brooklyn.

When Larry was watching cuts, he would often say, "Well, I would never say that, but TV Larry will say that." So TV Larry is Larry David unleashed, and the real guy controls the two.

Jeff Schaffer

Larry has always been able to take moments that he and other people have suffered through and make them funny. Like, "Oh God, that happens to me all the time!" The whole life of the show is wish fulfillment. Like, "I wish I had done what Larry did." "I wish I had told him off like Larry told him off." You know who else wishes that? Real Larry. It's wish fulfillment for him, too.

A contact sheet from "Chet's Shirt," S3, E1

"He gets to be Superman."

—ALEC BERG

Dave Mandel
Writer, director, and executive producer (Seasons 5–8)

TV Larry and real-life Larry have very similar thought patterns. But real-life Larry is smart enough not to say them out loud, or at least he waits until we're at the office.

Lauren Graham
Bridget (Season 9)

Before a *Curb* take with Larry, he was chewing gum, so when they yelled "Action!" he spit it out on the ground. I was like, "Larry, that's trash. That's gross." He was like, "No, gum is not trash." I was like, "What?! Gum is trash." And he was like, "No, gum is not trash." I said, "What constitutes trash?" He's like, "If a bird can eat it . . ." Then he just went down this rabbit hole. But it's like that blur between reality and the show, where every conversation feels like I'm in an episode of *Seinfeld* or *Curb*.

Alec Berg
Writer, director, and executive producer (Seasons 5–8)

When real Larry is in line at a frozen yogurt place and the person in front of him is taking too many samples, he stands there thinking, "This fucking asshole. I can't believe it." Then he writes it in his notebook as a funny thing for TV Larry to talk about. For years, Larry would carry this notebook around, and anytime he felt frustrated or uncomfortable or embarrassed, he would write it down. Those little moments became great *Curb* stories. Larry has these impulses that he knows he has to restrain because he has to live in civilized society, but on TV, he can act on all those. He gets to be Superman.

Jon Hamm
***Mad Men** star who guest-starred on Curb as himself (Seasons 10–11)*

It's all about degrees of separation. Both Larrys will sit at a dinner table and muse about how uncomfortable the chair is, or why the salt shakers are so small, or some sort of minutia that [they] find interesting or annoying or fascinating. But what I think real Larry has over fake Larry is an appreciation of people and life. He's not a misanthrope. He's engaged in life. He just finds certain things interesting and funny and has no compunction about sharing his opinion on this. That's where the similarity exists. But the negative aspect of [that attention to detail] is certainly played up for laughs. Anybody who's spent time with Larry can tell you, he's a joy to be around.

ON THE JOB WITH LARRY

Throughout *Curb*, Larry took on a variety of gigs. Here are some résumé highlights.

1. CAR SALESMAN Season two begins with Cheryl and Jeff encouraging a retired and rudderless Larry to get back to work. Returning to TV after *Seinfeld* feels like too much commitment— "I'm married, that's plenty of work," Larry tells Jeff. Instead, he challenges himself to fulfill a lifelong fantasy and takes a job as a car salesman at Toyota of Hollywood. But Larry gets fired on his second day when a showroom visit from Richard Lewis turns physical, costing him a sale.

2. *SEINFELD* REUNION SHOW COCREATOR NBC has been begging Larry for a *Seinfeld* reunion. Larry is against lame reunion shows, but in season seven, when he sees an opportunity to win Cheryl back (after their separation the season prior), he casts her as George's ex-wife and gets the gang back together. Jerry Seinfeld, Julia Louis-Dreyfus, Jason Alexander, and Michael Richards all return to a re-created *Seinfeld* set for a table read, rehearsals, and, eventually, the highly anticipated reunion special. Larry lets his jealousy over Jason and Cheryl's professional relationship get the best of him, however, and ends up quitting.

3. BROADWAY STAR The fourth season centered on producer Mel Brooks slyly casting Larry in the famed role of Max Bialystock in his production of *The Producers*, opposite Ben Stiller (in a two-episode arc) as Leopold Bloom, followed by David Schwimmer when Stiller's relationship with Larry turns antagonistic and he quits. Larry spends the season rehearsing and, much to Brooks's disappointment, the show does not flop. The producer had hoped the inexperienced Larry would kill the show, freeing him of *The Producers'* albatross. On opening night, stage fright does threaten Larry's performance, but he improvises and wins the audience back, and the show is a success. (The real David went on to star in his own show on Broadway, *Fish in the Dark*, when *Curb* later went on hiatus.)

4. RESTAURANT INVESTOR Larry and friends invest in a trendy new restaurant called Bobo's. Larry, however, fires their bald chef when he sees him wearing a toupee, and hires a last-minute replacement who has Tourette syndrome. On the restaurant's opening night, the chef has an outburst and screams, "Fuckhead-shitface-cocksucker-asshole-sonofabitch!" Larry saves the day by launching the patrons into an obscenities-filled scream-off.

5. COFFEE SHOP OWNER In a tenth season callback to Larry's *Seinfeld* reunion feud with Mocha Joe (Saverio Guerra), Larry launches a "spite store." He opens a rival coffee shop next to Mocha Joe's called Latte Larry's. In the finale, though, Larry gets "hoisted on his own spite store petard" when Latte Larry's burns to the ground. The ultimate germophobe, he had installed excess Purell bottles in the coffee shop, and they turned out to accelerate the blaze. When the episode aired amid the global COVID-19 pandemic, the imagery of burning Purell bottles proved to be quite prophetic.

6. HULU SHOW PRODUCER Larry returns with a new show idea in season eleven, called *Young Larry*, about his origins as a Brooklyn stand-up comic in his twenties. He pitches it to streamers, and the show ends up at Hulu. Later, he's blackmailed into hiring an inexperienced actress as his star, Maria Sofia (Keyla Monterroso Mejia), and he makes several attempts to kill the show, to no avail. The season twelve premiere reveals that *Young Larry* went on to become a hit and was renewed for a second season.

7. LIMO DRIVER Larry has a history of showing empathy for his drivers—once, even standing in on the job. In season two, sympathy for a hungry driver got him arrested for stealing a fork and ruined the chances of his CBS show with Julia Louis-Dreyfus, *Aren't You Evelyn?* This time, in season six, another gesture of kindness costs him when he invites his driver into Ted Danson's birthday party. The driver gets so drunk that Larry and Cheryl have to drive him home. The next day, Larry helps the hungover driver by posing as "Charlie" and picking up his VIP client, John McEnroe. McEnroe and Larry end up at a private party before the Paul McCartney concert, but get kicked out by Heather Mills.

HOW FAR IS Too Far?

He stole

a pair of shoes from an exhibit at LA's Holocaust Museum and wore them out the door. He wrote a musical inspired by the decades-long fatwa (death threat) against *The Satanic Verses* author Salman Rushdie. He inadvertently splashed urine on an image of Christ.

Nothing was sacred to *Curb Your Enthusiasm*'s problematic protagonist, Larry David. From 9/11 to January 6, antisemitism to authoritarianism, handicap parking to Parkinson's disease, Larry regularly wandered into sensitive subject matter with a stunning lack of awareness and decorum.

Curb Larry couldn't help but touch the proverbial hot stove over and over, laying waste to the old adage that with age comes wisdom. If the subject was taboo, or the timing too soon, he went there. But just how did he get away with it, week after week, decade after decade?

"That's a really good question," says David.

"If the real Larry ever figured that out, he wouldn't have had to do the show," says director Jeff Schaffer.

"Oh my God. Larry has done so many things that are just so wrong," says Susie Essman (Susie Greene). "Whether it's asking an interracial couple, 'Do you care if the baby looks more Black or more white?' or asking somebody with an adopted Chinese baby, 'Do they have a proclivity for chopsticks?'"

"There's the scene about all the packaging that Amazon stuff used to come in," says writer-director Dave Mandel. "Larry's complaining to Susie and Jeff at the dinner table about how he can't open this gift that they gave him. And they're like, 'Is there a tab?' 'No, there was no tab.' 'Was there a perforation?' 'There's no perforation.' And one of them says to him, 'Well, why don't you get a box cutter?' And Larry goes, 'A box cutter? Who am I, [9/11 hijacker] Mohamed Atta?' I can't prove it, but I'm guessing that was probably one of the first 9/11 jokes, or certainly one of the first Mohamed Atta jokes. It's a great example of Larry's fearlessness and willingness to just be fucking funny."

Larry asks if an adopted Chinese baby has "a proclivity for chopsticks" in "Denise Handicap," S7, E5.

They really knew

how to make a shoe

back then.

—Larry, pleased with the shoes that he stole from the Holocaust Museum

THE MORMON ADVANTAGE: S11, E.11

"Every rule is broken."

—TED DANSON

"In the *Seinfeld* reunion season, Larry and Jerry's assistant [Jillian Bell] wears these crop-top T-shirts, and she has a bit of a stomach roll," says Ted Danson. "Jerry and Larry keep talking about it between themselves and saying horrible, inappropriate things. Things you would not say about anybody, let alone a woman in the workplace. Every rule is broken. Later, she and Larry are on the roof of his office building. When he almost falls off, he spins around to grab hold of something, and it's her belly fat. He grabs her stomach roll with both hands. Her belly fat saves him. That scene is the essence of *Curb*: Do something horribly wrong, then double or triple down on it until your senses surrender and you go down the evil path with him."

To save himself from falling off a roof, Larry grabs on to his assistant Maureen's stomach roll (played by Jillian Bell) in "The Bare Midriff," S7, E6.

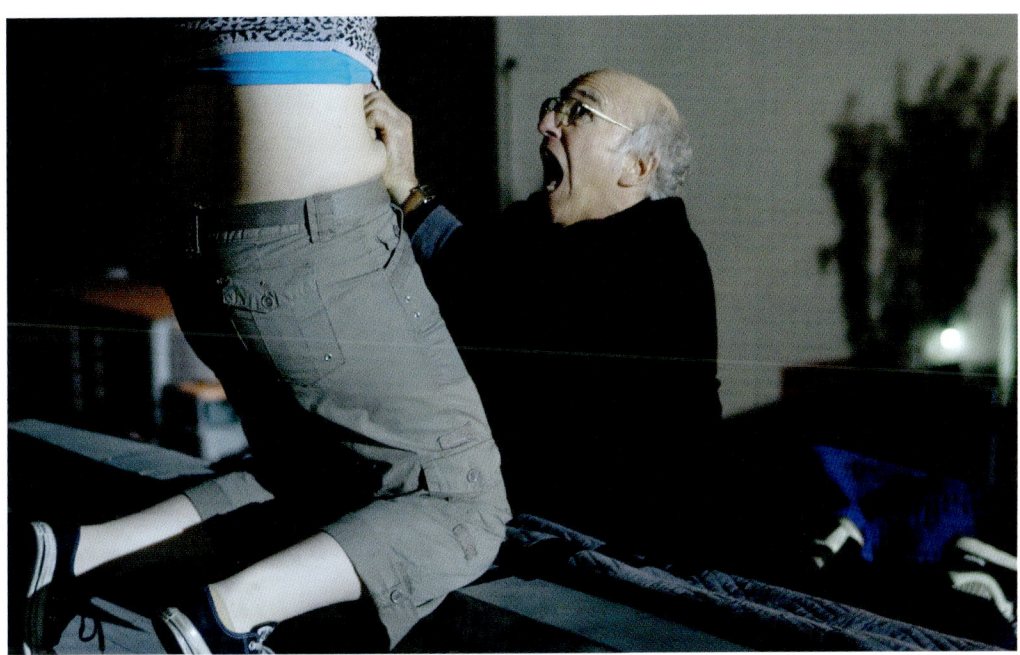

Scenes from "Palestinian Chicken," S8, E3.

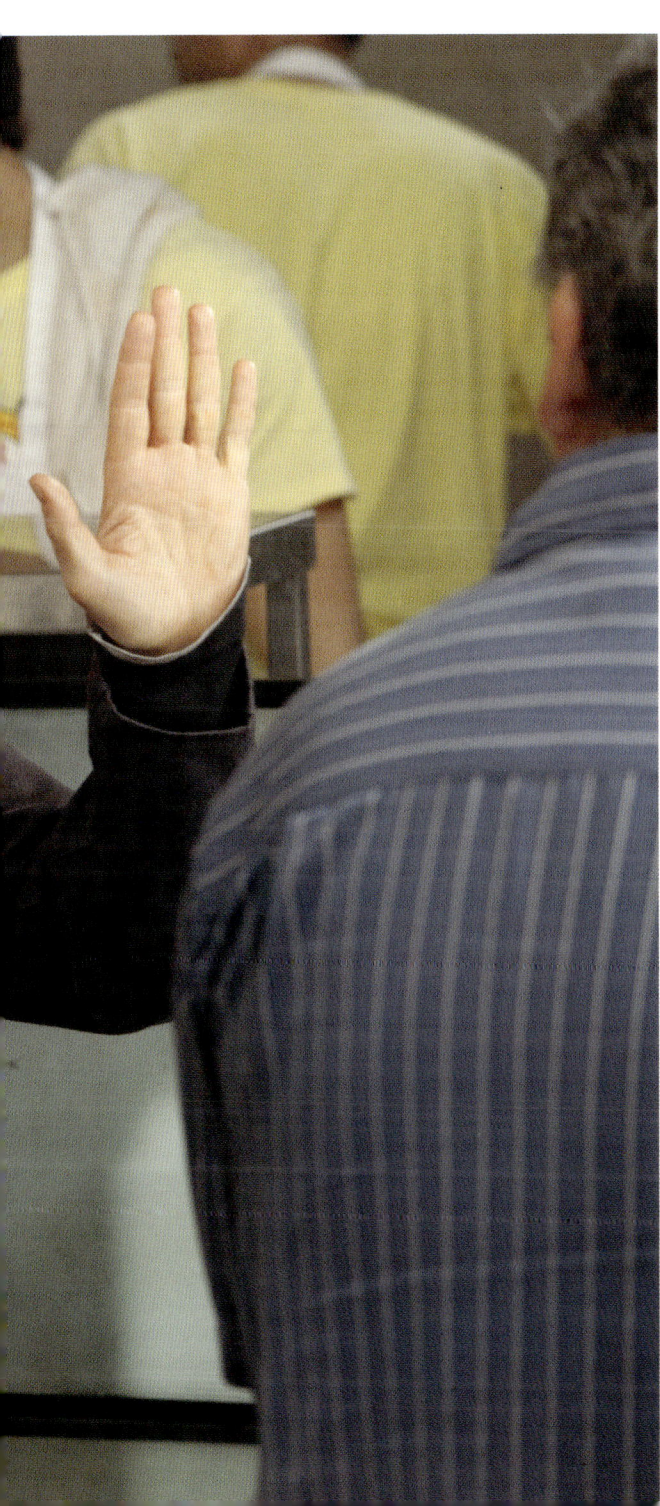

The very same path led to one of the show's riskiest and most beloved episodes, "Palestinian Chicken" (Season 8, Episode 3). In the story, Larry patronizes a Palestinian-owned diner, even though it's thought to be antisemitic. He's willing to forsake his people because the chicken is some of the best in LA. But there's more forbidden fruit than just the juicy kabob. A beautiful woman working at the restaurant, Shara, catches Larry's eye. The two end up having sex, which produces some of the best comedy ever to come out of the long-standing conflict between Arabs and Jews.

"Fuck me, you fucking Jew! You Zionist pig! You occupying fuck! Occupy this. I'm going to fuck the Jew out of you. You want to fuck me like Israel fucked my country? Fuck me, you Jew bastard! Fuck me like Israel fucks my people! Show me the promised land, Labe, son of Nat! You uncircumcised fuck!"

Marty Funkhouser, played by the late Bob Einstein, does not approve of the tryst, and later asks Larry, "When did you have your orgasm? When she said she'd fuck the Jew out of you?" Larry replies, "Let me tell you something. The penis doesn't care about race, creed, and color. The penis wants to get to his homeland. It wants to go home."

"Only Larry can stomp through the whole Jewish-Palestinian thing and come out unscathed," says Mandel. "It's full of heavy issues that comedy generally wants to run from. But it's funny because Larry never punches down. He'll have strange conversations, perhaps with a deaf person or somebody who is transgender. But the jokes are never belittling to the person he's interacting with. They're never attacking that person. The comedy is coming from somewhere else. His comments and questions come from a genuine curiosity, which I think is also very true of Larry David the person."

PALESTINIAN CHICKEN: S8, E3

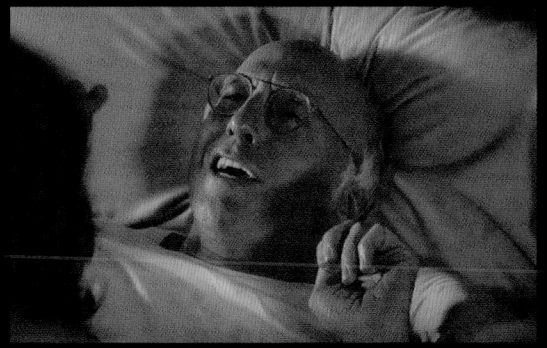

I'M AN OCCUPIER!

—Larry to Shara, in the midst of passionate lovemaking

ABOVE: Larry's warped sense of justice even extends to a KKK member in "The Watermelon," S11, E4. He offers to dry-clean the man's robe after accidentally spilling coffee on it and a chain of unfortunate events ensues. **OPPOSITE:** Larry celebrates his breakup with Irma Kostroski in "Fish Stuck," S12, E5.

Larry's inquisitiveness triggered embarrassing situations that might prove catastrophic in any other context, but for *Curb*, stepping on the third rail was the point.

"Larry is Lear, the crazy man railing in the storm," says Jason Alexander (*Seinfeld*'s George Costanza). "He's the guy screaming, 'Why is this happening?!' He knows that there's something brilliantly funny about that edge. If Larry were Ted Danson, he couldn't do it, because we equate Ted with a sophistication, a sexual quality, a ladies' man quality, a success quality. Larry is a frail, whiny, Jewish, bald guy who wears glasses and has a stoop. Yet he's walking around thinking he's a ladies' man who can handle himself in an altercation, and that he knows better about everything. There's something endearing and funny about a guy who is obviously lesser than, trying to be more."

"He can be reprehensible, or annoying, or pick your adjective," says Danson. "But it's also clear that Larry is not being held up as an example of how you should behave. He's the perfect misanthrope and there's something fun about that."

When an angry Klansman comes after him, Larry blows a shofar for help in "The Watermelon," S11, E4.

"NO ONE

"I think people have just come to expect it from him," says co-executive producer Laura Streicher. "He's Larry David. He's going to do crazy things and offend pretty much every single demographic. No one is safe. And yet somehow people are OK with that."

Even as the cultural landscape evolved and *Curb* continued to explore hot topics, Larry remained virtually fireproof. Take the overdue racial and gender equality reckonings of the 2010s. They were in full swing by 2017, when David returned from a six-year hiatus with *Curb*'s ninth season. Social media was brimming with #MeToo and #BLM. Culture wars had broken out around gender-neutral bathrooms. Everything was politicized, and the potential for inciting backlash was at a fever pitch. As the film and television industry gingerly stepped around just about every issue, *Curb* leaned into the tension.

Larry helps prepare the set (and an inflatable friend) for a scene in "Insufficient Praise," S10, E5.

IS SAFE.

AND YET SOMEHOW PEOPLE ARE OK WITH THAT."

—LAURA STREICHER

WHERE THE SACRED A

Everyone knows of sacrosanct subjects where comedy should never dare venture. Well, everyone but Larry. Here's a brief refresher of sanctified ground sullied by the wicked humor of *Curb*.

THE KAMIKAZE PILOT
KAMIKAZE BINGO, S5, E4

Larry offends Cheryl's Japanese friend Yoshi (Greg Watanabe) when he questions the validity of his father's claim that he was a World War II kamikaze pilot. Yoshi says his father's plane grazed an American ship. Larry argues that if his father survived, he's not a kamikaze pilot. Yoshi feels that Larry has insulted his father by calling him a coward and attempts suicide. Larry apologizes but re-offends him when, at a Japanese restaurant, the staff calls Larry "chicken teriyaki boy," and Yoshi thinks they are calling him a coward. He sends Larry a second suicide email. War, honor, and despair are not laughing matters . . . except when they're *Curb*ed.

RUINING A BAPTISM
THE BAPTISM, S2, E9

Cheryl's Christian sister Becky (Kaitlin Olson) is engaged to Barry, a Jew (Mitchell Whitfield). Barry is in the process of converting to her faith, but during the baptismal water dunk, Larry thinks his future brother-in-law is being assaulted and interrupts the ceremony, almost causing Barry to drown. The near-death experience changes Barry's mind about converting, and his Jewish family praises Larry for doing a mitzvah. Cheryl's family, on the other hand, is infuriated. No need to pray for Larry after this stunt. His fate is clearly decided.

SEX WITH A PALESTINIAN SHIKSA
PALESTINIAN CHICKEN, S8, E3

Larry and Jeff eat at a Palestinian restaurant known for its delicious chicken … and its anti-Israeli sentiments. But the two men see the cuisine as a potential olive branch and suggest the restaurant send their chicken to Israel as part of the peace process: "They would take down all those settlements in the morning." It's also a turn-on that the women working there "don't even acknowledge [their] right to exist." Larry hooks up with one of them, Shara (Anne Bedian), and when they have sex, antisemitic slurs double as dirty talk. If only the Mideast conflict were as funny.

> I CAN'T BELIEVE THIS GUY'S CONVERTING. YOU GUYS COME TO OUR SIDE, WE DON'T GO TO YOUR SIDE. —LARRY

AN ORTHODOX JEW, LARRY, AND A SKI LIFT
THE SKI LIFT, S5, E8

Larry poses as an Orthodox Jew to befriend the man (Stuart Pankin) in charge of the kidney transplant list, in hopes of getting Richard a kidney so Larry doesn't have to donate his. Larry asks Susie to pose as his Orthodox wife while they visit his ski lodge. This plan goes awry when Larry gets stuck on a ski lift with the man's single daughter (Iris Bahr) and she's forced to jump because her beliefs won't allow her to be alone with a man after sundown. Earlier scenes took aim at Orthodox customs when the daughter had to bury a plate because Cheryl wasn't aware of kosher laws. Oy.

THE KLANSMAN
THE WATERMELON, S11, E4

When Larry spills coffee on the robe of a Klansman (Marc Menchaca), he offers to dry-clean the garment. But the Jewish dry cleaner refuses to take the robe until Larry convinces him that he should not discriminate. Unbeknownst to Larry, Susie sews a Star of David onto the man's robe, causing the Klansman to be attacked by another KKK member during a rally. When the angry Klansman shows up at Larry's door, Larry blows a shofar (a horn used in Jewish religious ceremony), waking up his neighborhood and sending the Klansman running.

PEEING ON JESUS
THE BARE MIDRIFF, S7, E6

When Larry uses the bathroom in the home of his assistant (Jillian Bell), a recent change in his medication causes him to release an uncontrollable stream of urine, some of which splashes on a Jesus painting hanging above the toilet. The assistant sees the Christ "tear" and surmises she's witnessing a miracle. She quits her day job to tour the country and spread the word of this miracle, but eventually learns the truth and threatens to jump off the roof of Larry's office building. Another "miracle" ensues when the assistant's belly fat saves Larry from falling to his death.

ANGERING THE AYATOLLAH
FATWA! S9, E10

Larry messes with Iran's Ayatollah, the head of the Islamic state, when promoting his terrible idea for a musical, *Fatwa!* An actual fatwa, aka a death sentence, is issued against Larry. It's rescinded, but he still ends up running for his life because, well, he's Larry David.

ND PROFANE COLLIDE

> **YOU'RE NUTS ABOUT THIS JESUS GUY, AREN'T YOU?**
> —LARRY

THE PASSION OF THE CHRIST MEZUZAH
THE CHRIST NAIL, S5, E3

Larry uses the nail his father-in-law (Paul Dooley) bought as a collector's item from the *Passion of the Christ* movie to hammer in his mezuzah (a locket containing scripture that Jews affix to their doorposts) after his handyman quits. But his handyman, who happens to be named Jesús, returns to seek revenge on Larry for buying his wife, Larry's housekeeper, a bra. The handyman ends up chasing Larry with a cross-shaped stick. Religious Christian music swells, but Jesús is thwarted when he steps on a *Passion of the Christ* replacement nail. Jesus wept? Possibly.

LARRY'S MOTHER AND THE "SPECIAL SECTION"
THE SPECIAL SECTION, S3, E6

While Larry is filming a Martin Scorsese movie in New York, Larry's father (Shelley Berman) honors the dying wishes of Larry's mother, who asks him not to bother their son with news of her illness while he's busy. She dies, and Larry's father waits to tell Larry, causing him to miss the funeral. Larry later finds out that his mother has been buried in the "special section" at the cemetery due to a tattoo on her buttocks that he never knew about, which disqualifies her from being buried on consecrated ground. Larry bribes the gravedigger and he, along with Jeff, his cousin (Richard Kind), and father, dig up his mother's grave to put her in a better section.

> **MY MOTHER HAD A TATTOO ON HER ASS?**
> —LARRY

THE HOLOCAUST SURVIVOR MIX-UP
THE SURVIVOR, S4, E9

Larry meets with his rabbi to discuss his concerns about having sex with a woman outside of marriage (something Cheryl allows him as a tenth anniversary present). During the meeting, the rabbi asks if he can bring "a survivor" to dinner at Larry's house. Larry misinterprets this to mean a Holocaust survivor and tells his father to bring his Holocaust survivor friend (Allan Rich). But the rabbi's guest is actually a star from the reality TV show *Survivor: The Australian Outback* (runner-up Colby Donaldson). The two survivors get into an epic altercation over dinner. Everyone survives, but no one wins.

A CHRISTIAN SCIENTIST WITH PEANUT ALLERGIES
THE BENADRYL BROWNIE, S3, E2

Richard Lewis plans to take his date to the Emmys, but it's not looking hopeful since a peanut allergy has caused her face to swell—and she's a Christian Scientist who won't take medication to treat the severe reaction. Larry hatches a plan to hide Benadryl in a batch of brownies and feed them to her. It doesn't work (how very shocking). Later, when she and Richard walk the Emmys red carpet, Joan Rivers skewers his date on the E! preshow. "I've seen better faces on a hemorrhoid," cracks Rivers. "How are things in Loch Ness?"

THE BOWTIE-WEARING BLACK MUSLIM
THE BOWTIE, S5, E2

Larry assumes a private investigator (Mekhi Phifer) he hired to find out if he's adopted is Muslim because he's Black and wears a bowtie. Larry later asks Wanda Sykes her opinion. She berates him: "You think Farrakhan went out and bought all the bow ties or something? He's sitting there holding all the bow ties and only Muslims get them? What the fuck, Larry?" Larry eventually insults the investigator, who says he's only continuing with Larry's case because Muslims are a forgiving people. There's nothing halal about this episode, which is why it's so damn funny.

THE HOLOCAUST SHOES
THE MORMON ADVANTAGE, S11, E10

When Larry steps in dog poop outside of a Holocaust museum, he takes off his shoes and enters the building in socks. Inside is an exhibit of shoes belonging to those who died in the Holocaust, so Larry naturally helps himself to a pair. They become his footwear of choice until Trump whistleblower Lieutenant Colonel Alexander Vindman exposes Larry's crime. But there's more . . . It's revealed that the shoes belonged to the grandfather of Larry's girlfriend, Irma (Tracey Ullman), who died in the Holocaust. The discovery causes Irma, a recovering alcoholic, to relapse.

Larry struggles to help his assistant, played by Megan Ferguson, without inspiring a #MeToo moment when she chokes on a scone, in "Artificial Fruit," S10, E3.

In season ten, Larry's assistant accuses him of sexual harassment after he uses the shirt she's wearing to clean his eyeglasses. Making matters worse, Larry unintentionally touches a female server's chest later at a party when reaching for an hors d'oeuvre. The two women eventually compare notes, causing the assistant to confront Larry, but she finds him seated next to Jeff, whom she mistakes for Harvey Weinstein. Larry is inappropriately dressed in a robe and nothing else.

"Who jokes about #MeToo and gets away with it? Larry," says Joyce Lapinsky, wife of the late Richard Lewis. "Richard used to say Larry was like Archie Bunker. He's the only person who could say anything about everything without threat of being canceled. It's like, thank you, Larry. Somebody had to let the pressure out."

"Larry's blessed with a persona where the audience goes, 'Oh, he's so silly' as opposed to 'Oh, he's so mean,'" says Alexander. "If the audience understands from an entertainer that the intent of what they're doing is to delight, is to entertain, then the entertainer can get away with an awful lot. But if the intent is to diminish in some way, no matter how cleverly or skillfully done, you feel it. Like if a comedian is trying to make me laugh, I give them a lot of leeway. They can make short jokes, Jew jokes, bald jokes ... they can go really far because I don't think they're trying to hurt me."

Larry wasn't the only character on *Curb* to demonstrate poor judgment. The show's other characters often operated with their self-interest in mind, avoiding accountability at any cost.

"I worked on many shows before Jeff and I were hired by Larry, and every one of those series was a morality play," says writer-director Alec Berg. "A sitcom episode went like this: Somebody does something underhanded or selfish, and then in the end, they apologize and fix what they did. In *Curb*, the characters would act in petty and self-serving ways, screw somebody over, get somebody arrested, lie and shirk responsibility, then when they were caught, they would lie or double down on reprehensible behavior until they just were so cornered that they were exposed as a piece of shit, and that was the end of the episode. There was no moment where they went, 'I'm sorry. I shouldn't have done that.' That lack of morality is what governed all of *Curb*. *Curb* just felt like a much more honest way to do things. I mean, you go your whole life without learning anything. Why do you have to learn something in twenty-two minutes?"

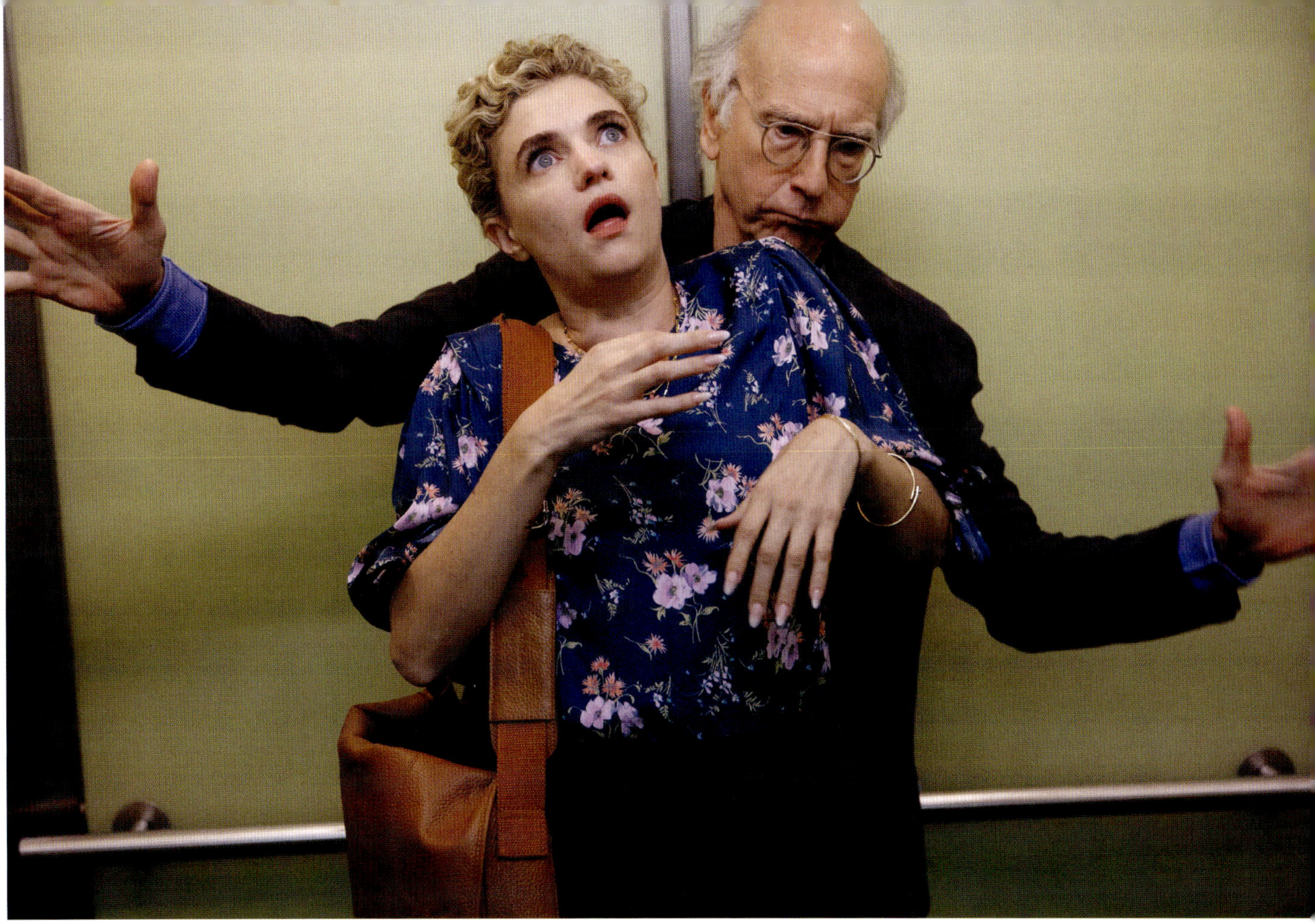

YOU SPRAYED ON JESUS!

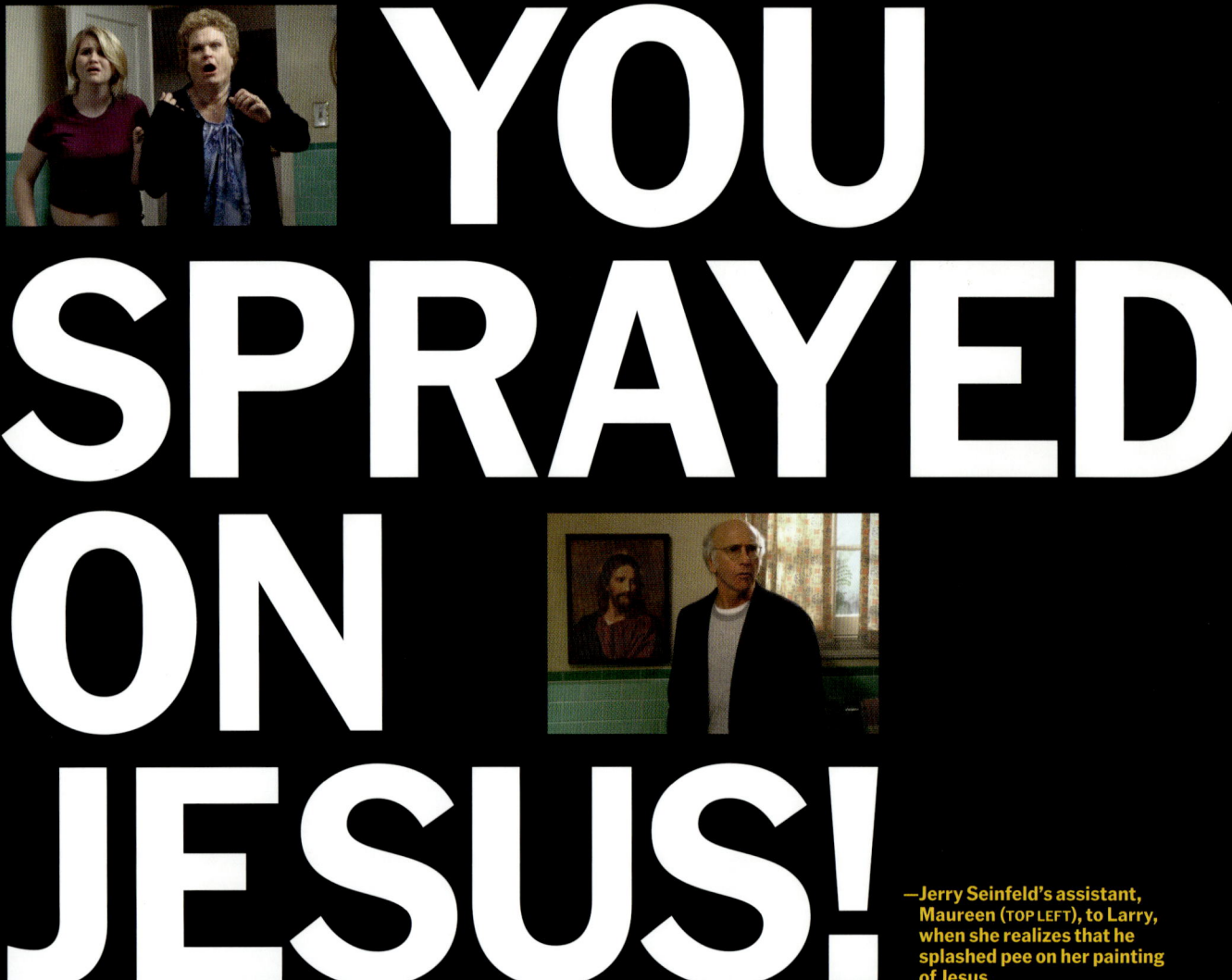

—Jerry Seinfeld's assistant, Maureen (TOP LEFT), to Larry, when she realizes that he splashed pee on her painting of Jesus

The crew and cast were not oblivious to *Curb*'s potential to offend. Those who worked on the show were aware that they frequently walked the line between public adulation and cancellation.

"We certainly danced around some explosive subjects, but because of the way they were handled, it was always kind of OK," says Mandel. "That being said, I'm sure with research you'll find somebody that's upset about something."

"I remember getting letters when he peed on the Christ painting," says David. "And when we killed the rat dog. It's funny, people love the show until you hit their one vulnerable nerve. They like everything else until you're in their wheelhouse, and there's that thing that they're most sensitive about. 'I've been with you for seven seasons, but when you stepped on that dog, that was it!' Now they hate you."

"There were times when I read the outlines and thought, 'This is really pushing it,' like the fatwa season. I was worried that the Ayatollah would come after Larry," says Essman. "But nothing happened."

"The only thing I remember anybody getting upset about wasn't even on *Curb*," says Streicher. "It was Larry's opening monologue on *SNL* about dating in prison camps, which was a hilarious bit, but some Jewish organizations didn't see the humor. But there were definitely times on *Curb*, where I was like, is this the one where HBO is going to say, 'No, we're not doing this!'? Is this the one that's going to really piss people off? But thankfully that never happened."

A scene from *Fatwa!* the musical in S9, E10.

FATWA!: S9, E10

Larry knocks down a cache of annoying electric scooters in "Happy New Year," S10, E1.

"*Curb*'s style of comedy sometimes required it to be cringey," says editor and music supervisor Steve Rasch. "Like there's an episode about a nurse with a big vagina that Jeff dates, and she claims Jeff has a small penis, but in fact, it's her. She has a big vagina. You could say that's offensive, they can't make jokes about that, but they somehow find a way to do it, and a lot of it has to do with using trained actors who are good at improv, they know how to keep it funny. And then, if it goes a little too far, we can pull it back in editing. Still some people will say, 'I can't watch that show. He's a sexist, he's a whatever.' So we crossed the line for a certain number of people, but you can't please everybody."

Rather than please folks, *Curb* gave viewers something even better by speaking for them. Larry's terrible judgment, tone-deaf responses, and knack for lying his way out of a tight spot represented little bits and pieces within all of us. *Curb* fans lived vicariously through Larry's actions, from telling teenagers they're too old to trick-or-treat to opening a spite store next to a place he abhors and wants to put out of business.

"There are two types of *Curb* stories," says Berg. "There are the ones where Larry is the asshole, and he's good at it. He's not the guy that fights for us. He's that guy that we want to fight. You know, *that* fucking asshole. Then there are the stories where Larry goes, 'You're not going to believe the fucking asshole I ran into.' Those are the ones where Larry speaks for all of us. He's a crusader for the rights of the downtrodden. 'Somebody needs to stand up to the assholes!'"

THE SKI LIFT: S5, E8

LARRY: BIG VAGINA?

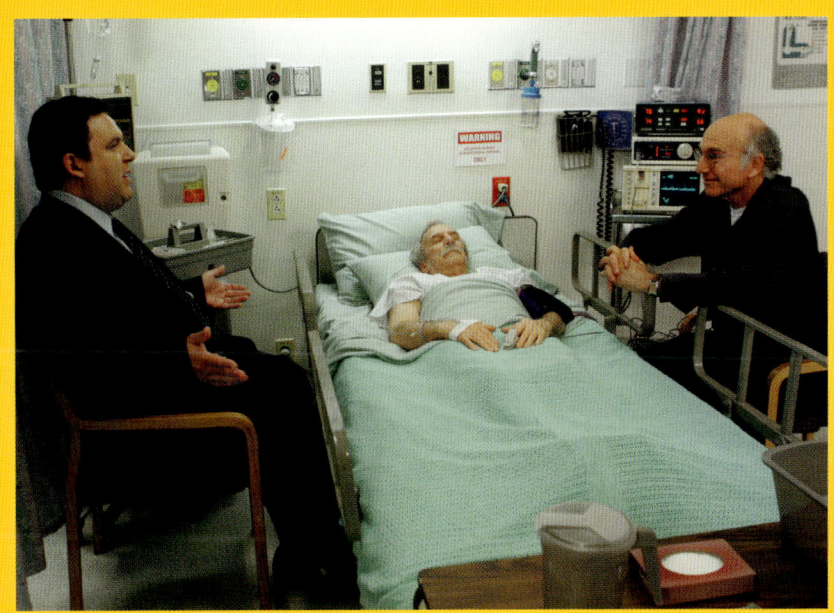

JEFF: GIGANTIC VAGINA.

—Larry and Jeff, after Jeff is accused by a former date of having a small penis

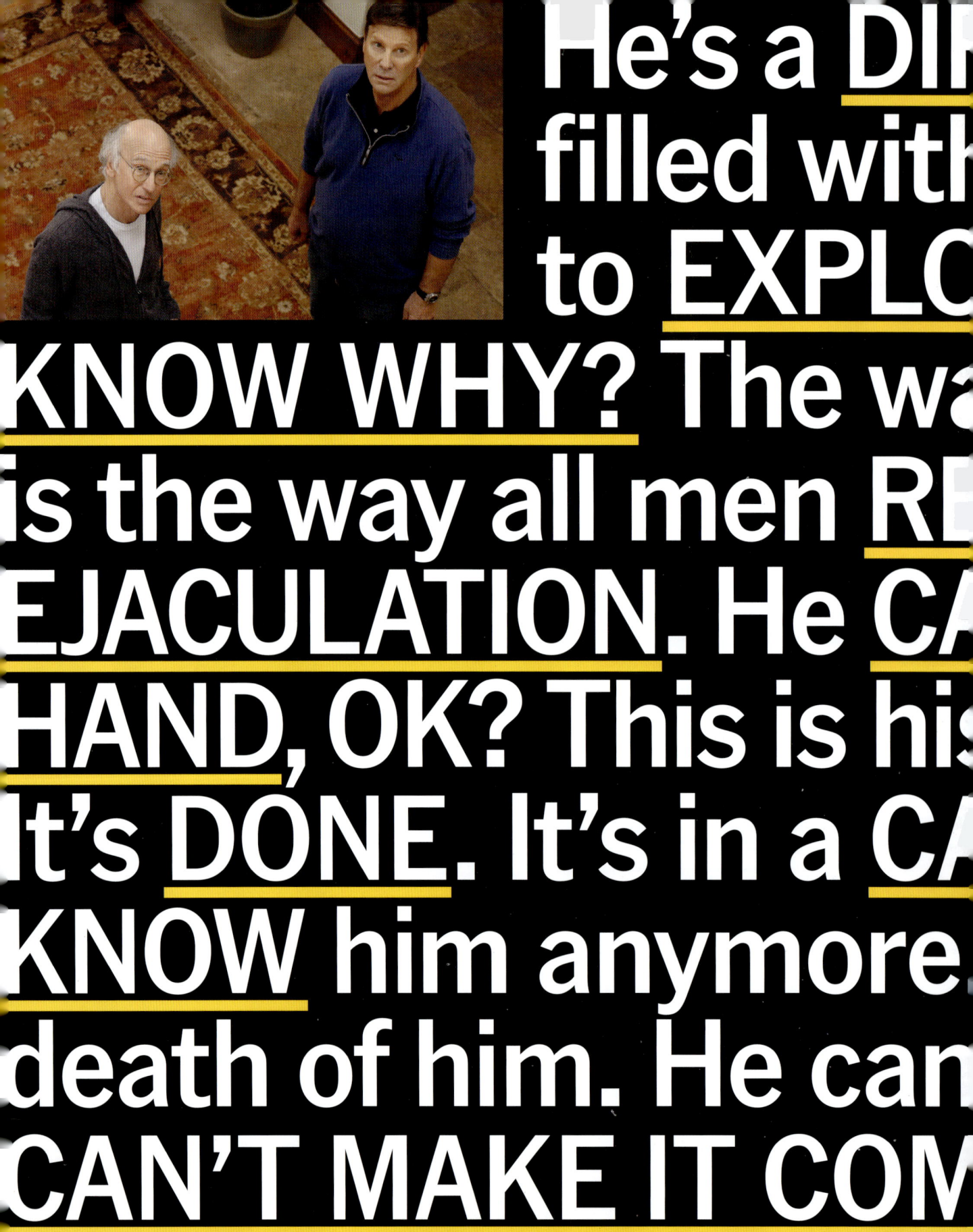

"[DIF]FERENT KID...He's [all] angst. He's READY [TO EXPLO]DE. You wanna [know why] he RELAXES? [HE REL]AX. It's called [MASTURBATIO]N'T USE HIS RIGHT [HAND HE'S A PR]EJACULATOR, OK? [HE'S LO]ST....I don't even [know why] I'm SCARED to [say it —] MASTURBATE! HE [HAS TO GET IT] OUT!"

—Marty Funkhouser to Larry, after his nephew, an All-American baseball player, breaks his elbow fighting with Larry over a pickle jar

THE PICKLE GAMBIT: S9, E2

"People are happy to hear it from somebody else," says David. "Like there's a dinner party at their house, and guests have stayed way too long, like well after dessert. They're thinking, 'Get out. What are you doing? Tomorrow's a school day. Get out!' They want to kick them out, but they can't do it. So I write a show where I have a dinner party and I can kick everybody out. Audiences want to see that because that's something they would like to do and say. I'm confronting people in a way that's very satisfying. They've had the exact same instinct but can't act on it, and neither can I. But I can in the show. That's why Larry gets away with so much."

The kicker? Larry failed to gain any sort of wisdom over twenty-four years of guffaws, fumbles, and transgressions. "You know how some bacteria are resistant to medicine?" says Schaffer. "Well, Larry is resistant to learning."

The arc of the series is proof enough: In season one, he infuriated his inner circle by mistakenly eulogizing his wife's "beloved aunt" as a "beloved cunt" in her obituary. In season twelve, Larry decides the best way to avoid conflict is to wear baggy shorts that expose his balls when he uncrosses his legs, and he does just that when confronting Mr. Takahashi. Does this sound like a man who's evolved?

Even when Larry tried to do the right thing, his Larry-ness would get in the way. Example: Season twelve finds Larry in Atlanta, Georgia, where he is appalled to see a Jim Crow–era, Black lawn jockey statue outside the Airbnb where he's staying with Susie and Jeff. He tries to move it, and it breaks. Attempting to hide his blunder from Susie, Larry looks for a replacement at the local garden center, but all the statues are white. He asks a Black employee (played by *The Bear*'s

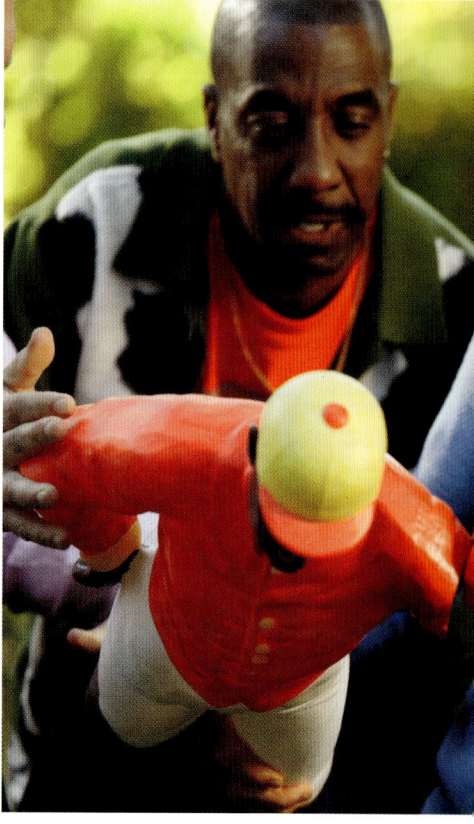

Larry accidentally breaks a dated ceramic lawn jockey statue at an Airbnb (and then gets in trouble trying to replace it) in "The Lawn Jockey," S12, E2.

Lionel Boyce) if there are any "darker ones." Boyce's character is clearly disgusted by the request. Larry tries to explain, then says, "It's a long story." The clerk snaps back: "Yeah, like 400 years long. Starts in Nigeria."

It's no wonder Jeff Greene once deemed Larry a "social assassin."

So is anything beyond the pale? How far, truly, is too far for *Curb*?

"We never asked ourselves that question," says David. "We don't avoid things because we're worried that we can't get away with it. That's not how it works. There's lots of execution discussions, like how do we do this in the funniest way? You can do anything. It's how you do it that matters."

Says Schaffer, "Never in my thirty years of working with Larry did I hear him say, 'I don't think we should do that because it might offend people.' Never. If we think it's funny, it's funny. If we don't think it's funny, we're not going to do it. Period."

When David's asked if cancel culture ever caused him to proceed with a little more caution, he says, "I don't think it did. In fact, it emboldened us."

"People must know that Larry doesn't seem to care, so they're like, why bother? Why put the effort in to cancel someone who doesn't care if he's canceled?" says Schaffer.

"Yeah, it never did happen that I was canceled," says David. "I was kind of hoping it would. That seemed like something I would have liked, especially for comedy. Not for anything else, but for comedy, yeah, that would have been great."

"Another regret," replies Schaffer.

"Maybe it's not too late," says David.

LARRY VS. KIDS

Larry said it best when in season twelve he proclaimed that he's "never spoken to a child without contempt." His awkward run-ins and feuds with kids represented some of *Curb*'s funniest moments.

1. THE ADOPTED GIRL In season seven's "Denise Handicap," Larry bumps into friends who adopted their daughter from China. Larry tactlessly asks the parents if she has a proclivity for chopsticks, and if they are worried that her biological parents might have mental issues, all while the young girl, Kelsey, sits silently in the stroller. The deeply offended wife later has the husband call Larry to disinvite him from a party. This is one of several examples where Larry offends parents.

"HAVE YOU NOTICED IF SHE HAS ANY PROCLIVITY FOR CHOPSTICKS?"

2. DRUNK SAMMI In season three's "The Corpse Sniffing Dog," Jeff has moved to a hotel because he is allergic to the family dog, Oscar, and his daughter Sammi picked the dog over her dad. Larry visits the house to try to convince Sammi to choose her dad, instead. When they have a chat, his glass of red wine is mixed up with her grape juice, and seven-year-old Sammi ends up very drunk. "She stinks like a fucking wino!" Susie later yells at Larry.

"SHE STINKS LIKE A FUCKING WINO!"

3. THE GIRL WITH THE JUDY DOLL At a party hosted by an ABC executive in season two's "The Doll," Larry obliges the man's young daughter and gives her collector's item doll named Judy a haircut—only to leave the girl distraught when she realizes it won't grow back. This leads to Larry finding a replacement by swapping the head of a doll belonging to Jeff and Susie's daughter, much to Susie's dismay. Later at the theater, Larry uses the women's bathroom because the men's room smells, and runs into the executive's daughter. She gives him a hug to thank him for fixing her doll. But Larry has hidden a water bottle in his pants, in an attempt to sneak outside water into the theater, and the girl runs out and tells everyone that Larry is in the women's bathroom "with something hard in his pants."

4. THE TATTLETALE In season five's "The Larry David Sandwich," when Larry scalps tickets for the Jewish High Holidays outside of his synagogue, a child spots the exchange. The kid tells on him and Larry (already in hot water for loudly arguing with Richard Lewis over sandwiches) and Cheryl are kicked out of Rosh Hashanah services.

5. THE TRICK-OR-TREATERS In season two's "Trick or Treat," Larry gets into a heated argument with two teenage girls when he deems them too old to be trick-or-treating on Halloween. He slams the door in their faces and they say, "Fuck you!" As revenge, the girls toilet paper his home and write "Bald Asshole" on his front door.

6. THE LEMONADE-STAND KIDS In season seven's "Officer Krupke," Larry argues with three kids who are selling lemonade near Susie's house. He tells them their lemonade tastes terrible and that he wants his $1 back. "You stink," yells the girl. "You stink!" he yells back. They call him a "loser" and a "bald asshole!" When the mom confronts him, he argues that the kids need supervision.

7. THOR'S KIDS In season two's "Thor," a driving Larry playfully mocks three kids who are making faces at him from the back of the car in front of him. This escalates into Larry pointing finger guns at the kids. The driver of their car, however, an unamused professional wrestler named Thor, threatens Larry over this "violent" behavior. "Have you heard of Columbine?!" he demands.

8. THE GIRL SCOUTS In season eight's "The Divorce," the thirteen-year-old daughter of the owner of the LA Dodgers (Kaitlyn Dever) goes to Larry's house to sell Girl Scout Cookies, and in bizarre bad timing, gets her first period while there. Larry gives her a tampon of Cheryl's, but she doesn't know how to use it, so he reads her the instructions through the door. The girl's father later hears of this and is so upset that Larry ends up losing out on his Dodgers tickets, which in turn leads Larry to back out of his cookie order when the Girl Scouts come to collect.

"REGARDING THE COOKIES, THERE'S BEEN A CHANGE OF PLANS."

9. THE WELL-ENDOWED BOY In season three's "The Nanny," while attending the pool party of a fellow restaurant investor named Hugh, Larry (along with Cheryl, Susie, and Jeff) ogles the endowment of his host's four-year-old son. Larry calls the child a "circus freak show," but also compliments the boy's penis size to his father, who is disgusted and offended by the comment. Larry later gets into a whisper argument with the same child, calling him "stupid" and "much, much stupider"—when his father brings the boy to a screening for Richard Lewis's special.

10. THE MAKE-A-WISH KID In season five's "The Smoking Jacket," Larry tries to wiggle his way out of donating his kidney to Richard Lewis. He visits Lewis's cousin, Louis Lewis, in the hospital and questions the doctor about his survival rate. A young patient (Grant Rosenmeyer) in the bed next door overhears and thinks Larry is trying to pull the plug. The critically ill kid then blackmails Larry into helping him with his Make-a-Wish, which is to see a naked woman. Larry ends up bringing him to the Playboy Mansion.

11. THE GIRL WITH THE RASH ON HER VAGINA In season seven's "The Table Read," the nine-year-old daughter of one of Larry's female colleagues, Emma, begins texting him while they're working on the *Seinfeld* reunion. It starts out friendly, but the texting goes sour when Larry loses his patience over her questions: "NO I DO NOT WATCH WIZARDS OF WAVERLY PLACE. I'M AN ADULT!!!" Her mother tells Larry that she's taking her to the doctor because she has a rash on her vagina. When he reports to others that he's talking to a young girl with a "rash on her pussy," red flags go up and a doctor ends up calling the police.

12. HIS GIRLFRIEND'S SON In season nine's "Namaste," Larry is smitten with Bridget, the NBC censor he's dating (played by Lauren Graham). But he's less enamored with her pre-teen son, who insults him when they first meet, saying his head is shiny. Bridget apologizes to Larry, explaining that her son has Asperger's, but Larry doesn't buy it. "I just think he's an asshole. The kid's an asshole!" he complains to Jeff. Susie calls out Larry for always having issues when he dates women with children, and suggests he foster a kid. He responds by laughing hysterically.

"THE KID'S AN ASSHOLE!"

13. THE MAGICIAN In season four's "The Blind Date," Larry argues with Cheryl's young cousin, played by Anton Yelchin, when he won't share his magic-trick secrets with Larry. Larry accuses him of being a one-trick magician.

14. THE KIDS AT BEN STILLER'S BIRTHDAY PARTY In season four's "Ben's Birthday Party," Larry joins Susie and a group of children, including Susie's daughter, Sammi, for a game of Telephone at Ben Stiller's birthday party. At the end of a round, Larry declares, "I love tits," alleging he is only repeating what the boy next to him just whispered in his ear. The child denies it, claiming he said, "I love pigs." "It's not funny, these are kids in here!" yells Susie.

Honey, We Have Gu

ests

Curb

Your Enthusiasm featured more high-profile guests than a vaunted Oscar party over its twelve-season run. Larry sparred with film and TV stars, alienated politicians, tripped sports figures, sickened musicians, stymied news anchors, alarmed whistleblowers, and vouched for felons.

As *Curb*'s notoriety grew, so too did its reputation for attracting some of the biggest names in entertainment and pop culture to guest-star on the show. Viewers looked forward to whomever might pop up on-screen each Sunday, be it Ben Affleck, Martin Scorsese, Meg Ryan, Shaquille O'Neal, or Bruce Springsteen. Prominent personalities vied for the chance to play heightened versions of themselves on the show, or to inhabit characters tailor-made for their specific talent or background.

A "guest" was anyone outside the circle of core cast members that included Larry, Cheryl, Susie, Jeff, and Leon. There were semi-regulars like Ted Danson, Richard Lewis, and Mary Steenburgen, repeat offenders like Wanda Sykes and Richard Kind, and one- or two-episode visitors like Alanis Morissette and Ben Stiller.

Emerging actors and less recognizable performers, brought in to play "real people," would often end up creating some of the show's most recognizable characters, like Krazee-Eyez Killa or Mocha Joe. Others might end up in a comedy master class with legendary figures such as Shelley Berman or Mel Brooks.

No matter their skill level, the world of Larry's pet peeves and particularisms was a playground for the adventurous.

Larry with Tracey Ullman (Irma Kostroski) in "Disgruntled," S12, E4.

The following accounts are culled from a selection of guests among the multitude of talent who appeared on *Curb* over its lifetime.

Ted Danson
Seasons 1–12
HIMSELF

Danson played an inflated version of himself, replete with the insecurities and ego associated with stardom. Curb Ted is handsome, well-liked, and far more famous than Larry, therefore Larry sees Ted as The Competition. The two men fight about everything, including naming rights for deli sandwiches and the length of Larry's running shorts. The Cheers *star ends up dating then marrying Larry's ex, Cheryl, intensifying Larry's disdain and jealousy for his nemesis, Ted.*

TD: "I literally went through an entire season not knowing that *Curb* Larry was calling *Curb* Ted the biggest asshole in the world and maligning my character behind his back. He couldn't stand me, but then he would be nice to my face. I didn't know he hated Ted until I hit my mark early by mistake. I was walking past him and Lucy Lawless, who were talking and hadn't finished their entire 'Isn't Ted an asshole' conversation yet. I heard it and went, 'Wait, what?!' I went to Jeff [Schaffer] later and said, 'Wow, that was a surprise.' And he said, 'You didn't know that [your character] is the biggest asshole ever this season? Larry hates you.' It's lucky that I'm oblivious, because I'm not that good of an actor to pretend I didn't know. If I knew I would have tried to find some way to make him like me."

"My function on the show then became clear, which was to make Larry a little crazy, irritate the shit out of him, push him into a verbal corner so he comes bursting out and acts even more Larry. Larry at his best is angry, irrational, and incorrect. I was good at pushing him around, so I was happy to do that."

"When he had me divorce Mary and hook up with Cheryl, that genuinely pissed me off. I showed up to work to find that I was divorcing Mary and hanging out with Cheryl. I did not like it. When the show came out, Mary and I would get calls from friends saying, 'Oh my God! I'm so sorry to hear . . .' And Mary was like, 'Yeah, right. That's how we chose to announce we're divorced. On *Curb*.' But it was so real on the show, and we were already walking the line of, 'Is this real Ted, or real Mary, or real Larry, or are they characters?' I know I'm an actor. I know I was playing a part, but I felt so upset."

Jerry Seinfeld
Seasons 4, 7, and 12
HIMSELF

The Seinfeld *cocreator, star, and Larry's former work partner was a master of winning pointless arguments about nothing in particular, often besting Larry at his own game.*

JS: "One of my favorite moments on the show was when Larry and I had that back-and-forth conversation about dating the bearded lady in the *Curb* finale. That was a very typical kind of way that we would talk, and I love that it was captured. Whenever Larry and I are together funny things just seem to happen."

Antoinette Spolar
Seasons 1–8
LARRY'S RECEPTIONIST, ANTOINETTE

Fictional Larry went through a lot of assistants over the decades, but Antoinette suffered through his peculiarities longer than anyone else on his payroll. She finally quit when Larry showed up at her father's funeral with a smiley face sunburned onto his balding head.

AS: "I get a lot of requests to do personalized Cameo videos, and the quote I'm asked for the most is from 'The Bat Mitzvah' episode [Season 6, Episode 10], when I say, 'Larry, do you still have that tickle in your anus?' It's not exactly 'Love means never having to say you're sorry,' but it did become a Giphy moment for me."

> "Whenever Larry and I are together funny things just seem to happen."
> —JERRY SEINFELD

Dana Lee
Seasons 2, 7, and 9–12
CUSTOMER IN CAR SHOWROOM/ MR. TAKAHASHI

Mr. Takahashi is the owner of the country club frequented by Larry and his golf buddies. He's known for running his establishment with an authoritarian-like need for order. Larry can't help but challenge and break Takahashi's strict rules (no cell phone usage in the dining room!). Takahashi would like nothing more than to ban Larry from the club forever, but Larry always finds a loophole in the rules, even after killing the club's mascot, the black swan.

DL: " 'The Black Swan' [Season 7, Episode 7]: It was a great way to introduce my character, Mr. Takahashi. And here's a little anecdote: The interrogation scene of Larry was supposed to be reminiscent of the interrogation scene in *The Bridge on the River Kwai*. The first time I was on the show, however, was in season two. I played a customer at Larry's car dealership. Mr. Takahashi was created later, in season seven. But since I'd worked on the show before, they did not want to see me audition at first. I was literally the last person they saw. But I got the part, and I gave the character the name Takahashi. I wanted something obviously Japanese but easy to pronounce and remember."

Jason Alexander
Seasons 2 and 7
HIMSELF

Jason Alexander steps into the *Curb* world more than once as Larry's disgruntled former *Seinfeld* colleague. On *Curb*, Larry is irked that Jason repeatedly refers to his *Seinfeld* character, George Costanza, as a "jackass" because the character was in fact Larry David's alter ego. In the most meta of meta seasons, when Jason joins his old castmates Jerry Seinfeld, Julia Louis-Dreyfus, and Michael Richards for a *Seinfeld* reunion, he has a falling-out with Larry over a pen, reigniting an old feud from a *Seinfeld* episode called..."The Pen."

JA: "In the episode where we do the table read of the *Seinfeld* reunion special, Larry got everyone that would have originally been at a real *Seinfeld* reading: all the execs, the crew, the producers. He brought them all into that scene, and he didn't have to do that. So it was not only the five of us, but it was our first director, our rep from Castle Rock, our rep from NBC. The sentimentality of Larry was also in the *Seinfeld* finale, but people shit all over that ending, so they didn't recognize it. But Larry found a way to bring in every actor that meant something to our success with *Seinfeld* so that they could celebrate our goodbye with us. And he did it for the *Curb* table-read scene, too, even though no one would have known if he'd just gotten background extras. That was extraordinary."

Chris Williams
Season 3
KRAZEE-EYEZ KILLA

In one of *Curb*'s most unforgettable guest spots, Chris Williams played Wanda Sykes's fiancé, rapper Krazee-Eyez Killa. Krazee warms up to Larry upon meeting him, trading racist terms of endearment that produced a shockingly memorable conversation (parts of which won't be repeated here): "Are you my Caucasian? Yeah, I'm your Caucasian!" Things hit peak *Curb* absurdity when Krazee takes advice from Larry regarding how many times he should or shouldn't say "motherfucker" in a song.

CW: "In the audition, I was like, 'So Larry David, you got two first names? Motherfucker, I like that shit. Where'd you get that shit?' And he says, 'My dad.' I was trying to be in character as much as possible, but Bob Weide knew I was just an actor. So did Jeff [Garlin]. But Larry didn't know shit. So I said to him, 'I like you. You my nigga, right?' It shocked him so much. Larry is always in control, so if someone can wrest control away from him and keep him off-balance, that's where the comedy is. If Larry David doesn't know what to do in a situation, that's comedy gold. I heard that after the audition, Larry asked if I was a good rapper. He was told, 'No, Larry. He's an actor.' But I still got the role over real rappers who auditioned for it."

"I researched for the role watching *MTV Cribs*. What do rappers say? What do they talk about? Like in *MTV Cribs*, Ghostface Killah had French colonial furniture in his mansion. Silkk the Shocker had a giant velvet portrait of himself and a hot tub in the middle of his house. So I was trying to incorporate all these things, and I was trying to be as hard as possible."

"While shooting, I knew I had to push the envelope and try to be outrageous. Larry was cracking up so much that we had to stop and do another take. Like in the first scene, when I'm talking to him at the party, and I was like, 'You were on *Steinfeld*, right?' He doesn't want to correct me, 'It's *Seinfeld*.' I'm like, '*Steinfeld*, whateva, muthafucka. So can you help me out with this song I'm writing?'"

Richard Kind
Seasons 3, 5, 7, 10, and 11
<u>COUSIN ANDY</u>

Viewers discovered that nit-picking, pettiness, and obsessing about unimportant details run in the David family when they met Andy David, Larry's cousin. He's the dull and unremarkable flip side of Larry, a guy who bores others to death with his low-wattage conversation. He's the guy you seat at the far end of the table during a dinner party—never in the middle.

RK: "You know, everybody goes, 'Oh, Andy's so annoying!' and he is, but he's only annoying if you know him for a long time. It's like, 'Wait, do I have to see him again?' At first glance, he's a terrific and lovely guy. But if you know him for a long time, it's just like, 'Ugh, enough already.'"

"I'd been friends with Jeff Garlin for years when he said *Curb* needed an actor to play Cousin Andy. It was early in the run of the show, so Larry didn't want to have famous people playing [other people]. They had to play themselves. The only exception at the time was Ed Asner. So Jeff mentioned me for the role of Cousin Andy, and Larry says, 'No, he's too famous.' [But I wasn't,] especially then. I told Jeff, 'Go tell Larry I'm not that famous. He thinks I'm famous because he knows me, but I'm not.' So they audition people and realize I may be the best guy for the part. So they gave me the part, and that's how I became Cousin Andy."

"I didn't have to audition. [Larry] just gave me the part, which was very nice. I remember him saying, 'Do you want to do it?' And I said, 'Yeah, sure.' It wasn't like, 'Oh dear God, I hope I get on *Curb*!' It was season two and *Curb* wasn't a commodity back then. But by the show's last season, when it *was* a commodity, I wanted to be on [season twelve], so I asked Larry. He's very kind. I mean, he's shockingly kind. You don't think that he is, but he is. He has great morality."

> **"I wanted to be on [season twelve], so I asked Larry. He's very kind. I mean, he's shockingly kind."**
> —RICHARD KIND

Lisa Arch
Seasons 3–11
<u>CASSIE</u>

Andy's wife, Cassie, has a knack for making hats . . . and making inappropriate requests. When Larry offers to pay for her young daughter's future college education, Cassie suggests that Larry instead pay for her—Cassie—to attend cosmetology school. Larry is incensed. Cassie pushes back, reasoning that it's best to spend the money now because they don't know what the future will bring for her daughter. "What if she turns out to be a drug addict or something?"

LA: "Cassie is a busy mom who is very involved with things that she finds important, like her charity. I also feel like she's a more simple person than a lot of people in that universe. But when I was first on *Curb*, she was all about her hats, and it felt like Andy and Cassie were kind of poor, or struggling a bit. Then when we came back in later seasons, all of a sudden we had this beautiful house and Cassie's working for a charity. So I'm not sure how that happened, but I'm very happy for them. Maybe she'd sold enough hats to make millions."

"I really love the 'middling' episode ["Happy New Year," Season 10, Episode 1] that I'm in. I got so many people calling me about that, so many emails saying that it was so relatable. For that dinner scene, the instructions were to have a really boring conversation with Andy. So he starts speaking as slowly as I am speaking. The fact that they gave us the space to do that was so much fun."

CLOCKWISE FROM TOP LEFT: *Curb Your Enthusiasm* welcomed acclaimed guest stars like Lucy Liu, Ashli Auguillard, Jon Hamm, Catherine O'Hara, Ted Danson, Hugh Hefner, Alanis Morissette, Chris Williams, John McEnroe, and Bill Hader.

Ann Ryerson
Seasons 4–8
NAN FUNKHOUSER

Nan is the long-suffering wife of Marty Funkhouser, Larry's self-proclaimed bestie played by the late Bob Einstein. Nan puts up with the infantile antics of both men, including decades of arguments and grudges about nothing of consequence.

AR: "[It was the early days] and I hadn't seen *Curb* because I didn't have HBO. But I'd heard how fun and wonderful the show was from my friends Paul Dooley and Julie Payne, who played Cheryl's parents in the first two seasons. Paul especially laid out how wild a scene in a restaurant had been and how much fun it was to film it."

"For my first scene, I only know that it's a dinner party. I am Marty Funkhouser's wife. After the first run-through, Larry tells us a few things not to say, but not much else. You learn on the fly. And there were many times when I would laugh. Like when Bob, who played Marty, gives a tribute to his dead father at his funeral and says outrageous things to us, completely deadpan. I laugh, but the camera isn't on me enough to upset the gist of the scene."

"Then at Sammi's bat mitzvah, when Larry goes to the front of the room and starts talking about a gerbil, again, I just scream. It is just so outrageous that I can't stop myself. I apologized to [director] Larry Charles, who was not far from me, but he said, 'Oh no, we like to know how far we've gone.' "

Ben Stiller
Seasons 4 and 6
HIMSELF

Ben Stiller is cast as Larry's costar in *The Producers* in "Ben's Birthday Party" (Season 4, Episode 2), but the two thin-skinned actors can't stop butting heads. There's the birthday bash for Ben, where Larry insults him when he asks, "Who celebrates their birthday so far from the actual date?!" Then there's the car ride, where the pair fight about the seating arrangement, causing Ben to explode and call Larry a "grown man-baby." But nothing in their pantheon of petulant spats tops the sneeze confrontation:

Ben: "You wouldn't even shake my hand the first time we met, Larry!"

Larry: "You sneezed . . . you had snot all over your hand!"

Ben: "That was a dry sneeze!"

Larry: "I can't assume dry, I gotta assume wet."

BS: "I knew there was an outline, and we would be going off of that. I loved doing *Curb*. It was the only time I did something fully improvised. The first take was the best because it was the total unknown. It's all actually happening for the first time. No rehearsal. It was fun times working with my wife [Christine Taylor] and Larry. Watching his process was fun."

Iris Bahr
Seasons 5 and 12
RACHEL HEINEMAN

Rachel unwittingly becomes wrapped up in Larry's scheme to get his friend Richard Lewis on a kidney transplant list. They wind up at a ski resort, where Rachel and Larry become trapped on a ski lift when it conks out halfway up the mountain. They're hungry, so Larry searches his pockets for food and finds edible underwear (it's a long story). Rachel, an Orthodox Jew, is appalled. But there's a bigger problem: According to Jewish law, a single woman can't be alone with a man after dark. As the sun sets, she says one of them must jump off. Larry refuses.

IB: "The first time Larry busted out the edible underwear [to eat when we were trapped on the lift], I had zero idea how this was happening. Full disclosure: I was not previously aware that edible underwear even existed. It just looked like a particularly festive fruit roll-up to me, and both my character and I have been avid fans of fruit roll-ups for many years."

"Riffing with Larry, Cheryl, Jeff, and Susie in the living room about Larry's Jewish band was a highlight for me, as was telling Cheryl and Larry to bury the plates, and Larry's answer to my question 'Do I smell bacon?' He replied, 'I lit a fart.' That killed me. And of course, just being stranded with Larry on the ski lift for hours shooting the shit was a highlight."

Ellia English
Seasons 6, 7, and 12
<u>AUNTIE RAE</u>

Auntie Rae moves in with the Davids after she and her family, the Blacks, are forced to relocate due to a hurricane. Rae makes herself at home in the upscale LA abode, displacing Larry in the process. She is a lovely, patient woman of faith . . . until Larry pushes her to the edge.

EE: "I grew up in a household where we did not curse. Now it wasn't like I hadn't been around people who were swearing. I had family members all around me, but my mom said I'd get in a lot of trouble if I swore. So when Auntie Rae had to really give Larry a good cursing out, it wasn't easy for me . . . I remember he came out of the room and I'm like, 'Fuck you and your monkey ass friend Bathsheba Munderman.' Something just came out of me. It was something I probably heard one of my relatives say. But there was a nervous energy with me doing it because I had my parents' voices in my head saying, 'Don't do it!' But I went all the way there. Once they said cut, my whole body was shaking. I felt like the kid who was going to get in trouble. I had to go into a back room and do some deep breathing exercises to get myself together. I kept saying, 'C'mon Ellia, you're a grown woman!'"

"Larry would see me on set and say, 'Here she comes.' Because I was always ready for my hug. I had to get my hug from my Larry. But that might have been why he came up with that scene where he was trying to get Auntie Rae to stop hugging him. Remember the scene when he is showing Auntie Rae the garden in the backyard that he had created for her because he knew that she loved gardening? She starts hugging him and telling him how much she appreciates him. And all of a sudden, everything down there in front of his pants starts doing some different things. And Auntie Rae lifts back, and says, 'Larry, you're disgusting!' then takes off running into the house. After that I wondered if it was real Larry's way of saying, 'Stop asking me for a hug!'"

Saverio Guerra
Seasons 7, 10, and 12
<u>MOCHA JOE & JOE D'ANGELO</u>

Mocha Joe dares to serve Larry a soft scone and cold coffee atop a wobbly table in his cafe, Mocha Joe's. Larry complains, Mocha Joe takes offense, and a bitter feud ensues. In retaliation for the poor service, Larry opens his own "spite store" next door called Latte Larry's. Ted Danson gets involved, and sides with Joe. Joe bests his enemy when he buys the house next door to Larry's. Skip forward to the final season. Larry needs a lawyer and Joe D'Angelo (also played by Guerra) shows up. But he looks remarkably like Mocha Joe. Larry finds the resemblance too disturbing and fires him.

SG: "When I was flying back in for season ten, I of course didn't know much about what Mocha Joe would be doing. But I ran into someone from the show at the airport in New York. She was in front of me in line boarding the plane, and she's like, 'Oh my God, you don't know? You're the whole fucking season! Don't tell Larry I told you.' When I got to LA and they brought me to the set, I saw that they rented a storefront in a strip mall and made an actual coffee shop, Mocha Joe's. And there was a Latte Larry's. They looked like real coffee shops. People kept coming up to buy coffee."

"I tease Larry that he both ruined and enhanced my life. Everywhere I go now it's 'Hey, Mocha Joe!' If I walk down the street in New York, people scream from their cars, 'Fuck you, Mocha Joe!' I was in a Starbucks and the guy behind the counter refused to serve me because he was a dedicated Latte Larry fan. And you know when you order coffee and they ask for your name so they can write it on your cup? I'll say Saverio, and it'll come back with 'Fuck you, Mocha Joe' written on the side. Now, if I go into a restaurant and the table is wobbling, I don't say anything. I just put my foot on the base instead to keep it steady. It's just easier."

> **"I tease Larry that he both ruined and enhanced my life. Everywhere I go now it's 'Hey, Mocha Joe!'"**
> —SAVERIO GUERRA

CLOCKWISE FROM TOP LEFT: Ben Stiller, Richard Kind, Shelley Berman, David Schwimmer, Isla Fisher, Woody Harrelson, Michael J. Fox, and Rosie O'Donnell all made appearances on *Curb*.

Anne Bedian
"Palestinian Chicken," Season 8, Episode 3
SHARA

"Palestinian Chicken" became an instant classic when it aired in 2011 and put an entirely new spin on Palestinian-Jewish relations. Shara works at Al-Abbas Original Best Chicken, a restaurant that's garnering rave reviews and concern because it's thought to have antisemitic politics and is opening near a Jewish deli. Larry dines there anyway, meets Shara, and the two end up having sex.

AB: "All I had to go on was a brief character description provided by my agent. It stated that the character was Palestinian, not politically correct, and that I needed to be comfortable with possible nudity—though it was specified as 'no front, back only.' That was it. There were no scripted lines, no detailed breakdown of the scene, and no sense of the storyline. That was literally all I had to work with going in."

"Between takes during the taping of the now famous sex scene, I told Larry, 'I'm so happy to be on the show but too bad we're doing this because it's not something I'm comfortable watching with my parents.' He looked at me and said, 'You know what? It's comedy. It's funny. You're not naked, we're not doing any nudity. It's OK.' He was trying to reassure me, showing me that it wasn't something vulgar or inappropriate. He wasn't being fatherly. He was being kind and thoughtful. He helped me make peace by pointing out the scene's comedic value rather than focusing on the discomfort I felt."

Jimmy Kimmel
Seasons 9 and 12
HIMSELF

Late night host Jimmy Kimmel invites Larry on the show to talk about Fatwa! The Musical. *During the interview, Larry impersonates the Ayatollah of Iran, causing an international incident. Iran's Supreme Leader then places a fatwa, or death threat, on Larry's life. Larry suggests to Jimmy that he should return as a guest on the show to apologize. Jimmy's answer? A hard no.*

JK: "*Curb* was a show that I loved right away. And once we knew Larry's character and his personality, we were able to laugh at the situations he's in before the scene even gets going. When you create a character that gets laughs without the character having to even say anything, that's a rare and impressive thing."

"I always secretly hoped they would ask me to be on the show. I love the show but I certainly wasn't going to reach out and force myself on anyone. So I was quite delighted when they did ask. But with that said, the whole thing seemed like Larry was doing me a favor."

> **"I always secretly hoped they would ask me to be on the show."**
> —JIMMY KIMMEL

"When I was on the 'Foisted!' episode [Season 9, Episode 1], I was getting hung up on playing myself. Like, 'Oh, what would I really do in this situation?' I started talking to Larry about it, and I said, 'What I would really say here is . . .' He listened and then said, 'Yeah, yeah, yeah. Just do what we wrote in the thing.' He couldn't have cared less about what I would do in real life, even though I was playing myself. He wanted to get it down and get out of there."

"On a number of occasions, I've had to restrain myself from pitching my own *Curb Your Enthusiasm*–type situations to Larry. Like, 'Oh, this would be great for *Curb*!' I know he gets bombarded with that stuff. Also, knowing Larry, it wouldn't mean more coming from me than it would from any stranger on the street."

Bryan Cranston
Season 9
DR. TEMPLETON

Bryan Cranston plays Larry's passive-aggressive therapist, Dr. Templeton. During a session, Larry becomes obsessed with the difference in their respective chairs and complains that the therapist's seating arrangement is better. The doctor doesn't see a difference and says, "Interesting. You are the first and only patient who has found something negative about that chair." Larry replies, "I don't find that interesting at all." Dr. Templeton responds, "Well I do and that is my job, to find things interesting. [Jots down 'chair issues' on his notepad.] *I think there's something deeper here."*

BC: "I get a call from Larry saying, 'I'd love to have you come on the show.' I've been a fan of Curb and I know friends who have been on it. They said it's great fun. It's a little crazy, and you're kind of flying without a net, but in a fun way. And the best thing is you don't have to really memorize anything. I was like wow! Fantastic. Larry basically said, 'You'll be my therapist.' And I thought, 'Oh my God, wouldn't that be fantastic to be Larry David's therapist? You could just have the one patient your entire career, and have enough time and enough billable hours to live in a nice place.' So I was very excited about that."

"I was surprised to be on the show because I gave [real] Larry some really bad advice, he took the advice, and I think he hates me for it. We were at a funeral of a friend's parent. Larry said to me, 'Hey. You've done Broadway before. Did you like it?' And I said, 'I did. I loved the performing aspect. It's tiring, but I loved it.' He said, 'Do you think I should do it? I have a play in mind.' I said, 'You should absolutely do Broadway, Larry David!' And so he did. He wrote this play [Fish in the Dark] and went on Broadway. I went backstage after the play one night, and I said, 'Larry, that was fantastic.' And he said, 'Oh my God, I'll never listen to you again. I hate doing this!' It was his own show and his own material, but just the idea of going on night after night, eight performances a week, doing the same thing over and over—he hated it. It was like I fed him a load of garbage."

> ## "And I thought, 'Oh my God, wouldn't that be fantastic to be Larry David's therapist?'"
> —BRYAN CRANSTON

Vince Vaughn
Seasons 10–12
<u>FREDDY FUNKHOUSER</u>

Vince joined Curb in season ten as Marty Funkhouser's half-brother, Freddy. His ownership of a thriving bed company earned him the nickname "The Mattress Champ," but he was also a trusty sidekick who could be as petty as Larry. Freddy's greatest regret: consulting Larry on the potential contents of his new hotel's minibars. (In-room snacking was never as fraught.)

VV: "Freddy is a fun character to play. He's not like a guy who has balance and self-reflection. He's fun for comedy because his self-interest is always at play. That's the joy of the show. All of the characters are these imperfect people. They give in to their impulses, so it's not the better side of themselves, but it's an honest side of themselves. It's fun to watch them in this world where they muddle things up and get into conflicts with each other. They're flawed, which makes the show pretty reflective of humanity."

> ## "That's the joy of the show. All of the characters are these imperfect people."
> —VINCE VAUGHN

Tracey Ullman
Seasons 11–12
<u>IRMA KOSTROSKI</u>

Ullman plays the brusque and graceless Santa Monica City councilwoman Irma Kostroski. She's a hard-to-love, local-ordinance wonk whose utilitarian hairdo and clothing are the antithesis of LA chic. Larry cozies up to her, literally, in hopes of getting a local zoning law changed to his benefit. Irma gets under Larry's skin, and eventually under his sheets, when he resorts to sleeping with her to get what he wants. When Irma and her CPAP machine move in with Larry, he's afraid he'll never get rid of her.

TU: "They sent me the outlines of things they wanted to do in the season. And I just thought, 'I'll play this totally unattractive woman. Brilliant!' I love that Irma wasn't into show business, and I really played to that. She'd never watched the Oscars. I teased Larry and said, 'You always have these gorgeous women on the show, Sienna Miller, your beautiful wife, Cheryl. Now you're finally going for a woman your own age. A sexy senior!' "

"Larry has to put up with her because he wants something. She doesn't realize that he doesn't really fancy her. So when she's saying to him, 'You want to come up and take a shower with me?' it was like James Mason and Shelley Winters in Lolita. The real Larry loved it. I think he felt very challenged. I was one of the first characters that he couldn't just get rid of or trash or dismiss."

CLOCKWISE FROM TOP LEFT: Jane Krakowski, Albert Brooks, F. Murray Abraham, Saverio Guerra, Jimmy Kimmel, Clive Owen, and Lauren Graham also guest-starred on Curb

Alexander Vindman
Seasons 11–12
HIMSELF

Vindman, the retired US Army lieutenant colonel whose 2019 testimony before Congress regarding the Trump-Ukraine scandal helped bring about an abuse of power charge in Trump's first impeachment trial, overhears Larry trying to bribe a local Santa Monica city councilwoman and exposes him. In the series finale, Vindman takes the stand in court to testify against Larry's character: "I will not tolerate corruption from Trump, Putin, or Larry David," says Vindman.

AV: "There are a lot of people who love *Curb*. It has a cult following. But I never really watched the show. I don't know if it was just Larry being off-putting or what, but I never really got into it. So my preparation [to be a guest] was watching the preceding season to get a little bit more background. It was very similar to my preparation for meeting President Zelensky of Ukraine and watching his hilarious *Servant of the People* sitcom. Having shows like these meant I could prep properly."

"I had to pause over the storyline in that season because of Larry stealing shoes from the Holocaust Museum. It set me back a little, but I had to rationalize it in my mind. That was him being on-brand, versus me playing it myself as a goodie two-shoes. So it all kind of seemed to come together."

Sienna Miller
"Fish Stuck," Season 12, Episode 5
HERSELF

Film and television star Sienna Miller plays a version of herself, a film and television star who has a fetish for all things Jewish, including Larry himself. Larry notices she can't seem to act out a scene without a piece of fruit in her hand.

SM: "I laughed in every single scene. It was impossible not to, because Larry cracks up in almost every take, and as soon as you see that laugh he does, where the jaw goes up and down, it's over for everyone."

"There was a moment when he visits my trailer [on the set of my character's film] and slowly raises a piece of fruit into frame while saying, somewhat accusatory, 'Siennaaaaa.' We actually couldn't look at each other. The scene took way too long because we had tears streaming down our cheeks. It was hands down the most fun I have ever had at work."

> ## "I laughed in every single scene. It was impossible not to."
> —SIENNA MILLER

Lori Loughlin
"The Gettysburg Address," Season 12, Episode 6
HERSELF

Full House star Lori Loughlin, who was indicted by the FBI for fraud and bribery in the Varsity Blues scandal, plays herself. She's costarring with Ted Danson in a play about Abraham Lincoln. Ted asks Larry to sponsor Lori for a country-club membership because she's been blacklisted from every country club in the area since her arrest. Larry vouches for her only to find that Lori's bribery skills know no bounds.

LL: "They reached out to my manager and said, 'Listen, we have an idea for Lori if she's up for it. If she doesn't respond to it, we totally understand. We're not offended.' They pitched the idea of me trying to get into a country club, but I can't because of the college admissions scandal. Ted Danson goes to Larry and says, 'Would you help her?' And Larry's like, 'Yeah, I'm all for the underdog. I'll do it.' So I try to join this club with Larry's help, and I'm cheating, and I have a handicap placard in my car but I'm not disabled. When my manager told me the premise, I couldn't stop laughing. I was like, 'This is the greatest thing I've ever heard.'"

"I knew that it would be funny because look at the history of that show. I knew it was a great opportunity for me. It's always good to be able to make fun of yourself and take responsibility with humor. So for me, it felt like a win-win all the way around."

"The first time I went to do a scene, I was like, 'Holy smokes.' Improv is new and different for me, but you just remind yourself, it's Larry's show. Larry's going to carry the scene. You're a guest, not the star. You're never going to come in and try to one-up the lead of a show. So I said to myself, 'OK, take a deep breath and follow Larry's lead.'"

"I was nervous when I first met Larry, but he was very sweet. He walked over to me and he said, 'Loughlin, that's Irish, right?' And then I said something stupid that I still think of to this day. I said, 'Yeah, I'm mostly Irish, but my grandfather was from Germany, so a little bit German.' And he stops, looks at me, and he goes, 'Oh, a little German? Good to know, good to know.' And he walks away. And I'm like, 'Why did I tell him that?!'"

Bruce Springsteen
Season 12
HIMSELF

Bruce Springsteen publicly praises Larry David for supporting voting rights in Georgia by bringing water to Auntie Rae when she was waiting in a long line at the polling station. Springsteen meets Larry in person during a tour stop in LA, and while chatting, the Boss accidentally drinks from Larry's water glass. Larry doesn't know it but he's coming down with COVID, and ends up giving it to Springsteen. The singer has to postpone the rest of the tour, angering his fans, who publicly denounce Larry. It's one more strike against Larry ahead of his trial in Atlanta for breaking voting laws.

BS: "*Curb* and Larry are unique. They are a mirror, showing that we all have a petty, irascible side. Before *Curb*, you really hadn't seen that on TV. I mean, on *Seinfeld* they touched on it, but there's never been a character quite like Larry David. He's constantly transgressive and it's so satisfying to watch."

"I've spent a reasonable amount of time in front of cameras, but it's not quite the same as being in an acting situation. So before we went on, Larry came upstairs where I was in a little dressing room and he said, 'We just keep going till we get it.' So he was sort of reassuring me that, like, no matter how lousy you are, this is going to end up funny. No matter what. So that was comforting and it made me comfortable on camera."

"If I had to memorize actual lines when I appeared on the show I probably couldn't have done it because my memory is shot. So it was perfect for me. They say, 'OK, in this scene, Larry's going to do this, and you're going to do that,' and then they start and you just riff. It was a lot of fun though I did break and laugh. At least I laughed in all the right spots."

> "*Curb* and Larry are unique. They are a mirror, showing that we all have a petty, irascible side."
> —BRUCE SPRINGSTEEN

Keyla Monterroso Mejia
Seasons 11–12
MARIA SOFIA ESTRADA

The perpetually off-kilter Maria Sofia was a terrible actor, but Larry cast her in his new series "Young Larry" anyway to avoid being sued for an accidental death in his pool. Maria Sofia irked Larry throughout season eleven and some of season twelve with her wooden delivery and terrible performances. Then fame made her ego swell, and she wouldn't give him the time of day. Lucky Larry.

KM: "I was not a *Curb* fan, but not because I didn't like the show. It's because I didn't even realize it existed until I booked a role on it! It used to come on HBO at 10 p.m. and at the time, I was relatively young so I had a bedtime. It also wasn't appropriate for me to watch [laughs]. But after landing the role and doing my research, I became a huge fan, which honestly in the long run, ended up making the experience a lot more nerve-racking."

"The first [season] all I can truly remember is how nervous I felt. But I was really lucky to go back the following season and one of the things that will stay with me is watching a mastermind at work and seeing how these scenes and loglines took life. I was very aware that I was watching some of the greatest to ever do this format—comedy geniuses. So to see a scene ping-pong and come to life from what Larry had imagined is truly otherworldly."

CLOCKWISE FROM TOP LEFT: Bryan Cranston, Tracey Ullman, Ricky Gervais, Julia Louis-Dreyfus, Vince Vaughn, Lori Loughlin, Lin-Manuel Miranda, Harry Hamlin, and Julie Bowen are among the familiar faces that appeared on the show.

Lauren Graham
Season 9
BRIDGET

In Graham's first gig after reprising her role as Lorelai on the Gilmore Girls *revival, she guest-starred as Larry's new girlfriend, Bridget. Bridget happens to be a censor at NBC, making things complicated for Larry, who spent years battling her kind during his* Seinfeld *years. The irony? Bridget is a foul-mouthed, swearing machine.*

LG: "Larry called me and asked, 'How do you feel about saying things that are really dirty?' I said, 'Well, not fantastic.' It's off-brand for me, but I'd never been on the show and I was dying to do it so I said, 'Yes. I'll do it.'"

"There's a scene where we're all at a dinner party. Ted Danson, Cheryl David [Hines]—everybody's there. Afterward Ted said, 'You know, this is HBO. You can be dirtier.' And I'm like, 'Ted, that is as dirty as I can be.' So I was open to suggestions, and I took many suggestions. They had to feed me some of the more risqué lines just to get what they wanted."

> **"There's a nostalgia and a familiarity to *Curb* that I would have stuck with for ten more seasons if I could have."**
> —LAUREN GRAHAM

"Now we're saying goodbye to shows that really defined eras of TV and HBO, where we'd all sit down to watch TV at a certain time and then talk about it the next day. There's a nostalgia and a familiarity to *Curb* that I would have stuck with for ten more seasons if I could have. And after I was on the show, Larry told me that he thought our characters might get married. And I was like, 'Larry, don't tell me that!' That would have been so fun. I don't know why it didn't happen. But I was almost married to Larry."

Jon Hamm
Seasons 10–11
HIMSELF

Season ten found Madmen *star Jon Hamm shadowing Larry as research for an upcoming movie where he'd play a character based on Larry. A note-taking Hamm follows Larry around, aping every action and mannerism. He wears the same brand of shoes as Larry, squeezes his lime into his water like Larry, and accuses Richard Lewis of going over his appetizer allotment—just like Larry did to Christian Slater in season seven.*

JH: "The genesis of the idea that I'd shadow Larry? I don't know where it came from other than it was something Larry thought would be funny, and it did make us both laugh. You can tell when you watch the show that everybody on it is having fun. I think people experience that thrill vicariously. And watching somebody trying to be Larry . . . that's funny for everyone."

"[*Curb*] is mostly improv, and that can be a very daunting prospect. You don't know if it's going to work until you get in there and start chopping it up. It's like, OK, this could really go sideways. But with *Curb* you're in tremendously good hands. You're with people who know what they're doing and feel comfortable. And that extends to the other side of the camera as well with [directors] Jeff Schaffer and Alec Berg. They have a sense of people's strengths and how it's going to play and how not to paint yourself into a corner narratively. Like, 'Don't go down that road, because it's a dead end—let's instead make a left turn here.' I found it freeing to be given a loose road map and also have the freedom to go off-road."

> **"With *Curb* you're in tremendously good hands. You're with people who know what they're doing and feel comfortable."**
> —JON HAMM

Bailey Thompson
"The Doll," Season 2, Episode 7
TARA MICHAELSON

Bailey Thompson was eight years old when she starred as Tara Michaelson in one of Curb's *most beloved episodes, "The Doll." Tara, the daughter of a TV exec, asks Larry to cut her doll's hair. When he obliges, she becomes very upset. To placate her and ward off a confrontation with her mom, Larry and Jeff steal another head from Jeff's daughter's doll and Frankenstein it onto Tara's. The episode ends in the bathroom of a movie theater, where Larry has stuffed a water bottle down the front of his trousers in order to sneak it into the venue. Tara sees him and gives him a hug for "fixing" her doll, creating another terrible situation for Larry when she screams, "Mommy, mommy! The bald man's in the bathroom and there's something hard in his pants!"*

BT: "When we shot 'The Doll,' I knew nothing about the show. I didn't know *Seinfeld* at that time. I didn't know who Larry David was. I was watching Nickelodeon. I also didn't really understand what I was saying [when I delivered that line about Larry's pants]. My mom had told me, 'Hey, we're not really going to talk about the context. You're just going to say this line, and I'm going to explain it to you when you're older.' Since I was the young little professional, I was like, 'Yes, ma'am. I'll just say the line.' And I did. I had no idea what it meant until I was around thirteen and I was like, 'Oh, my God, I can't believe that I said that!' But I was very taken care of on the set. My parents were there, and everyone made sure that I was comfortable. There was a lot of extra attention and care."

"I didn't know 'The Doll' became such a popular episode until my high school improv coach emailed me a *Time* magazine article about the top 100 episodes of television of the past fifteen years. 'The Doll' was in there. It was the first time that it clocked for me that it was a big deal because—even at that age—I still didn't watch the show since it was more for adults. I remember going to IMDb and looking it up and seeing the rankings of it. Every time I would tell someone who was a fan of the show, they'd be like, 'That's the best episode!'"

Sean Hayes
"Fish Stuck," Season 12, Episode 5
CHRISTOPHER MANTLE

Hayes of Will & Grace *fame played a defense attorney Larry chose largely on the basis of his last name (it's the same as Larry's favorite baseball player, Mickey Mantle). Larry discovers Mantle's plans to give his child his husband's last name, Zeckelman. Naturally, Larry has to say something, causing a rift in the couple's marriage.*

SH: "I loved every second of *Curb* [when the series premiered in 2000] and was very impressed. I was fortunate enough to be asked to participate in the 2004 season but my schedule didn't allow [it]. Luckily, I ran into Larry at a party during his last season of the show and I'm glad I made it on the show just under the wire."

"I knew the general idea of the episode but not too many details. I knew Christopher Mantle was married and that he and his husband were in the middle of trying to have a baby via a surrogate, but the rest was pretty much discussed on set . . . which was great since I'm not a huge fan of reading."

"Improv is only fun and easy when you're doing it with people who are funny. It's really difficult to improvise with people who aren't. That said, it's sometimes a bit terrifying to jump on a set at 6:00 a.m. and force that part of your brain to kick in gear. It's much easier after lunch with a plate of spaghetti in your stomach."

"I just remember savoring the permission to say and do anything I wanted to Larry while he sat across from my desk. Those were some of the most side-splitting laughs I've ever had on a set."

> **"Those were some of the most side-splitting laughs I've ever had on a set."**
> —SEAN HAYES

LARRY'S RULES

Why was Larry irritated all the time? Because the overly observant protagonist followed a set of rules and etiquette that he believed everyone else understood. Example: When a patron in front of him in line at a frozen yogurt kiosk asks for too many samples, Larry notes the infraction in a subsequent meltdown: "She wasn't following the rules of society!" he rails. "The unwritten rules that we have!" Cheryl says it best when she tells her irate husband, "Not everyone knows your rules, Larry. You think everyone is going to adhere to them, but they're not because nobody knows them." Enter a handy guide to Larry Etiquette.

1. RESPECT WOOD.

SEINFELD, S7, E10

"I respect *all* wood," says Larry to Jerry Seinfeld about a coffee ring stain on his desk after Jerry shrugs it off. "I respect pine. I respect walnut. I respect oak... You don't."

2. THERE'S AN AGE LIMIT ON TRICK-OR-TREATING.

TRICK OR TREAT, S2, E3

Larry refuses to give candy to a group of uncostumed teenagers who show up at his door on Halloween, deeming them too old to trick-or-treat: "There's got to be some sort of cutoff—shouldn't there be—for Halloween? What are you gonna be, forty? Trick-or-treating at forty?!"

3. ADHERE TO A SET APPETIZER ALLOTMENT.

THE HOT TOWEL, S7, E4

"You're really going to town on that caviar," says Larry to Christian Slater at a party. "I think you're going over your allotment a little bit, no?"

4. SORRY WINDOWS ARE NOT OPEN INDEFINITELY.

THE SMILEY FACE, S8, E4

"With all due respect, don't you think the sorry window has closed on that?" Larry says to a friend who is looking for some sympathy about her father's somewhat recent death. "Two years and you're still getting sorries? I don't think so."

5. AVOID THE STOP AND CHAT.

THE MASSAGE, S2, E10

"He wanted to stop and chat with me and I don't know him well enough for that," says Larry. "For him, all I need to do is just say hello."

6. ESTABLISH HUG TIME LIMITS.

THE N WORD, S6, E8
Larry explains why Auntie Rae's embrace exceeds the hug time limit: "She went over the appropriate amount of time that I can have human contact without getting aroused. I only have five seconds. After that it's out of my control."

7. ONE "THANKS FOR YOUR SERVICE" IS ENOUGH.

THANK YOU FOR YOUR SERVICE, S9, E5
"They thanked him. Three people thanked him. Why do I have to thank him? Does everybody have to thank him for his service?" says Larry about a war vet.

8. REFRAIN FROM USING SMILEY FACE EMOJIS OUTSIDE OF TEXTS.

THE SMILEY FACE, S8, E4
"I told her about the smiley faces—that I can't stand it," says Larry. "Everybody uses them! What, are they going to be in newspapers soon? The *New York Times* headline: 'Unemployment Drops, smiley face?'"

9. SAY NO TO NAMASTE AND OTHER COMMUNAL SALUTATIONS.

NAMASTE, S9, E7
"Not a namaste guy," explains Larry. "I don't participate in group activities. I don't sing birthday songs . . . There is no light within me."

10. TEXT CHAINS ARE FOR IDIOTS.

THE DREAM SCHEME, S12, E7
"Every two minutes, it's 'ding'—too many dings! And what is it? It's just these ridiculous inspirational sentiments that amount to nothing. They're all trite. I don't even know why people bother to write them. And you want me to give it a 'haha'? A 'haha'?!"

11. "HAPPY NEW YEAR!" HAS A CUTOFF DATE.

HAPPY NEW YEAR, S10, E1
"It's a little late, frankly, for the Happy New Year's, ya know?" says Larry to a friend at the gym. "Statute of limitations has kind of run out on the new year . . . Three days is plenty."

12. HONK GENTLY.

HONKING IS VERY DANGEROUS.

THE BARE MIDRIFF, S7, E6
Larry only honks softly and refers to a regular honk as "dangerous." His thesis is proven when a rude honk from Jerry Seinfeld earns an angry verbal barrage from a fellow driver.

Pretty Pretty Pretty Good

Just
as every awkward dinner party, contentious lunch date, and competitive golf game must come to an end, the same is true for *Curb Your Enthusiasm*. The show's final episode aired April 7, 2024, capping twelve seasons of hilariously divergent comedy from Larry David, *Curb*'s cast, and an impressive roster of guests.

TV's funniest show ended with the aptly titled episode "No Lessons Learned," assuring viewers that seventy-six-year-old Larry had gained no wisdom over his lifetime or the show's two-and-a-half-decade run. It was also clear he would not be embarking on a redemptive journey or apology tour to atone for a lifetime of transgressive behavior. *Curb*'s protagonist instead flew off into the sunset with Susie, Jeff, Cheryl, and Leon, arguing about in-flight window-shade etiquette. How perfectly *Curb*.

Larry, taking a breath behind the scenes, during the final season of the show.

SUSIE ESSMAN (SUSIE GREENE): "No one learned their lesson in *Curb*, and that's one of the reasons why it's so funny. Look at comedy greats like Ralph Kramden in *The Honeymooners*. He tried a new scheme week after week after week. He never learned his lesson, because learning is not funny. Funny is repeating the same mistakes over and over again, and Larry is a master at that."

The final scene of the series finale, "No Lessons Learned," S12, E10.

DAVE MANDEL, WRITER, DIRECTOR, AND EXECUTIVE PRODUCER (SEASONS 5-8): "Larry was never worried about looking bad. All he cared about was that the show was funny. He wasn't worried about offending anyone. It's a credit to the audience's intelligence, like hey, guess what? You make a really funny show and we'll seek it out. That's *Curb*'s legacy."

"Hey, you didn't like it the first time? Well I'm doing it again."

—LARRY DAVID

Larry's old foes, including Mocha Joe (Saverio Guerra) and Mr. Takahashi (Dana Lee) testify against him in the series finale.

The final chapter of *Curb* also drew heavily from another legacy: *Seinfeld*. The NBC sitcom's finale caused an uproar when the wildly popular show ended in 1998 with Jerry, Elaine, George, and Kramer serving time for their bad behavior. Reactions from fans ranged from flummoxed to furious, and critics had a field day. David wouldn't dare repeat the same mistake with *Curb*, or would he? He would.

The show's finale found Larry's character on trial. People he'd wronged over the show's 120 episodes testified against him, detailing his worst moments. The list of the aggrieved included Tara (Bailey Thompson), the little girl whom Larry terrorized when he cut her doll's hair, now in her thirties. Also there were country-club owner Mr. Takahashi (Dana Lee), archnemesis Mocha Joe (Saverio Guerra), and whistleblower Alexander Vindman. Larry is sentenced to a year in prison, just like the characters in the disputed conclusion of his former show.

But *Curb* took an unexpected turn when Jerry turned up at the jail to inform Larry that a juror broke sequester, and his sentence has been commuted. Larry's stunned, then Jerry drops this *Seinfeld*-referential gem: "You don't want to end up like this. Nobody wants to see it. Trust me."

David stayed on-brand by repeating his mistake *and* proving that it wasn't such a bad idea for a finale after all.

LARRY DAVID: "The idea was a little crazy on its face. 'You didn't like it the first time? Well I'm doing it again.'"

In the finale's court sequence, prosecutor Earl Mack (Greg Kinnear) calls out many of Larry's past transgressions, including **(CLOCKWISE FROM TOP LEFT)**

breaking into a graveyard, pretending to be an incest survivor, burning down Mocha Joe's coffee shop, and bringing a sex offender to a Passover Seder.

JERRY SEINFELD: "It was a funny thing to do, and I was thrilled with how it came out.

JEFF GARLIN (JEFF GREENE): "I started reading the outline for episode ten and my initial response was, 'What the fuck are you doing?! This makes no fucking sense.' And then as I got further along I was like, 'OK.' And then by the end, I was yelling, 'Fucking amazing!' I knew it was really the end of *Curb* this time, because you cannot top that ending. We really are done."

LAURA STREICHER, CO-EXECUTIVE PRODUCER: "It was a genius idea, and the ultimate nose-thumbing to everyone who'd given Larry a hard time about the *Seinfeld* finale. But I think his biggest concern for season twelve was, 'Are people going to figure it out?' And what we came to realize is that even if uberfans anticipated it, there was no way they'd predict the Jerry ending. That twist was just everything."

JEFF SCHAFFER, WRITER, DIRECTOR, AND EXECUTIVE PRODUCER (SEASONS 5-12): "When people realized we were redoing the *Seinfeld* series finale, they were thinking, 'I can't fucking believe you're going there.' And that was the point—to steer the *Titanic* right back at the iceberg. That made the finale bigger than *Curb*. It was about Larry's consistent and brilliant intransigence. But the story was so strong that it sort of forced the show's hand to end. Although I do always tell Larry there's nothing more Larry David than having a whole bunch of hoopla about the last season of *Curb*, only to come crawling back."

THIS PAGE AND OPPOSITE: Jerry Seinfeld visits Larry in jail and alerts him that there has been a mistrial.

Larry and Jerry behind the scenes during the taping of the finale episode.

12 SEASONS, 24 YEARS. I'LL BE 77.

But after several false stops, David contends that this time it's for real.

DAVID: "It just seemed like the right time. I didn't want the audience to take the show for granted. I thought twelve seasons, that's a lot for a comedy. And we had this idea for the finale, and it could only work if it was a finale. It had been twelve seasons, twenty-four years. I was about to be seventy-seven. I just thought it was enough."

Susie on set during the series finale.

HBO's little show that could was more than enough. It entered the fray on its own terms, exceeded all expectations, broke barriers, and exited on a high note. Among the fifty-five Primetime Emmy Award nominations *Curb* received over its lifetime, the final season landed nods for best comedy series and lead actor in a comedy. David's responses to the two honors: "Misanthropy is finally being recognized as an art form," and "This is a sad day for actors everywhere. See? Anyone can do it."

But not just anyone can do it. In fact, no one but David has been able to pull off a comedy coup like *Curb*.

SCHAFFER: "Most people still don't understand why *Curb* worked. It's like how *Seinfeld* was misnamed 'a show about nothing,' when it was actually the most story-driven sitcom on television. The common misconception about *Curb* is that people think it's just about Larry's life. But it's not. If that was the Real Larry's life, he'd be friendless, penniless, in jail, or dead. The show is about Larry's *ideas*. It's wish fulfillment. For the audience. And for Larry too. But there's such a fundamental misunderstanding of why it even worked, and that's why it can't be repeated."

VINCE VAUGHN (FREDDY FUNKHOUSER): "It's an original in a time when everything else is saying, 'How do we take what's worked before and do it again, slightly differently?' *Curb* is its own animal. You can see how it's extended from *Seinfeld*, how there's an evolution there. But the setting, the circumstances, the world that they live in—there's really nothing else that runs alongside Larry and the show. That's what makes it stand out. Its original thought."

TOP: Jeff Schaffer and Larry behind the scenes of the final episode. BOTTOM: The outline for the final episode of Curb.

CASEY BLOYS, CHAIRMAN AND CEO, HBO AND MAX CONTENT: "*Curb* set the standard for our brand-defining, auteur-driven comedies. Larry paved the way for Issa Rae, Danny McBride, and Bill Hader, among many others."

Curb influenced and outlasted many comedies that followed in its wake. It's no wonder viewers and those involved in the show became emotionally attached. Nevertheless, there was no way David was going out on a sentimental note.

CHERYL HINES (CHERYL DAVID): "I remember when *Friends* was ending and the actors from that cast were vocal about how hard it was to say goodbye and how much they all meant to each other. Our finale was not like that. We had moments, but Larry does not particularly like to indulge in that sort of emotion. He does not appreciate it. He did not want us showing up sad."

"Some days would start where we would look at each other and say, 'Wow, this is our last episode, I can't believe it,' and we'd hug each other. Then by the end of the day, it was like, 'Oh, this chair is killing my back. How much longer is this scene? When are we going to eat? I'm starting to feel faint.' Everyone wanted to go home. It was so *Curb*."

"We'd start out with emotional sentiments, then the reality of being uncomfortable would kick in—but that was my experience during the whole series. Anytime we'd be nominated for an Emmy or a Golden Globe, it'd be exciting for a minute. Then there would be a chorus of complaining: 'I don't want to have to wear a tux. That's a long night.' I would always think they can't be saying this over on *Everybody Loves Raymond*. They must be excited over there."

ESSMAN: "The finale was so emotional for me on so many levels, starting with Richard Lewis's death [on February 27, 2024] a couple months before the finale aired. I'm welling up now talking about it. It was also emotional because it was the finale of twenty-four years of my life. And in the finale, what Larry tried to do is give each of us something special to leave with. Jeff had that scene with the salad dressing. I was in a wheelchair. Richard had that whole storyline about the car. JB had the whole storyline of his family in Georgia. They were giving us all these little parting gifts. When I read the finale outline, I cried my eyes out. I just felt like, 'This is a gift.'"

GARLIN: "I had a very pragmatic approach to it. I really did. That was my feeling the whole season, but when we shot the last scene, after Jeff Schaffer said, 'That's a wrap on the greatest comedy of all time,' I was completely inconsolable. Larry left the set pretty quickly when everyone was making their speeches. But he came back looking for me, because he heard I was sobbing. He gave me a hug, which is not something he's known for. I mean, he's hugged me before, but that was a really warm embrace, and he thanked me."

THIS PAGE: A camera view of Larry during the trial. **OPPOSITE:** Laura Streicher, *Curb*'s co-executive producer, on set while filming the series finale.

"That's a wrap on the greatest comedy of all time."

—JEFF SCHAFFER

STREICHER: "For a few weeks after we wrapped, it felt like I'd been hit by a truck. First of all, you're exhausted by working on the season. It's very long. But there was also the emotional aspect of the show ending for good. And of course soon after we wrapped, we lost Richard... which added another layer to everything. It really was the end of an era, but ultimately the right decision. It was time. Afterwards, I remember asking Larry how he was feeling, and he said something along the lines of, 'I feel like I've died, and I'm now seeing the afterlife.' And I think that summed things up perfectly."

JOYCE LAPINSKY, WIFE OF THE LATE RICHARD LEWIS: (Lapinsky made an appearance as Lewis's date in episode eight of the final season.) "When we shot 'The Colostomy Bag' episode in March of 2023, Richard was declining, but we didn't know that he was not going to be around in a year. We just thought, 'Wow, look at us. We get to be together forevermore.' And I thank Larry profusely for that because when it aired, Richard had already passed. It was hard to watch, but it was everything. We're together forever for the world to see. And who gets to have that? It was a really sweet moment, even though it stinks in that car."

Curb was never known for its big feelings, or its sense of generosity, but the show did change lives and livelihoods.

SAVERIO GUERRA (MOCHA JOE): "I'm honored that Larry let me be part of *Curb*. I knew that it was a show that everybody in Hollywood wanted to be on or make a cameo in. Larry could have had anybody he wanted, so the fact that he invited me to play that character is amazing. He sent me a beautiful email, saying, 'You created one of the most memorable characters on the show. Thank you so much.'"

RICHARD KIND (COUSIN ANDY): "Cousin Andy didn't make it into the final season, so Larry wrote me the most beautiful note saying, 'You know how much I love you. You know how much I love Cousin Andy. But there's just no place for him in the final season.' I knew it had nothing to do with my talent, or that he didn't like me or appreciate what I'd done for the series. Larry is slavish to the material and to the story he wants to tell. If he had to impose a character in the story just because he wanted to put me in, it would be like putting a round peg in a square hole. He just can't do it. There's a purity to that kind of comedy, to what he writes. I thought that was the most gracious thing in the world that he wrote to me and said, 'I wish I could put you in, but there is no place.'"

TED DANSON: "When I joined *Curb* [in 2000], I had just done a pilot that hadn't gotten picked up and I felt like I'd stayed at the half-hour comedy party too long. Other people were way funnier than I was, and I was slightly demoralized. And I said, 'OK, no more. I'll just do films and leave the funny to other people.' And then Larry invited us to play ourselves that first season, and it was so rehabilitative. My desire to be part of the joke, to find the giggle, and to have fun. And it was so much fun. It was so relaxed. And it kind of changed my life. And I do credit him. Being part of *Curb* was so cool and it gave energy to my career, and for that I am forever grateful."

Larry sitting with JB Smoove and the crew during season twelve.

"It was the right time to end things. And we ended on top." —JEFF GARLIN

And so, too, are the fans of the show for delivering a quarter century of rib-tickling, taboo-smashing, boundary-bending comedy with Larry and the cast of *Curb*.

BOB WEIDE, DIRECTOR (SEASONS 1-5, THEN PERIODICALLY THEREAFTER): "Larry David is in the comedy pantheon and can take his place among Jackie Gleason, Lucille Ball, Dick Van Dyke, and those immortals. I can use such a pretentious word, 'pantheon,' because he's made his mark on camera, and he's hit it out of the park now—twice as a creator. Who even does that once?"

ALEC BERG, WRITER, DIRECTOR, AND EXECUTIVE PRODUCER (SEASONS 5-8): "I'm so curious to see what Larry does now. I don't think he's just going to go play golf. He'll find something to pour his creative energy into because that's just who he is. He didn't have to work a day after *Seinfeld* was done, yet he chose to. And that's what I love about *Curb*, it truly is an offering to the gods. He didn't do it for a paycheck. He didn't do it because somebody ordered it and he had an obligation. He designed it outside of the system. It's obligation-free comedy."

GARLIN: "I know people have fond memories of the show. I have fond memories. It means the world to me. I spent most of my adult life on *Curb*. But it was the right time to end things. And we ended on top."

Remembering Three Comedy Greats

Curb Your Enthusiasm lost three great performers and beloved friends over its twenty-four-year run. Respected stand-up comedian Richard Lewis, who rose to fame with his unique brand of dark, self-effacing humor in the 1970s and '80s, was a lifelong friend of Larry David and an integral part of the *Curb* universe. Fictional Lewis played fictional Larry's lifelong friend from the series' inception to its finale. Shelley Berman, one of America's most successful stand-up comedians of the 1950s and '60s, portrayed Larry's father in seasons two through seven. Comedic actor, producer, and writer Bob Einstein of the 1980s and '90s show *Super Dave* assumed the role of Larry's long-suffering pal, Marty Funkhouser, in seasons four through nine. They all made the world a funnier place, leaving behind unparalleled legacies and indelible memories. *Curb* remembers Richard Lewis, Shelley Berman, and Bob Einstein.

Richard Lewis

June 29, 1947–February 27, 2024

"Richard used to come home from shooting *Curb*, and I'd ask, 'How'd it go?' A totally rhetorical question, but nonetheless something to ask. He would say, 'I went. Larry and I got into an argument. I left. Now I'd like to take my makeup off.' He made it seem easy because it was so in line with who he was. He knew his character. But Richard was not that hyperbolic, exaggerated version of himself that you saw on TV. He was very emotional. He wore his heart and mind and soul on his sleeve. And not just his sleeve—it was coming out of his pores. He was very disarming, so he brought [those attributes] out in people. When you watched him with Larry, he'd be asking for more, whether it was more information, more feeling, more engagement. He wanted to feel it all." **—Joyce Lapinsky, Richard's wife**

"It's hard to come up with words because Richard means so much to me on a professional and a personal level. Professionally, I got to work with one of my comedy heroes. I got to watch somebody work who had definitely a strange approach to the work. I just adored Richard. On a personal level, he has helped change many people's lives for the better." **—Jeff Garlin**

"Richard was an influence on me comedically because he was so free and such an open wound onstage. People always compared him to Lenny Bruce, who was one of Richard's influences, but Richard took what Lenny was doing to a very intimate and personal place. He ripped his heart open onstage in a way that was very moving and always funny." **—Susie Essman**

"I listened to Richard on the radio when I was at my first after-school job, when I was a perfumer apprentice. He'd be on the *Howard Stern Show* and that guy was something else. He was so smart, and his humor was so cutting edge. He wasn't afraid of his faults. He let his faults breathe. And later watching the real friendship between him and Larry. To see it up close . . . I'm telling you, I couldn't tell the difference sometimes if it was a damn scene or it was just them hanging out. They were so comfortable around each other. You're watching these knuckleheads, thinking, 'Wow, these dudes are pros.' And that last season, when we got Richard back for a little bit, he got a chance to shine and do more scenes together with Larry. Coming from a place where we didn't think we would ever get him back, it was amazing." **—JB Smoove**

"I had admired Richard for decades. I had a huge crush on him in my twenties. I loved watching him run his fingers through his long dark hair as he paced around stage performing his neurotic, self-deprecating stand-up routine. His gift was transforming his neurosis and his acute sense of persecution and paranoia into a source of hilarity for the rest of the world. He was my favorite. To have had the extraordinary experience of working with him, loving him, and being loved by him was more than I could've ever dreamed of. Sometimes he'd send me a text just to let me know he was thinking of me. Pure joy." **—Cheryl Hines**

"My closest friend for fifty years. What I loved about our friendship was we could say anything to each other, and no matter how insulting it was, we would never get offended, a dynamic that also carried over into our relationship on the show. The best example of this was a scene from season eleven's 'Irma Kostroski' when we were attending a political fundraiser. We were mocking each other unmercifully, as was our wont, when at some point I turned to him and asked, "When are you going to die?" (The irony is not lost on me.) There's no other person on Earth I could've said that to. He just laughed and continued the scene.

Not only was Richard hilarious, but he was also sweet and kind and generous. That's a rare combination for a comedian, because most of us are egomaniacs who don't care about anything except getting a laugh. Sweet and kind and generous are totally incompatible with funny . . . except for him." **—Larry David**

Shelley Berman

February 3, 1925–September 1, 2017

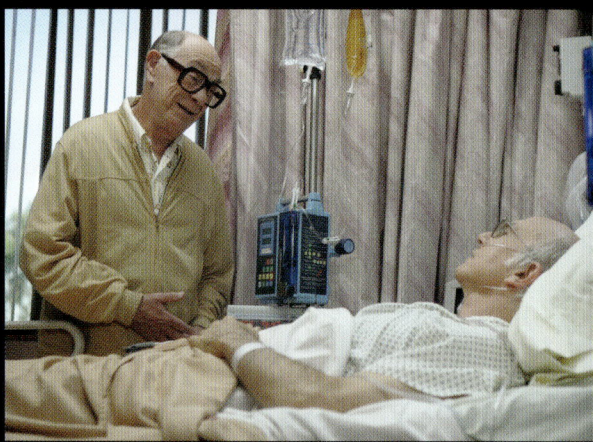

"Shelley Berman was not only a gifted comedian, he was also a sweet friend. He brought a photo album to the set one day so he could show me pictures from some of his iconic performances. I basked in his laughter as he shared his life's journey with me. I felt so lucky to have had the opportunity to spend time with him." —**Cheryl Hines**

"I got to work with one of the all-time great comedians, Shelley Berman. He was a brilliant improviser, actor, and comedian. He was a joy to work with." —**Jeff Garlin**

"Shelley was absolutely perfect casting for Larry's father. He was the perfect fit physically, comedically, intellectually, emotionally . . . Everything about him was perfect for that character. I can't imagine anybody else playing that role but Shelley." —**Susie Essman**

"I had a lot of respect for Mr. Berman. He's a comedy legend, and for me coming from an improv background, I think of that time we had him on the show as golden." —**JB Smoove**

When he came in to audition, he had on a toupee—and not a very good one. (Are any of them?) We did the scene from "The Special Section" where I find out my mother died and he never told me about it because she told him in the hospital that she didn't want him to bother me. He was perfect in the scene, except for one thing: his hairpiece. Afterwards, I caught up with him in the hallway and told him how great he was and that I wanted him to play my father, but without the piece. In a trice, he took it off his head and said, "How's this?"
—**Larry David**

Bob Einstein

November 20, 1942–January 2, 2019

"Any day on the set with Bob was guaranteed to be entertaining. He'd spend the majority of his time telling . . . let's call them 'off colored' jokes to try to get a laugh from Larry. He was very successful." —**Cheryl Hines**

"Bob Einstein was one of my best friends. After we filmed every day he would call and tell me how excited he was about what we just filmed and how great it was. Bob would tell me stories that left my jaw on the ground. He just was a great, great pal." —**Jeff Garlin**

"Bob was irreplaceable. He was a completely original comedic voice and there will never be anyone else like him. He came to the show a little later, and he died too soon, but he fit into the wacky *Curb* family in a way that nobody could have ever imagined, and he added so much to it." —**Susie Essman**

"Bob Einstein's show *Super Dave* was the greatest TV show ever. I loved it so much growing up, so I'd always be like, 'Man, you know, you're a legend, right？ He told me all these amazing stories from his life. I loved the guy." —**JB Smoove**

"Bob was my first and only choice to play Marty Funkhouser. Often, while we were in the middle of a scene, apropos of nothing, Bob would tell a joke—or more to the point, Marty Funkhouser would tell a joke. Of course I would look at him like he was nuts. I knew it was a complete waste of time and that we'd never end up using it on the show, but nobody in the world could tell a joke like him, so it was always worth it. I'd say to him, 'OK, Bob, you got it out of your system. Don't do it again.' But of course he would, with a different joke. In season seven during 'The Table Read,' we were doing a scene with Jerry Seinfeld when out of the blue, as always, Bob told perhaps the most memorable joke in TV history, ending with, 'Your cunt is in the sink.' That one I kept in the show."
—**Larry David**

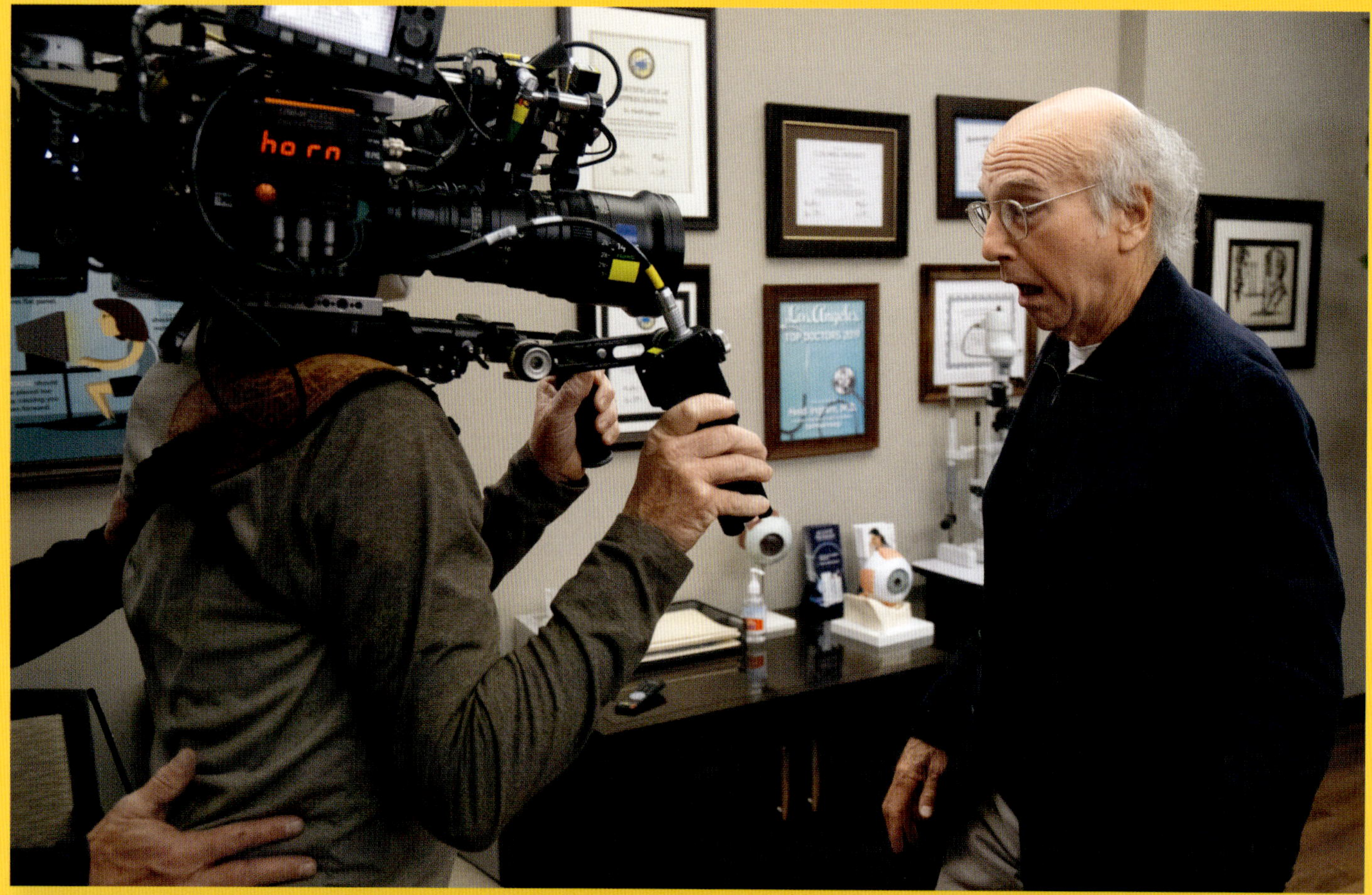
horn
Los Angeles
TOP DOCTORS 2017

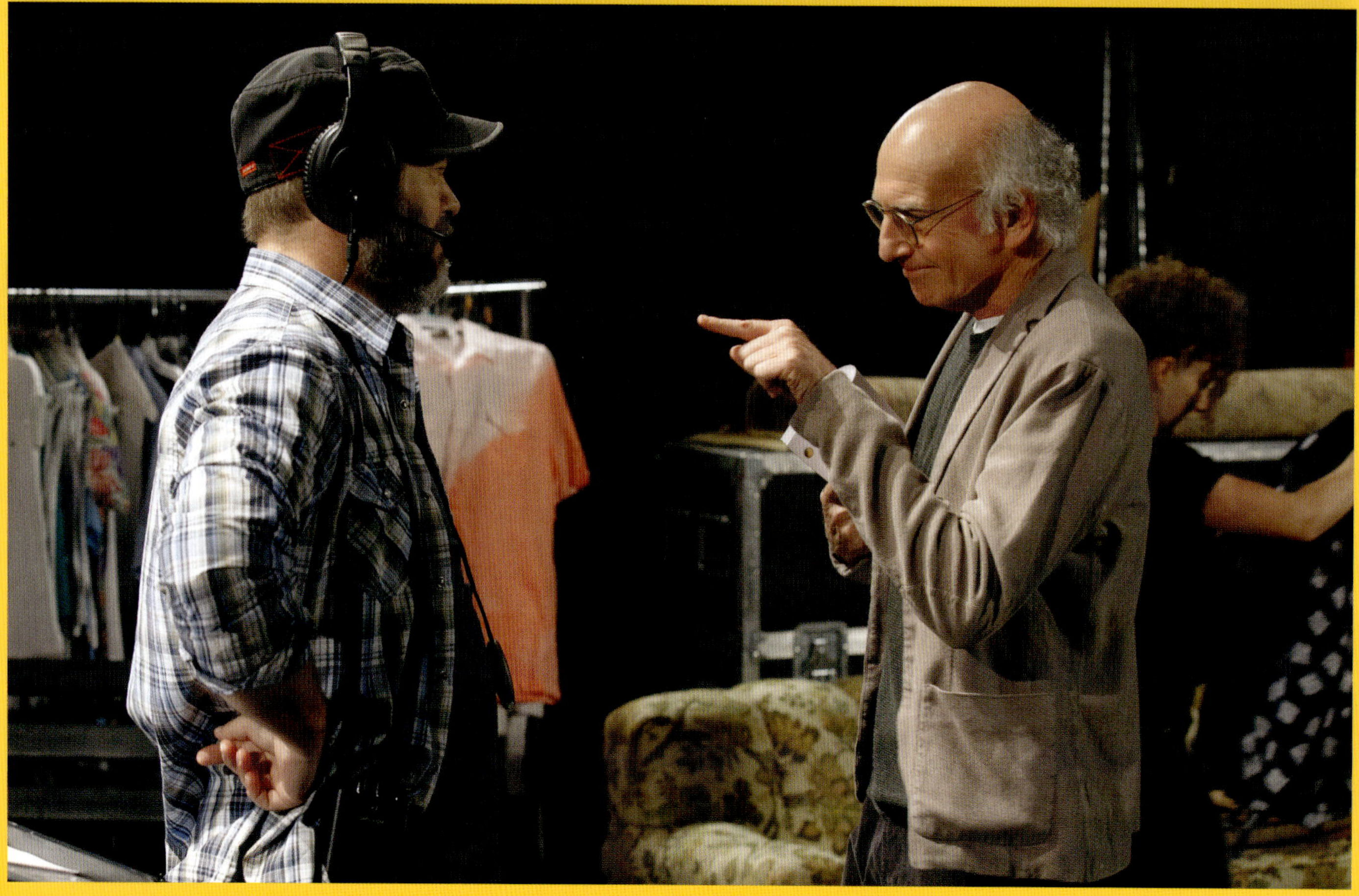

Episode Guide

Special: Oct. 17, 1999

LARRY DAVID: CURB YOUR ENTHUSIASM
DIRECTED BY *Robert B. Weide*
STORY BY *Larry David*

The cocreator of TV's *Seinfeld* exposes his George Costanza–like personality in this delightfully deadpan comedy special.

Season 1: Oct. 15, 2000

E1: THE PANTS TENT
DIRECTED BY *Robert B. Weide*
STORY BY *Larry David*

In the pilot episode of this hit comedy series, an innocent bunch-up in Larry's trousers gives rise to an embarrassing situation.

E2: TED AND MARY
DIRECTED BY *David Steinberg*
STORY BY *Larry David*

Larry and Cheryl's fun-filled bowling date with Ted Danson and Mary Steenburgen ends with Larry's shoes missing.

E3: PORNO GIL
DIRECTED BY *Robert B. Weide*
STORY BY *Larry David*

Larry sets off a bizarre chain of events (as he always does) in which he is forced to attend a party at the home of a porno businessman.

E4: THE BRACELET
DIRECTED BY *Robert B. Weide*
STORY BY *Larry David*

Larry is continually thwarted in his effort to buy a bracelet as a peace offering for Cheryl.

E5: INTERIOR DECORATOR
DIRECTED BY *Andy Ackerman*
STORY BY *Larry David*

An act of kindness results in Larry missing a meeting with an actress whose phone number he just can't get!

E6: THE WIRE
DIRECTED BY *Larry Charles*
STORY BY *Larry David*

Larry and Cheryl befriend their odd neighbors in order to get their approval to bury an unsightly phone wire.

E7: AAMCO
DIRECTED BY *Robert B. Weide*
STORY BY *Larry David*

A radio commercial causes Larry to crash Jeff's prized car.

E8: BELOVED AUNT
DIRECTED BY *Robert B. Weide*
STORY BY *Larry David*

Larry's offer to help with Cheryl's recently deceased aunt's obituary results in a shockingly profane misspelling.

E9: AFFIRMATIVE ACTION
DIRECTED BY *Bryan Gordon*
STORY BY *Larry David*

Larry insults a Black dermatologist while on the way to fill a prescription for Cheryl's skin condition.

E10: THE GROUP
DIRECTED BY *Robert B. Weide*
STORY BY *Larry David*

In the season one finale, Larry gets in trouble with his wife, a stage director, an old flame, and an incest survivors' group!

Season 2: Sept. 23, 2001

E1: THE CAR SALESMAN
DIRECTED BY *Robert B. Weide*
STORY BY *Larry David*

In the season two premiere, Larry shocks everyone by taking a job as a car salesman.

E2: THOR
DIRECTED BY *Robert B. Weide*
STORY BY *Larry David*

Larry seeks revenge against pro wrestler Thor Olson, who he believes slashed his tire after a road-rage incident.

E3: TRICK OR TREAT
DIRECTED BY *Larry Charles*
STORY BY *Larry David*

Larry experiences the trick side of Halloween when he questions the age of two girls who want candy.

E4: THE SHRIMP INCIDENT
DIRECTED BY *David Steinberg*
STORY BY *Larry David*

Larry's suspicion that an HBO executive has lifted some shrimp from his Chinese food leads to trouble.

E5: THE THONG
DIRECTED BY *Jeff Garlin*
STORY BY *Larry David*

Larry and Richard Lewis plot to end their relationships with a shrink after Larry sees the doc in a thong.

E6: THE ACUPUNCTURIST
DIRECTED BY *Bryan Gordon*
STORY BY *Larry David*

An acupuncturist agrees to waive his $5,000 fee if he can't cure Larry's back problems.

E7: THE DOLL
DIRECTED BY *Robert B. Weide*
STORY BY *Larry David*

The daughter of a TV exec gets Larry to cut the hair off her beloved doll—and then throws a fit.

E8: SHAQ
DIRECTED BY *Dean Parisot*
STORY BY *Larry David*

Larry is villainized for accidentally tripping Shaquille O'Neal at a Lakers game, but the debacle winds up bringing him good luck.

E9: THE BAPTISM
DIRECTED BY *Keith Truesdell*
STORY BY *Larry David*

Larry is shocked when he discovers that the Jewish man who is marrying Cheryl's sister is converting to Christianity.

E10: THE MASSAGE
DIRECTED BY *Robert B. Weide*
STORY BY *Larry David*

In the season two finale, Larry lands in hot water when Cheryl's psychic busts him for getting a naughty massage.

Season 3: Sept. 15, 2002

E1: CHET'S SHIRT
DIRECTED BY *Robert B. Weide*
STORY BY *Larry David*

Larry and Jeff invest in a restaurant with Ted Danson.

E2: THE BENADRYL BROWNIE
DIRECTED BY *Larry Charles*
STORY BY *Larry David*

Larry finally enters the world of cell phones, but poor reception leads to a big mix-up.

E3: CLUB SODA AND SALT
DIRECTED BY *Robert B. Weide*
STORY BY *Larry David*

Larry, Jeff, and Ted scramble to find a new chef when Randy quits.

E4: THE NANNY
DIRECTED BY *Larry Charles*
STORY BY *Larry David*

Larry, Cheryl, Jeff, and Susie encounter a nanny from hell, while Larry commits a faux pas at a pool party.

E5: THE TERRORIST ATTACK
DIRECTED BY *Robert B. Weide*
STORY BY *Larry David*

A rumored terrorist threat overshadows a benefit performance by Alanis Morissette.

E6: THE SPECIAL SECTION
DIRECTED BY *Bryan Gordon*
STORY BY *Larry David*

Larry receives bad news, but it offers him an excuse to turn down some unappealing invitations.

E7: THE CORPSE-SNIFFING DOG
DIRECTED BY *Andy Ackerman*
STORY BY *Larry David*

At dinner with the Braudys, Larry ponders a ridiculous question—with predictable results.

E8: KRAZEE-EYEZ KILLA
DIRECTED BY *Robert B. Weide*
STORY BY *Larry David*

Larry is accused of betraying the confidence of Wanda's rapper boyfriend.

E9: MARY, JOSEPH, AND LARRY
DIRECTED BY *David Steinberg*
STORY BY *Larry David*

Larry proves to be an incompetent Christmas tipper and a lousy liar.

E10: THE GRAND OPENING
DIRECTED BY *Robert B. Weide*
STORY BY *Larry David*

Larry figures out a way to fire a chef and alienate an important restaurant critic.

Season 4: Jan. 4, 2004

E1: MEL'S OFFER
DIRECTED BY *Larry Charles*
STORY BY *Larry David*

Larry reminds Cheryl of a tenth-anniversary present she promised him when they got engaged.

E2: BEN'S BIRTHDAY PARTY
DIRECTED BY *Robert B. Weide*
STORY BY *Larry David*

Larry reconnects with Michael, his blind tormentor, with bad results.

E3: THE BLIND DATE
DIRECTED BY *Larry Charles*
STORY BY *Larry David*

Larry mends fences with Michael by setting him up on a blind date.

E4: THE WEATHERMAN
DIRECTED BY *Robert B. Weide*
STORY BY *Larry David*

Larry inadvertently traumatizes the Greenes' daughter and has a problem with a local weatherman.

E5: THE 5 WOOD
DIRECTED BY *Bryan Gordon*
STORY BY *Larry David*

Larry's working relationship with David Schwimmer and his golf-club membership are threatened.

E6: THE CAR POOL LANE
DIRECTED BY *Robert B. Weide*
STORY BY *Larry David*

Larry finds an innovative way to use the HOV lane to get to a Dodgers game.

E7: THE SURROGATE
DIRECTED BY *Larry Charles*
STORY BY *Larry David*

Larry's decision to buy a surrogate mother a baby-shower gift backfires . . . as do his efforts to pass a routine physical.

E8: WANDERING BEAR
DIRECTED BY *Robert B. Weide*
STORY BY *Larry David*

A surreptitious video purchase endangers Larry's relationship with his assistant, Antoinette.

E9: THE SURVIVOR
DIRECTED BY *Larry Charles*
STORY BY *Larry David*

Larry contemplates a tempting offer from his Hasidic dry cleaner.

E10: OPENING NIGHT
DIRECTED BY *Robert B. Weide*
STORY BY *Larry David*

In the season four finale, Larry opens in *The Producers* on Broadway.

Season 5: Sept. 25, 2005

E1: THE LARRY DAVID SANDWICH
DIRECTED BY *Robert B. Weide*
STORY BY *Larry David*

In the season five premiere, Larry is changed by a near-death experience, a revelation, and a sandwich.

E2: THE BOWTIE
DIRECTED BY *Larry Charles*
STORY BY *Larry David*

Larry hires a private investigator to uncover a personal secret and adopts a racist dog.

E3: THE CHRIST NAIL
DIRECTED BY *Robert B. Weide*
STORY BY *Larry David*

Larry buys his housekeeper a bra, and is saved from the wrath of her vengeful husband by orthotics and a special nail.

E4: KAMIKAZE BINGO
DIRECTED BY *Robert B. Weide*
STORY BY *Larry David*

Larry dishonors an art dealer at a Japanese restaurant and accuses a nursing-home resident of a Bingo fix.

E5: LEWIS NEEDS A KIDNEY
DIRECTED BY *Robert B. Weide*
STORY BY *Larry David*

Larry and Jeff debate how far they're willing to go to help out a friend in need.

E6: THE SMOKING JACKET
DIRECTED BY *David Steinberg*
STORY BY *Larry David*

Larry is blackmailed into making two wishes come true, and swaps smoking jackets with an icon.

E7: THE SEDER
DIRECTED BY *Robert B. Weide*
STORY BY *Larry David*

Larry ruffles feathers by inviting a sex offender to a seder.

E8: THE SKI LIFT
DIRECTED BY *Larry Charles*
STORY BY *Larry David*

Larry and Jeff befriend the head of a kidney-transplant consortium.

E9: THE KOREAN BOOKIE
DIRECTED BY *Bryan Gordon*
STORY BY *Larry David*

Larry suspects his Korean bookie of kidnapping Jeff's dog.

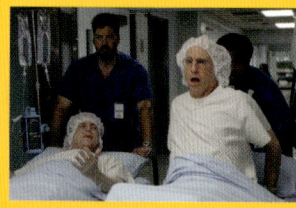

E10: THE END
DIRECTED BY *Larry Charles*
STORY BY *Larry David*

In the season five finale, Larry is changed by a trip to Arizona.

Season 6: Sept. 9, 2007

E1: MEET THE BLACKS
DIRECTED BY *Larry Charles*
STORY BY *Larry David*

In the season six premiere, Cheryl talks Larry into adopting the Blacks, a family displaced by a hurricane.

E2: THE ANONYMOUS DONOR
DIRECTED BY *Robert B. Weide*
STORY BY *Larry David*

The Davids and the Blacks move into a new house and take in a guest. Larry alters a dry-cleaning rule.

E3: THE IDA FUNKHOUSER ROADSIDE MEMORIAL
DIRECTED BY *David Mandel*
STORY BY *Larry David*

Larry argues with Susie and Richard Lewis over condolences and is accused of pinching flowers by Marty Funkhouser.

E4: THE LEFTY CALL
DIRECTED BY *Alec Berg*
STORY BY *Larry David*

Larry regrets getting Richard Lewis's girlfriend Cha Cha a job near the office bathroom.

E5: THE FREAK BOOK
DIRECTED BY *Bryan Gordon*
STORY BY *Larry David*

A book about freaks, coupled with a chauffeur's incapacity, sets Larry up for a string of ejections.

E6: THE RAT DOG
DIRECTED BY *David Steinberg*
STORY BY *Larry David*

Larry tests the limits of sick sex, and Loretta and Leon's job prospects are burned by a slow toaster.

E7: THE TIVO GUY
DIRECTED BY *Jeff Schaffer*
STORY BY *Larry David*

A malfunctioning TV device puts Larry's marriage with Cheryl into crisis mode.

E8: THE N-WORD
DIRECTED BY *Tom Kramer*
STORY BY *Larry David*

Larry tries to do Auntie Rae a favor, but ends up offending her. Jeff's hospital stay opens a door for Larry.

E9: THE THERAPISTS
DIRECTED BY *David Mandel*
STORY BY *Larry David*

Larry tries to curry favor with Cheryl by influencing her therapist.

E10: THE BAT MITZVAH
DIRECTED BY *Larry Charles*
STORY BY *Larry David*

In the season six finale, a bat mitzvah provides Larry with a chance to clear up his recent domestic travails.

Season 7: Sept. 20, 2009

E1: FUNKHOUSER'S CRAZY SISTER
DIRECTED BY *Larry Charles*
STORY BY *Larry David*

In the season seven premiere, Larry attempts a preemptive breakup with an ailing Loretta and learns a lesson.

E2: VEHICULAR FELLATIO
DIRECTED BY *Alec Berg*
STORY BY *Larry David*

Larry deliberately tries to annoy Loretta, against the advice of a renowned doctor, and dooms Richard Lewis's new relationship.

E3: THE REUNION
DIRECTED BY *Jeff Schaffer*
STORY BY *Larry David*

Larry resists Jeff's suggestion to do a *Seinfeld* reunion special—until he figures out a compelling personal reason to do so.

E4: THE HOT TOWEL
DIRECTED BY *Alec Berg*
STORY BY *Larry David*

Larry rats out Christian Slater at Ted and Mary's anniversary party, but later gets his payback at a restaurant rendezvous.

E5: DENISE HANDICAP
DIRECTED BY *David Mandel*
STORY BY *Larry David*

Larry learns to embrace the upside of disability without actually being disabled, and looks to disprove a rumor.

E6: THE BARE MIDRIFF
DIRECTED BY *Larry Charles*
STORY BY *Larry David*

Larry and Jerry Seinfeld consider incorporating Larry's latest real-life experience into the reunion show.

E7: THE BLACK SWAN
DIRECTED BY *Bryan Gordon*
STORY BY *Larry David*

Larry twice encounters bad luck on the same golf hole.

E8: OFFICER KRUPKE
DIRECTED BY *David Steinberg*
STORY BY *Larry David*

Jeff's indiscretion forces Larry to embrace his feminine side, and one of Jeff's clients competes with Cheryl for a *Seinfeld* role.

E9: THE TABLE READ
DIRECTED BY *Larry Charles*
STORY BY *Larry David*

Larry gets frustrated by a nine-year-old's emails, Leon poses as a dead man, and Jerry befriends Funkhouser.

E10: SEINFELD
DIRECTED BY *Jeff Schaffer and Andy Ackerman (Seinfeld segment)*
STORY BY *Larry David*

In the season seven finale, a returned favor costs Larry quality time with Cheryl.

Season 8: July 10, 2011

E1: THE DIVORCE
DIRECTED BY *David Steinberg*
STORY BY *Larry David, Alec Berg, David Mandel, and Jeff Schaffer*

In the season eight premiere, Larry learns his divorce lawyer isn't kosher, and rescinds a cookie order from a Girl Scout.

E2: THE SAFE HOUSE
DIRECTED BY *Bryan Gordon*
STORY BY *Larry David, Alec Berg, David Mandel, and Jeff Schaffer*

Larry becomes an unlikely role model for battered women, and Richard Lewis's relationship with a burlesque performer is put to the test.

E3: PALESTINIAN CHICKEN
DIRECTED BY *Robert B. Weide*
STORY BY *Larry David, Alec Berg, David Mandel, and Jeff Schaffer*

Larry plays social assassin to the hilt at a dinner party, on the golf course, and at a Palestinian restaurant with chicken to die for.

E4: THE SMILEY FACE
DIRECTED BY *Jeff Schaffer*
STORY BY *Larry David, Alec Berg, David Mandel, and Jeff Schaffer*

Larry vows to topple a sacred dating taboo, and regrets making concessions to his new office neighbor.

E5: VOW OF SILENCE
DIRECTED BY *Alec Berg*
STORY BY *Larry David, Alec Berg, David Mandel, and Jeff Schaffer*

A failed alibi has coastal consequences, and the Greenes' dog is denied a last meal. Larry confronts a buffet-line transgressor.

E6: THE HERO
DIRECTED BY *Alec Berg*
STORY BY *Larry David, Alec Berg, David Mandel, and Jeff Schaffer*

Larry plays the hero in the sky and underground, and Jeff's courtship of Ricky Gervais is sabotaged by a nosy waiter.

E7: THE BI-SEXUAL
DIRECTED BY *David Mandel*
STORY BY *Larry David, Alec Berg, David Mandel, and Jeff Schaffer*

Larry competes with Rosie O'Donnell for the same woman, and explores the nuances of Japanese bows.

E8: CAR PERISCOPE
DIRECTED BY *David Mandel*
STORY BY *Larry David, Alec Berg, David Mandel, and Jeff Schaffer*

Larry and Jeff weigh an investment opportunity, and Wanda Sykes preempts Larry's training schedule.

E9: MISTER SOFTEE
DIRECTED BY *Larry Charles*
STORY BY *Larry David, Alec Berg, David Mandel, and Jeff Schaffer*

An ice-cream truck triggers a painful childhood memory for Larry that has a huge impact.

E10: LARRY VS. MICHAEL J. FOX
DIRECTED BY *Alec Berg*
STORY BY *Larry David, Alec Berg, David Mandel, and Jeff Schaffer*

Larry accuses NYC neighbor Michael J. Fox of harassment, and Jeff takes a bullet for Susie.

Season 9: October 1, 2017

E1: FOISTED!
DIRECTED BY *Jeff Schaffer*
STORY BY *Larry David and Jeff Schaffer*

In the season nine premiere, Larry tries to rid himself of an inept assistant, offends Jeff's barber, and gets into hot water over a new project.

E2: THE PICKLE GAMBIT
DIRECTED BY *David Steinberg*
STORY BY *Larry David, Jeff Schaffer, and Justin Hurwitz*

Larry reaches out to a familiar face, gives a hotel guest sartorial advice, and looks to create a diversion to help a friend's nephew.

E3: A DISTURBANCE IN THE KITCHEN
DIRECTED BY *Jeff Schaffer*
STORY BY *Larry David and Jeff Schaffer*

Larry turns to a writer for advice; searching for Susie's missing little sister, he gets ticketed by an overzealous cop.

E4: RUNNING WITH THE BULLS
DIRECTED BY *Bryan Gordon*
STORY BY *Larry David and Jeff Schaffer*

Larry's therapist accuses him of overstepping; Susie grows suspicious of Jeff and Larry, and bribes an usher at a funeral.

E5: THANK YOU FOR YOUR SERVICE
DIRECTED BY *Larry Charles*
STORY BY *Larry David and Jeff Schaffer*

Larry commits a faux pas with Sammi's fiancé, and tries to start over with his mail carrier and a golf-club security guard.

E6: THE ACCIDENTAL TEXT ON PURPOSE
DIRECTED BY *Larry Charles*
STORY BY *Larry David, Jeff Schaffer, and Jon Hayman*

Larry invents an ingenious ploy for getting his friends out of relationship jams. Larry upsets Funkhouser's new girlfriend.

E7: NAMASTE
DIRECTED BY *Jessie Nelson*
STORY BY *Larry David and Jeff Schaffer*

Larry angers a hot-yoga teacher, has an auspicious first date, and seethes over a run-in with an unfair Uber driver.

E8: NEVER WAIT FOR SECONDS!
DIRECTED BY *Robert B. Weide*
STORY BY *Larry David and Jeff Schaffer*

Bridget asks Larry for a favor on behalf of her son. Larry earns unexpected gratitude in a buffet line.

E9: THE SHUCKER
DIRECTED BY *Jeff Schaffer*
STORY BY *Larry David, Jeff Schaffer, and Justin Hurwitz*

Larry is blackmailed by an employee and tormented by someone from his past. Jeff and Larry pitch a new creative venture.

E10: FATWA!
DIRECTED BY *Jeff Schaffer*
STORY BY *Larry David, Jeff Schaffer, Justin Hurwitz, and Jon Hayman*

In the season nine finale, Larry has a scheduling conflict, takes issue with some work associates, and hosts a pair of ungrateful houseguests.

Season 10: January 19, 2020

E1: HAPPY NEW YEAR
DIRECTED BY *Jeff Schaffer*
STORY BY *Larry David, Jeff Schaffer, and Steve Leff*

Larry makes a new enemy and gets into hot water at a cocktail party.

E2: SIDE SITTING
DIRECTED BY *Jeff Schaffer*
STORY BY *Larry David and Jeff Schaffer*

Larry's lawyer tries to settle the Alice situation. Larry gives Susie an extravagant gift.

E3: ARTIFICIAL FRUIT
DIRECTED BY *Cheryl Hines*
STORY BY *Larry David, Jeff Schaffer, and Carol Leifer*

Larry gets the chance to clear the air with Alice and goes to extreme lengths for a lunch with Richard.

E4: YOU'RE NOT GOING TO GET ME TO SAY ANYTHING BAD ABOUT
DIRECTED BY *Jeff Schaffer*
STORY BY *Larry David and Jeff Schaffer*

Larry brings an impromptu date to a destination wedding and finds himself in a sticky situation when he goes searching for a toothbrush.

E5: INSUFFICIENT PRAISE
DIRECTED BY *Jeff Schaffer*
STORY BY *Larry David and Jeff Schaffer*

Larry receives a problematic gift and causes trouble with Richard's new girlfriend.

E6: THE SURPRISE PARTY
DIRECTED BY *Erin O'Malley*
STORY BY *Larry David and Jeff Schaffer*

Larry enlists the help of a new friend to ensure Jeff's surprise party doesn't go awry.

E7: THE UGLY SECTION
DIRECTED BY *Jeff Schaffer*
STORY BY *Larry David and Jeff Schaffer*

Larry capitalizes on a friend's death and notices a discrepancy at a new restaurant.

E8: ELIZABETH, MARGARET, AND LARRY
DIRECTED BY *Jeff Schaffer*
STORY BY *Larry David and Jeff Schaffer*

A prominent actor studies Larry for an upcoming role, while Larry stokes a sibling rivalry and helps Leon with a new app.

E9: BEEP PANIC
DIRECTED BY *Jeff Schaffer*
STORY BY *Larry David and Jeff Schaffer*

Larry finds himself indebted to a struggling waitress and draws the ire of Mocha Joe.

E10: THE SPITE STORE
DIRECTED BY *Jeff Schaffer*
STORY BY *Larry David, Jeff Schaffer, and Justin Hurwitz*

Larry runs into an old acquaintance and causes a rift between expectant parents.

Season 11: October 24, 2021

E1: THE FIVE-FOOT FENCE
DIRECTED BY *Jeff Schaffer*
STORY BY *Larry David and Jeff Schaffer*

While his latest venture is threatened by forces outside his control, Larry attends an unprecedented event at Albert Brooks's house.

E2: ANGEL MUFFIN
DIRECTED BY *Jeff Schaffer*
STORY BY *Larry David and Jeff Schaffer*

Larry has a work meeting that backfires and sets out on a sting operation for Jeff.

E3: THE MINI BAR
DIRECTED BY *Jeff Schaffer*
STORY BY *Larry David and Jeff Schaffer*

After enlisting Cheryl's help in a last-ditch effort, Larry has an idea that could save his latest project.

E4: THE WATERMELON
DIRECTED BY *Jeff Schaffer*
STORY BY *Larry David and Jeff Schaffer*

Larry hangs out with Woody Harrelson and cashes in on Susie's favor.

E5: IRASSHAIMASE!
DIRECTED BY *Robert B. Weide*
STORY BY *Larry David, Jeff Schaffer, and Carol Leifer*

After enlisting both Jeff and Freddy's help for the occasion, Larry's hot date goes south.

E6: MAN FIGHTS TINY WOMAN
DIRECTED BY *Jeff Schaffer*
STORY BY *Larry David and Jeff Schaffer*

Larry's uncomfortable with his chauffeur, his roofer, and his chiropractor.

E7: IRMA KOSTROSKI
DIRECTED BY *Jeff Schaffer*
STORY BY *Larry David, Jeff Schaffer, and Nathaniel Stein*

Ahead of Election Day, Larry gets involved in local politics while mediating a conflict on his set.

E8: WHAT HAVE I DONE?
DIRECTED BY *Jeff Schaffer*
STORY BY *Larry David and Jeff Schaffer*

Larry does damage control to remain in Irma's good graces while encouraging Leon to monetize his knack for husbandly counsel.

E9: IGOR, GREGOR, AND TIMOR
DIRECTED BY *Jeff Schaffer*
STORY BY *Larry David and Jeff Schaffer*

Larry seizes an opportunity to avoid Irma as he's roped into Jeff's latest apology tour.

E10: THE MORMON ADVANTAGE
DIRECTED BY *Jeff Schaffer*
STORY BY *Larry David and Jeff Schaffer*

With the city council vote rapidly approaching, Larry gives some unsolicited marriage advice and hosts an event for an American hero.

Season 12: Feb. 4, 2024

E1: ATLANTA
DIRECTED BY *Jeff Schaffer*
STORY BY *Larry David and Jeff Schaffer*

Larry heads to Atlanta to attend a birthday party for a prominent businessman.

E2: THE LAWN JOCKEY
DIRECTED BY *Jeff Schaffer*
STORY BY *Larry David and Jeff Schaffer*

Still in Atlanta, Larry finds himself stuck at a rental home with a questionable lawn ornament.

E3: VERTICAL DROP, HORIZONTAL TUG
DIRECTED BY *Jeff Schaffer*
STORY BY *Larry David, Jeff Schaffer, and Justin Hurwitz*

While at the range, Larry eavesdrops on a lesson that improves his golf game a little too much.

E4: DISGRUNTLED
DIRECTED BY *Jeff Schaffer*
STORY BY *Larry David and Jeff Schaffer*

A note in the men's locker room sparks controversy at Oceanview. Larry and Irma's couple's counselor crosses a professional line.

E5: FISH STUCK
DIRECTED BY *Jeff Schaffer*
STORY BY *Larry David, Jeff Schaffer, and Carol Leifer*

After an incident at temple, Larry asks friends to vouch for his character.

E6: THE GETTYSBURG ADDRESS
DIRECTED BY *Jeff Schaffer*
STORY BY *Larry David and Jeff Schaffer*

Larry tries to make better use of his time in the bathroom. Susie starts a new business, and her advertising has unexpected results.

E7: THE DREAM SCHEME
DIRECTED BY *Jeff Schaffer*
STORY BY *Larry David, Jeff Schaffer, and Nathaniel Stein*

An acquaintance from the club asks too much of Larry.

E8: THE COLOSTOMY BAG
DIRECTED BY *Robert B. Weide*
STORY BY *Larry David and Jeff Schaffer*

Richard enlists Larry's help to buy a vintage car, but his careless behavior leads to an unwanted outcome.

E9: KEN/KENDRA
DIRECTED BY *Jeff Schaffer*
STORY BY *Larry David and Jeff Schaffer*

A misunderstanding with a masseuse threatens Larry's precarious public image.

E10: NO LESSONS LEARNED
DIRECTED BY *Jeff Schaffer*
STORY BY *Larry David and Jeff Schaffer*

Larry returns to Atlanta, where he gets involved in Richard's love life and reveals a secret about Cheryl.

Image Credits

ALL IMAGES COURTESY OF HBO UNLESS OTHERWISE INDICATED

Courtesy of Larry David: pp. 2–3; pp. 4–5; p.7; p.12; pp. 56–57; p. 86; pp. 88–89; pp. 94–95; pp. 96–97

Courtesy of Susie Essman: p. 157: top right; p. 158: middle (Susie Essman, Jeff Garlin); pp. 158–159: bottom middle (JB Smoove, Susie Essman); p. 159: middle (Jeff Garlin, Larry David, JB Smoove); p. 159: bottom right; p. 159: top right; p. 159: top middle (Susie Essman, Jeff Garlin); p. 262: bottom left

Courtesy of Roger Nygard: p. 114: top left, top right

Courtesy of Erin O'Malley: p. 101

Courtesy of Jeff Schaffer: pp. 90–91; pp. 102–103: #20; p. 109; p. 209; p. 231

Courtesy of Bob Weide: p. 20

Getty Images: p. 6: Getty Images/Silver Screen Collection; p. 8: Getty Images/ABC Photo Archives; p. 9: GettyImages/Bob D'Amico; pp. 16–17: Getty Images/David Hume Kennerly; p. 27: Getty Images/David Hume Kennerly

John Johnson/HBO: pp .ii–iii: left, second from left, third from left; p. 1; p.37: Bruce Springsteen; p. 37: Susie Essman; pp. 44–45; p.52; p.55; p. 58; p. 59: bottom right; pp. 62–63; pp. 68–69; p. 79; p. 80; pp. 102–103: #3, #18, #19; p. 110; p. 119: top right; pp. 128–129; pp. 130–131; pp. 132–133; pp. 154–155: Hallway Hog; pp. 158: bottom (Susie Essman, Larry David, Cheryl Hines, Ted Danson, JB Smoove, Jeff Garlin); pp. 158: middle left (Larry David, Jeff Garlin); pp. 158–159: top left, middle (Jeff Garlin); pp. 162–163; p. 164: top left, bottom right; pp. 168–169: right; pp. 170–171: left, right; pp. 178–179; pp. 184–185; pp. 188–189: top left, middle right; pp. 190–191: middle images (Cheryl Hines, Larry David in car); p. 196: bottom left; p. 199; pp. 200–201; p. 213: #5 (right); pp. 218–219; p. 233: Holocaust Shoes (left); p. 235; p. 239; p.240; pp. 242–243; pp. 244–245; p.250; p. 251: Ted Danson; p. 251: Jerry Seinfeld; p. 253; pp. 254–255: bottom left; p. 256: Iris Bahr; p. 263: top right; pp. 262–263: Jimmy Kimmel, Larry David; pp. 262–263: bottom right; p. 264: Lori Loughlin; p. 264: Alexander Vindman; p. 264: Sienna Miller; p. 265; pp. 266–267: Larry David, Lori Loughlin; p. 269: Sean Hayes; p. 271; pp. 278–279; pp. 284–285; p. 301: left; p. 302; p. 308: S9E2, S9E3; p. 309: S9E5, S9E7, S9E8, S9E9, S9E10, S10E1, S10E2, S10E3, S10E4, S10E5; p. 310: S10E6, S11E1 S11E2, S11E8; p. 311: S12E2, S12E4, S12E5, S12E6, S12E7, S12E9

Joe Pugliese/HBO: p. 39; pp. 50–51; p. 83; pp. 84–85; p. 106: top; p. 111; p. 114: bottom; pp. 274–275; pp. 276–277; pp. 282–283; pp. 286–287; pp. 288–289; p. 291; pp. 292–293; pp. 294–295; pp. 296–297; p. 299: top right

Art Streiber/HBO: p. 121; p. 193; pp. 272–273; p. 312, back cover (full-body image of Larry)

Courtesy of Laura Streicher/HBO: pp. 112–113

![blink logo]

First published in the UK in 2025
by Blink Publishing
An imprint of Bonnier Books UK
5th Floor, HYLO, 105 Bunhill Row,
London, EC1Y 8LZ

HBO ORIGINAL

Copyright © 2025 Home Box Office, Inc. All Rights Reserved. HBO and related trademarks are the property of Home Box Office, Inc.

Page 313 constitutes an extension of the copyright page.

No part of this publication may be reproduced, stored or transmitted in any form or by any means, electronic, mechanical, photocopying or otherwise, without the prior written permission of the publisher.

A CIP catalogue record for this book is available from the British Library.

Hardback ISBN: 9781785124334

Also available as an ebook

MELCHER MEDIA

This book was produced by Melcher Media, Inc.
melcher.com

Founder and CEO: Charles Melcher
Vice President and COO: Bonnie Eldon
Editorial Director: Lauren Nathan
Production Director: Susan Lynch
Executive Editor: Christopher Steighner
Senior Editor: Megan Worman
Editorial Assistant: Sonia Menken
Editorial Intern: Grace Luckett

Print book cover and interior design by Laura Palese

Additional text contributions by Jackie Strause

Thanks also to Amélie Cherlin, Rebecca Karamehmedovic, Lynne Palazzi, Kayt Sukel, and Laura Wallis.

Printed and bound in China

Every reasonable effort has been made to trace copyright holders of material reproduced in this book, but if any have been inadvertently overlooked the publishers would be glad to hear from them.

The authorised representative in the EEA is Bonnier Books UK (Ireland) Limited.

Registered office address: Floor 3, Block 3, Miesian Plaza, Dublin 2, D02 Y754, Ireland

compliance@bonnierbooks.ie

www.bonnierbooks.co.uk